INDONESIA

INDONESIA

Bruce Grant

Fellow in Political Science
University of Melbourne

MELBOURNE UNIVERSITY PRESS

LONDON AND NEW YORK: CAMBRIDGE UNIVERSITY PRESS

First published 1964
Reprinted 1964, 1965
Printed and bound in Australia by
Melbourne University Press, Carlton N.3, Victoria
Registered in Australia for transmission
by post as a book

Text set in 10 point Fairfield type

Preface

Everything flows. Indonesians have often said this to me, adding that the western anxiety to halt reality and examine its meaning is a cause of unhappiness. It is also, however, a cause of understanding. This small book is dedicated to the proposition that it is possible to halt the processes of a country in order to test them, and, even if this were not possible, that the writer ought to be allowed to try. From an Indonesian's point of view it is therefore an outsider's book.

Indonesians tend to say: 'Oh, you don't understand. You *can't* understand'. What they mean is: 'You can't be me'. This also may be true, but it is a request for sympathy, not for understanding. My sympathies for Indonesia were easily engaged and are lasting. I have wanted in the pages that follow, however, to examine the country more closely than I have been able to do in the past as a sympathetic —and rather hurried—observer.

I went first to Indonesia expecting to contemplate Scott Fitzgerald's 'fresh, green breast of the new world'. When I found that the lovely land had been pawed for centuries, I became absorbed in the political corrective to this sordid affair: nationalism as a form of idealism, nationalism as rebirth. Indonesia did not beckon with a mysterious past, as China, India and Japan do, but writing urgently of what was taking place I was always aware of the country itself, untouched by cabled dispatches, breathing softly in the available distance.

I came to realize that there are three Indonesias. There is an Indonesia, the first, which is defined by political events: what the President says and does publicly, what decisions are taken by the government. In this sense, Indonesia is an important nation with a voice in world affairs, attitudes and opinions concerning the big issues of our time, problems of defence, trade and so on. The second is defined by the resources of the people: their attempts to understand life and death, their humour, their social relations, their style of thought and dress. These things may be uneventful for journalism, but they 'happen' all the time. It is hard to find a national meaning in a beautiful face in the street, the sound of betjak bells at night, the sombre colours of a batik sarong, yet they are as much the mark of a country as the insignia of politics. The third Indonesia is defined not by nationalism or culture but by ecology. To the ecologist the reticulated Indonesian rice terraces are more impressive than the artistic galleries of ancient monuments or the edifices of the modern nation. Can Indonesia show that it is a nation able to keep a safe balance between land and people?

This is a book of political interpretation, which means that it is about the first Indonesia. I have tried to use the other two Indonesias, however, to inform and enlarge the study. As much as possible I have tried to keep the information open and dispersed, rather than marshalled in support of a viewpoint, in the hope that the book will serve a more general purpose than that of argument. There is a great deal of outside political judgment about Indonesia but very little knowledge of its politics.

As I am not a scholar this is not a scholarly book. The information is often raw and the judgments made without reference to previous authority. There are no footnotes. On occasions (for example the visits of the Australian Minister for External Affairs to Manila in March 1963 and to Djakarta in September 1963 and the reference on page 160 to the late President Kennedy's intervention in the West Irian crisis) the main public sources are articles I wrote at the time and I have based myself, without attribution, on them. Sometimes I have used statements made in conversation by leading Indonesians which have not been used before. Generally, however, I have tried to keep the level of source material even and non-controversial.

A special word, therefore, about chapter 9. I advise readers not to play 'spot the victim' as they will find themselves to have been deliberately misled. The words in these conversations are real; the people are composites designed to lose the scent. The reasons for this subterfuge are obvious enough, although the Indonesian security police is no more active than its counterparts in other Asian countries. There is opposition to the Sukarno government, even if growing weaker, and I wanted in some of these conversations to show the kind of opposition it is. The chapter also shows an acceptance, short of fervent support, for Sukarno. I would not claim any sociological value for it: the people interviewed are English-speaking and Djakarta-based and this gives them a bias. Politically, however, an élite of a few thousand people manipulate Indonesian politics and with few exceptions they live in Djakarta and speak English.

A word, also, about Indonesian names and titles. I have tried to keep the text readable, which has meant sometimes disregarding the refinements and elaborations of Indonesian proper names. Indonesians themselves are casual about this: Dipa Nusantara Aidit is

Aidit, Ali Sastroamidjojo is Ali, Tan Malaka is neither Tan nor
Malaka but always Tan Malaka. Some, like Sukarno, have only one
name. Javanese in particular sometimes change their names to cele-
brate an event. Wherever possible I have simply followed common
Indonesian usage. Titles offer such a technical tangle that I have
generally not used them, especially as they are in the process of
change. Such aristocratic titles as Raden (Javanese) and Sutan
(Minangkabau) are still in fact used, as is the Muslim title of Hadji
(for one who has made the pilgrimage to Mecca). Academic titles are
doubly confusing to the English reader because they have been
inherited from the Dutch. 'Mr' (*Meester*) is a graduate in law; 'Ir'
(*Ingénieur*) is a graduate in engineering, architecture or agriculture;
'Drs' is used by graduates in economics or literature while 'Dr' is
reserved for higher degrees in all fields and for medical and dental
graduates. The Indonesian president is sometimes called Dr Sukarno
but he is more strictly Ir Sukarno. The Foreign Minister, Dr
Subandrio, uses his correct title—as a graduate in medicine. Like
most people, Indonesians use the respected title 'Dr' rather loosely.

Many Indonesians helped me to write this book, although most
were not aware of it at the time. Rather than create an unnecessary
mystery over names excluded, or embarrassment—as this is a critical
book—for the owners of those included, I have decided not to
acknowledge their indispensable assistance. I would like to thank Dr
Herbert Feith, of Monash University, Melbourne, who put his
enormous mental filing system at my disposal and helped in innumer-
able small ways. Mr W. E. Purnell, formerly director of the South-
east Asia Science Co-operation Office of Unesco in Djakarta
(now executive secretary of the Royal Australian Chemical Institute) read the manuscript with a sharp eye. He is the kind of critic
who, in addition to a world-wide reference for his knowledge of
Indonesia, can say whether it was possible for Shrivajaya to have
shipped naphtha to China in the fourteenth century—a handy man
to have around. My wife, Joan, did some of the research, edited and
typed (at least twice) everything I wrote. As the book had to be
completed quickly, her help was much more than that of an
assistant: sometimes she seemed to be working harder than I was.

Melbourne
February, 1964

Contents

Illustrations

CHAPTER ONE

The Beginnings

On the plains of central Java stands the pyramid temple of Boro-budur. It is one of the great relics of tropical Asia, where only solid stone survives the heat and rain. Mount Merapi rises in the near-distance, but the surrounding land is even, a pattern of shrub-trees and fields of rice and sugar cane. Borobudur does not pierce the un-dulating landscape like the religious spires of rural Europe. It is an impassive monument, with a contemplative style befitting a Buddhist place of worship. It is set broadly on its base of six hundred feet square, rising solidly at a low gradient to a central stupa shaped like a giant bell. When you stand on the higher terraces watching the steamy morning coming to life in the heartland of Java you may feel that the monument is floating. Sometimes at night, when moon-light falls on the calm-faced buddhas in its galleries, you may catch the spirit that the men who made Borobudur were trying to preserve. It is less dramatic than the relics of its contemporary, Angkor, the ruined Hindu-Buddhist temple civilization of the Khmers in Cam-bodia, but it is evidence in today's underdeveloped Indonesia of a level of art and engineering two centuries before the French pro-duced the cathedrals of Notre Dame and Chartres. (As a matter of perspective, all followed nearly two thousand years after the Egyptian pyramids.)

Today, President Sukarno and other Indonesian leaders refer often to Borobudur as proof that their country has a civilization of depth and variety. 'We object to the description of ourselves as under-developed', Sukarno has said. 'Qualify the expression! Call it eco-nomically undeveloped or technically undeveloped and, with some reservations, I would agree. But spiritually, mentally, culturally, I disagree wholly and completely.'

Borobudur was built between 760 and 820 A.D. and among its fourteen hundred bas-reliefs, in addition to serene buddhas, are Hindu gods such as Shiva, and images which spring from the primi-tive beliefs of the people before the religions of the Asian mainland reached the South-east Asian archipelago. Borobudur embodies the

1

now well-known Indonesian talent for blending religious doctrines—
the totality of religious beliefs and practices which in Java is called
agama Djawa, the 'religion of Java'. It was built just as another
religion, Islam, appeared on the scene and was in fact buried by
Javanese Buddhists during Islam's penetration of the East Indies.
Discovered by an English colonel during the brief British seizure of
Indonesia from the Dutch during the Napoleonic Wars (1811-16)
it was excavated and restored under the supervision of Sir Thomas
Stamford Raffles, then Lieutenant-Governor of Indonesia and later
founder of Singapore. When you stand on Borobudur you touch the
physical evidence of Indonesia's ancient history.

An hour's drive away is even more ancient history. In 1891 the
bones of 'Java man' (Pithecanthropus erectus) were discovered near
what is now the city of Solo. We do not know what happened to
the Java men, although we have no reason for believing, especially in view of the later reputation of their island-home as a breeding
ground for the human race, that they did not multiply. But the evidence of the bones has convinced anthropologists that one of the
earliest races of mankind began in this Indonesian island. The direct
ancestors of today's Indonesians came to the archipelago hundreds of
centuries later, first as a negrito race now found in only a few parts
of Africa, southern Asia and Australia, and then in waves of people
belonging to the Malay-Polynesian language group. They arrived
over an unknown period of centuries before the birth of Christ.

Java has been civilized longer than England, for these people practised complicated techniques of rice cultivation and developed from
them forms of social organization. The climate of central Java, with
its hot, even temperature, plentiful rainfall and volcanic soil, was
ideal for the wet-field method of rice growing, known as *sawah*
cultivation, and the society it demanded may explain why the
Javanese developed a more sophisticated civilization than the inhabitants of the other islands. On islands with less favourable climate
and soil, dry-field or *ladang* rice cultivation, in which the fields are
prepared by burning down forest, was used. No elaborate social
structure was necessary for this simple agriculture, which was also
migratory.

The Javanese, at any rate, apparently began to live in towns and
cities close to their rice fields well before the time of Christ. Little
is known of the lives of these early Indonesians. They grew rice,
worked metal—bronze, copper and gold—and had a knowledge of
the stars and navigation. They lived in co-operative communities,
perhaps even at that stage organized as bureaucratic states imposed

on the village headmen. The people were animists, believing in the liveliness of inanimate objects as well as trees and living creatures, and practising ancestor and spirit worship. Terraced hillsides, topped by small stone pyramids and rough wooden or stone figures, which were used as places of worship, have been found in east Java and south Sumatra. The chants and ritual dances which invoked ancestral souls can still be traced in folk masques and plays. Most important, the social and religious duties of the rice-growing communities were gradually refined to form a body of behaviour which became the basis of *adat*, or customary law. *Adat* has persisted through successive waves of imported religious and social beliefs—Hinduism, Buddhism, Islam and 350 years of Dutch overlordship—and remains today a force in Indonesian culture.

Without written records, it has been difficult for scholars to agree about the strength of this civilization; whether, in fact, it was a civilization or merely isolated tribal societies which flowered under civilizing influences from the outside. 'Whoever approaches the history of Indonesia enters into an unknown world', wrote the Dutch historian J. C. van Leur, who nevertheless trenchantly argued, before his death at the age of thirty-four in the World War II battle of the Java Sea, that the basis of Indonesian civilization was laid before the first outside influence, Hinduism, came from India around the time of Christ. Van Leur, who based his approach on the work of the German sociologist Max Weber, fought a running battle with some of the most respected Dutch scholars. But modern scholarship, especially in America, has tended to support him, as, of course, has nationalist sentiment in Indonesia. The distinction between being 'primitive' and being 'civilized' has become blurred as we have become less dependent on criteria of material wealth.

What is certain is that by the first century A.D. trade with other parts of Asia, however motivated and managed, was firmly established. A report in the court annals of the Chinese Han Emperor Wang Mang (1-23 A.D.) tells of a mission sent to 'Huang-tche' or Atjeh in northern Sumatra, to acquire a rhinoceros for the Imperial Zoological Garden. In 166 A.D. Indian and Indonesian 'embassies' were in China, at the same time that a representative of Marcus Aurelius arrived in the Celestial Kingdom. Numerous pieces of Han Dynasty ceramics excavated in south Sumatra, west Java and east Borneo suggest that a vigorous trade existed with China in the first century. Apart from rhinoceros horn, prized by the Chinese as an aid to potency, gold and precious stones found their way to China and silk cloth came back. The early trade with India, which was probably more active, involved spices, drugs, expensive woods and exotic birds. In Edward Gibbon's description, it was a trade 'splendid and trifling' and it linked India, China and Indonesia with the ancient world of Greece and Rome.

Religion and culture followed trade. The increasing influence of Brahmin priests in Indonesian courts during the first centuries A.D. brought with it the art of writing, which for the first time made the civilization 'vocal'. The oldest works of Hindu art so far discovered, in Celebes (now called Sulawesi) and Sumatra, are statues of Buddha which date from the third century, and the earliest inscriptions, in Sanscrit, are of the beginning of the fifth century in east Borneo. The ruler mentioned in the inscriptions presumably governed a kingdom in which Hindu culture was superimposed on an Indonesian framework of customs and beliefs, because sacrificial animal pillars, common in old Indonesian cults, are mentioned. Another inscription of the same period, at the foot of mountains south of today's Djakarta, is surrounded by two sets of footprints—those of the king, 'the powerful ruler, the illustrious Purnavarman, King of Taruma, whose footsteps are like those of Vishnu', and those of the king's elephant.

But until about 700 A.D. information about life comes mainly from Chinese court chronicles, which tell of the tribute offered by 'Kings of the Southern Islands', and from reports of Chinese Buddhist scholars who visited the Indonesian islands on their way to India, adding their influence to the Buddhist doctrines and practices which were already arriving from India. In 414 A.D. Fah Hsien, a Buddhist pilgrim, visited the island of 'Ye-p'o-t'i', probably a transliteration of Yavadvipa, or Java, and commented that only a few of its inhabitants were followers of Buddha. A sixth-century Chinese traveller, describing probably a coastal state in the vicinity of Kedah on the Malayan peninsula, wrote, 'The king half-reclines on a golden bed in the form of a dragon. The nobles in his retinue are on their knees before him, their bodies erect and their arms crossed in such a way that their hands lie on their shoulders. At his court one sees many . . . Brahmins who came from India to profit from his munificence and are much in his favour.' I-Tsing, a pilgrim, stayed for four years some time between 671 and 692 on his way home from India at 'Bhoga', a city on an island in the 'Southern Ocean', and found 'more than one thousand Buddhist priests studying and working'.

This island was probably Sumatra, because its early Hindu kingdoms, first Malayu and, by the seventh century, Shrivajaya, were

centres of Buddhist learning and regular stopping places for pil-
grims, as well as being important trading states. The Sumatran
coastal state of Shrivajaya was perhaps the first of the great Indonesian commercial sea powers, handling the international trade of
South-east Asia under the royal authority of rulers who demanded
tribute from overseas dependencies and controlled the Strait of
Malacca.

In Java, on the other hand, Buddhist influence was much slighter,
and the major central Javanese state of Mataram, which was supreme
between the eighth and tenth centuries, remained predominantly
Hindu, although its kings were related to Shrivajaya's rulers. Shrivajaya's trade brought it wealth, but Mataram possessed greater manpower, and the two states seem to have been both rivals and partners,
crowning their partnership with the erection of Borobudur, for
which they enlisted the help of artists from India.

At this stage in Indonesia's history, two types of state had emerged.
One, typified by Shrivajaya, was coastal and commercial, based on
the international trade. Smaller, without the reserves of manpower
available in Java, these coastal principalities, found mainly in Sumatra, did not build monuments like Borobudur to their greatness.
But they seem to have been wealthy and predatory. Van Leur describes the city of Shrivajaya, on a foundation of stilts in the Palembang River like many towns in the region today, as 'turbulent and
cosmopolitan'. In the tenth century, Shrivajaya shipped as presents
to the Emperor of China ivory, frankincense, rose-water, dates, preserved peaches, white sugar, crystal rings, coral, rhinoceros horn,
perfumes and condiments. Glass bottles, naphtha and cotton cloth
were trans-shipped; it was clearly a centre on the world trade routes.
One authority supposes that Tamil, Persian, Arabic and Greek would
have been heard in its market-place and a twelfth-century visitor
described 'eight hundred money changers' apparently busily engaged.
Supported by this active commerce, a tight aristocracy seems to have
ruled, with a display of warships and warriors. One twelfth-century
report describes the funeral of a ruler who is followed in death on
the pyre by his retinue. Mercenaries of the Shrivajaya kingdom
served as far afield as Persia and Mesopotamia.

The second kind of state was situated inland, especially on the
plains of Java separated by volcanoes from the sea; Mataram was
based on the Solo River region. If the Sumatran coastal principalities
recall the Phoenician city states, these inland Javanese states are
reminiscent of the mountain fastnesses of early Peru and Mexico.
Relying on an agrarian civilization, they were bureaucratic and con-

servative, with already a marked capacity to absorb and transform the Indian influences. One of east Java's inland rulers had the Indian epic the *Mahabharata* translated into East Javanese in the eleventh century, and it was later rewritten, using Javanese customs and settings, and introducing new characters such as the buffoon Semar, who as the guardian spirit of the Javanese people has become one of the major figures in the *wayang* (the Indonesian theatre). The kings of Kadiri, in east Java, stopped using the Hindu title Maharajah and adopted the Javanese title *Panji*. Temple architecture began to show local forms of design. This is the period when Javanese culture comes into its own, spreading its influence to Bali, where the courts began to use the Javanese language in preference to their own, and to culturally separate Sunda (west Java) where east Javanese styles and titles were imitated.

Kadiri is remembered today for the famous prophecy attributed to its soothsayer King Jayabaya, who predicted in one popular version that 'a white buffalo will come to rule Java, and will remain for a long time; he will be supplanted by a yellow monkey, who will remain only for the lifetime of the maize plant; then, after a period of chaos, Java will come back to its own people'. The Indonesian sociologist Seloseomardjan in *Social Changes in Jogjakarta* says the prophecies, in which the buffalo was believed to represent the Dutch and the monkey the Japanese, were 'an inexhaustible source of spiritual strength and faith' to the Javanese during the Japanese occupation of 1942-5, and the subsequent military attempts by the Dutch to return. Sutan Sjahrir, nationalist leader and intellectual, mentions the prophecies during the period before the Japanese occupation in his autobiographical *Out of Exile;* he was unhappy that they should have been so widely believed. Another of Jayabaya's predictions is that momentous events are destined in years whose digits are reversible. Nothing happened as far as is known in 1691 and 1881, but as 1961 approached a ripple of half-believed gossip spread in Indonesia about impending national catastrophes.

When modern Indonesians refer to the glories of their past, they are certain to mention Majapahit. Founded in 1293 with its capital on the Brantas River in east-central Java, it lasted almost a century and is now described in Indonesian schools as Indonesia's Golden Age, comparable with the Elizabethan Age of England and the Tang Dynasty of China. The most powerful personality of its history was not a king but a prime minister or *patih* named Gajah Mada, whose fame as a unifier of Indonesia has made him one of the symbols of the present Indonesian Republic. He codified the laws and customs of the kingdom, and the administration he established was so solidly based that it remained essentially the same into the nineteenth century. The name Gajah Mada is said to mean 'an elephant; powerful, impassioned, but with wisdom unswayed by passion'. The university established by the Republic of Indonesia at Jogjakarta is named after him as is one of Djakarta's main streets, in homage to the last man until President Sukarno to unite 'Indonesia' under a single ruler.

Much of the information about Gajah Mada and Majapahit comes from a history by the court poet Prapanca. It is unreliable, being a paean of praise as much as a record of events, but the rise of Majapahit called for lofty phrases. In addition to conquering Bali and establishing a Javanese dynasty on the island, Majapahit's army enthroned a new king, Adityavarman, in Malayu (Sumatra), who actually ruled with relative independence and laid the foundations of the kingdom of Minangkabau. Prapanca includes among Majapahit's vassal states almost all the coastal districts of the archipelago—west, east and north Sumatra, south, west and north Borneo, Celebes, Moluccas, Sumbawa and Lombok, and reports that areas which neglected their tribute were 'visited' by Javanese fleets. Timor sent tribute, and after a fierce struggle the Sundanese kingdom of west Java was conquered. In addition, Prapanca says that Majapahit maintained regular relations with China, Champa (Vietnam), Cambodia, Annam and Siam. He also describes a royal dinner at which the king sang—'lovable as the call of the peacock sitting in a tree, sweet as a mixture of honey and sugar, touching as the scraping noise of the reeds'—and acted in a masquerade, the king's uncle played in the *gamelan* (Indonesian orchestra), and the queen sang while wearing 'a funny wig'.

By the time Gajah Mada's last king died in 1389, twenty-five years after his prime minister, Majapahit was in decline. The cause may have been malaria and its related fevers, which upset many of these ancient kingdoms. Or it may have been the removal of a strong personal influence, needed to extract support from the hard-worked people and land of central Java for the grand strategies of the courts, with their machinery of officialdom and heavy establishment of priesthood, their armies and their expensive diplomatic habits, such as the gift of pearls (and slaves) to powerful neighbours. The coastal dependencies in northern Java rebelled against the administrative hierarchy and began themselves paying tribute to China, taking up arms against Majapahit to support their independence. At this time, too, the first penetrations of a three-fold invasion—Islam, Chinese settlers and European explorers—had taken place in the archipelago, and the stage was set for a new and startling development in Indonesia's history.

The first part of the East Indies in which Islam took hold was northern Sumatra, where traders from Gujarat (the west coastal Indian State) stopped on their way to the Moluccas and China. Settlements of Arab traders were mentioned on the west coast of Sumatra as early as 674 A.D., but religion followed trade at a distance. In 1292 Marco Polo noted that the inhabitants of the town of Perlak on Sumatra's north tip had been converted to Islam, adding, on rather slender knowledge, that it was 'the only Islamic place in the archipelago'. Islam spread steadily; the first Muslim states were Atjeh, in northern Sumatra, and Malayu. By the time of Majapahit's final collapse at the beginning of the sixteenth century, many of its old satellites had declared themselves independent Muslim states, enriched by their position as trans-shipment points for the growing spice trade with India and China.

The Moluccas had begun their fabled story as 'the spice islands' at the beginning of the twelfth century. They had nothing to offer except their clove and nutmeg trees, which originally grew nowhere else. The trade was monopolized until the fifteenth century by the Gujarati, who had been introduced to Islam by Persian merchants in the ninth century, but the Moluccas natives were not socially organized and appeared uninterested in the new religion. Another port affected by this spice trade was Malacca, on the Malayan peninsula. Its rulers accepted Islam in the fourteenth century and by the sixteenth century it was the principal port of the region. A European traveller to Malacca in the sixteenth century guessed that more ships harboured there—the large vessels ranging between two hundred and four hundred tons—than in any other port in the world.

A new Muslim kingdom—the last Javanese power—arose in the region of present-day Jogjakarta, calling itself Mataram after the great Hindu state. Also, by the end of the sixteenth century a naval power had risen in the archipelago—the twin principalities of Makassar and Gowa in south-west Celebes, which had been settled by Malay traders who sailed to Johore, the Moluccas and later to 'Australia'. The Australian historian C. M. H. Clark in the first volume of his *A History of Australia* says that the establishment of a Muslim kingdom at Makassar brought Islam 'to the frontiers of civilization, from which, if they had pushed further . . . they would have moved on into New Guinea and from there across to the north coasts of Australia. They had begun to do this just when the coming of the European ended the spread of Islam, for when Torres first sailed through the strait which still bears his name, in 1607, he met Moors in west New Guinea.' According to missionary reports from Arnhem Land, Matthew Flinders met some of a fleet from Makassar while charting the Arnhem Land coast in 1803. Their ancestors are said to have been visiting the coast for hundreds of years and to have introduced the aborigines to steel, pottery and tobacco.

As with Hinduism and Buddhism centuries earlier, Islam was accepted gracefully. It was not the austere religion of the Middle East but a mystic, salvation-conscious variant called Sufism, brought to India from Persia. It seems to have fitted without doctrinal upheaval into the animist beliefs of Indonesia's *agama* and the mystic Tibetan Tantrism into which Java's Buddhism and Shivaism had merged. The syncretic result was tolerant of all the gods. It saw Buddha, Brahma, Vishnu and the Javanese messiah Erucakra as equal principals of order, manifested in kings in the world of men. It was tolerant, too, of Islam, which had only one God, not to be reproduced in graven imagery; Islam responded amiably by permitting its sultans to be worshipped as saints after death. Islam at times showed its fire in the Indonesian chapter of its world saga, but its success in adapting to local conditions is one reason why today it maintains at least a nominal hold over ninety per cent of the population. It was also spurred by a holy, bloody war with the foreign, Catholic Portuguese and a commercial struggle with the foreign, Protestant Dutch.

First reports of Chinese settlements in the archipelago come from the end of the thirteenth century, referring perhaps to the descendants of shipwrecked sailors. In 1382 a fleet of the first Ming emperor found a Chinese pirate ruling Palembang (whom they arrested and took back to China). These were the scattered beginnings of Chinese immigration in Indonesia. The immigrants, usually men, married local women but maintained their own customs and language. They did not play a major part in determining the course of Indonesian history, but they grew in private economic power until, with the tacit consent of the Dutch, they became the middlemen of the economy. Their clash with the new Indonesian nationalism is still in process.

Marco Polo and a few early missionary-travellers aside, the first Europeans to visit Indonesia were the Portuguese, spearheaded by Vasco da Gama, who came to the east to find the spice islands and to crusade against the 'Moors'. In 1511 Alfonso d'Albuquerque conquered Malacca, which was then paying homage to China, be-

ginning a tradition of terrible European blunders: he captured and
looted all Muslim vessels he encountered; he demanded that the
Sultan of Malacca let him build a Portuguese fort; when he built the
fort, he destroyed Muslim graves for building materials; and he sum-
marily executed the leading Javanese trader. This and subsequent
Portuguese behaviour made St Francis Xavier say that their knowledge was restricted to the conjugation of the verb *rapio* (to steal), in
which they showed 'amazing capacity for inventing new tenses and
participles'. Not surprisingly, they could not get local support for
their ambitions in the spice islands, although until 1641 when
Malacca fell in turn to the Dutch they had some successes, building
forts on Ternate and Ambon in the Moluccas and obtaining a temporary monopoly of the clove trade and a share in the west Javanese
state of Bantam's pepper trade. The Portuguese were surprised at the
sophistication and size of Indonesian arms. When d'Albuquerque
took Malacca after a long battle, he found three thousand artillery
pieces, including two thousand bronze cannon. The Sultan of Atjeh
was sent skilled artillery troops and guns and ammunition by the
Turks to fight the Portuguese.

In June 1596, Holland made its appearance on the scene when
four Dutch ships sailed along Sumatra's west coast and anchored at
Bantam, on the western tip of Java. The commander, Cornelius de
Houtman, concluded a treaty of friendship after finding all of Ban-
tam's trading community kindly disposed. A Dutch account of
Bantam at that time gives a lively picture:

> There came such a multitude of Javanese and other nations as
> Turks, Chinese, Bengali, Arabs, Persians, Gujarati, and others
> that one could hardly move . . . they . . . came so abundantly
> that each nation took a spot on the ships where they displayed
> their goods the same as if it were on a market. Of which the
> Chinese brought of all sorts of silk woven and unwoven, spun and
> unspun, with beautiful earthenware, with other strange things
> more. The Javanese brought chickens, eggs, ducks, and many
> kinds of fruits. Arabs, Moors, Turks, and other nations of people
> each brought of everything one might imagine.

Within three years Dutch ships frequented the archipelago, trading
with the Moluccas and finding acceptance everywhere except in
Madura and in Atjeh, where de Houtman was later killed.

Dutch trade expanded quickly because the Indonesian sultans enjoyed the higher prices which Dutch-Portuguese competition brought,
and also because Portuguese attempts to drive out the Dutch were

thwarted by a British blockade of Lisbon. Indeed, the Indonesian attitude was so unsuspicious that a Balinese king wrote to the 'king of Holland' expressing the wish that 'Bali and Holland should become one' (a Balinese expression meaning they should have a close alliance), and presented a Dutch admiral with a nubile girl. The first Indonesian visit to Holland occurred at about this time, when the king of Atjeh, after concluding a trade agreement with the Dutch, sent two ambassadors to the Netherlands.

But unlike the Buddhist-Hindu and Muslim penetrations of Indonesia, which were peaceful and left lasting effects, the impact of Europe was violent and had little cultural influence. We are accustomed to speak of the Netherlands' three hundred and fifty years in Indonesia as if it were an established period; in fact only the beginnings and the end are clear. Throughout the seventeeth century the Dutch East India Company with its superior arms and Buginese and Ambonese mercenaries (who had transferred their service from Java's kings) fought off attacks everywhere in the islands.

Probably the Dutch action which brought a major confrontation between the Company and the Javanese and began the Indonesian hostility which ceased only at the end of Dutch rule was the founding of Batavia at the town of Yacatra in 1619. This provided the only fruition during his lifetime of the great schemes of Jan Pieterszoon Coen, who had become the Company's 'Governor-General of the Indies' the year before. (His other ideas included the monopolization of the spice trade, the conquest of Manila and Macao, using Japanese mercenary soldiers offered by the emperor of Japan, the takeover of spice production by Dutch settlers and colonists from Madagascar, Burma and China, who would be kidnapped if necessary—he preferred Chinese as 'industrious and unwarlike'—and the complete annihilation of Asian and rival European shipping.)

As a first step he ordered the Company storehouse at Yacatra to be secretly fortified, because he thought the English, who were losing their competition with the Dutch for trading advantage in the region, were about to attack his fleet. The prince of Yacatra discovered the fortification, built a battery opposite (by the sixteenth century the Javanese were casting their own cannon and making their own muskets, bullets and powder, though reported not to be very good at their use), and asked the English for help. Coen attacked first, conquering the battery and burning down Yacatra's English tradingpost. Then, with a fleet and a thousand troops, he burned down the town—losing only one man—and occupied its land for the Company, building a bigger fort and a small Dutch town complete with today's canals. He called it Batavia after the Germanic tribe the Batavi, who fought the Romans and settled in Europe's lowlands.

Years of warfare followed, with Bantam and Mataram united in their attempt to conquer Batavia. In addition to their muskets, the Javanese foot-soldiers were armed with *kris* (swords with undulating blades) and shields, and the cavalry used long pikes, guiding their horses with knees and body so as to have both hands free for fighting. The soldiers wore armour of buffalo hide and coats of mail, and marched behind royal banners and pennants which they believed had a magical significance. During the first siege of Batavia, the tide of battle was temporarily turned by the favourite Javanese military tactic of amok-running. During the second siege the Javanese armies spent thirty days trying unsuccessfully to build a river dam to cut off Batavia's drinking water. They also sent the Dutch letters of challenge to battle in traditional form, containing huge exaggerations of the number, strength and imperviousness to wounds of the attackers, describing the terrible destruction to follow and declaiming the greatness of the kingdoms, their rulers and their historical conquests. Gongs, drums and shouting were used during advances as another tactic of intimidation. Finally, Sultan Agung of Mataram called his whole empire to the colours for the third siege, and 'tens of thousands' slowly gathered around Batavia. Unfortunately, this so terrified the sultan of Bantam that he made peace with the Dutch. Sultan Agung continued his preparations, but the troops had to be supplied by sea and the Dutch destroyed two hundred rice-laden Javanese ships so that when the army finally attacked, it was near starvation and was forced to retreat after five weeks of siege.

Some of the above information comes from the *Babad Tanah Djawi*, which was written by Sultan Agung's court poets and revised and enlarged several times during the seventeenth and eighteenth centuries. Its name means 'The Clearing of Java' and it has been called a mixed history and Javanese creation myth. In it, Mataram's defeat at Batavia was transformed into a tale in which the leader of the Mataram armies was a traitor to the sultan, and the Dutch in killing him served the sultan's will, then sending an embassy to the court of Mataram (which in fact they did, after the battle) to thank Sultan Agung for his spiritual leadership. The Dutch historian Vlekke comments: 'The interpretation made Batavia a vassal state of Mataram and it also made further violence unnecessary. The Dutch may have attributed the end of the fighting to their own prowess, but the Javanese attributed it to the fact that their superiority had been acknowledged.' The *Babad* also turned Coen into a hero of Javanese descent, named Mur Jangkung, whose mother was a princess of the old Hindu Mataram and whose father was a brother of 'Sikender', the Javanese name for Alexander the Great, who symbolized the 'western conqueror'. (The Minangkabau genealogy also incorporates Alexander, as 'Iskandar'.)

In the eighteenth century, until its charter expired on 31 December 1899 and its affairs, in a state of deterioration, were taken over by the Netherlands government, the Company was forced to defend its trading privileges against constant attack. Although the Dutch created a close alliance with the west Javanese princes—who were now called regents and appointed by the Governor-General—important areas of Indonesia remained independent, including Bali, Lombok, Atjeh and Borneo.

Even on Java the Dutch found the situation by no means in control. Unrest continued into the nineteenth century and a revolt was sparked in 1825, turning into a full-scale war when its leadership was taken by Prince Diponegoro, son of the first Sultan of Jogjakarta. Diponegoro had frequented religious schools and meditated on the Koran in sacred caves. As a religious mystic of royal blood he was an ideal Javanese leader and the people told stories of him as a 'Prince Liberator' with a magic sword, who would free them. From the hills of central and east Java Diponegoro conducted a guerilla war, which the Russian ambassador in Brussels described to his government: 'They avoid battles with the troops and have adopted a plan of undermining the strength of the Europeans with the help of the unhealthy climate and fatigue. Such a method of warfare may in the end give them superiority.' The Dutch recruited additional soldiers from Holland as well as troops from Madura, north Celebes and Surakarta (now Solo), but were unable to overcome the rebels, who routed several Dutch attacks. During this period the Hague seriously considered abandoning Java.

After five years of fighting the Dutch captured Diponegoro's closest adviser and the prince offered to negotiate. In March 1830 he went by appointment to one of the Dutch generals and was arrested and deported to Makassar where he died in exile twenty-five years later. There are no official records of the 'Java War' casualties but it has been estimated that two hundred thousand Javanese were killed as well as eight thousand Dutch and seven thousand of their Indonesian mercenaries. Diponegoro became not only a Javanese but a national hero and Jogjakarta gained a reputation as a stronghold of Javanese independence which was upheld by its activities in the post-World War II fight with the Dutch, under the leadership of the present Sultan of Jogjakarta, a direct descendant of Diponegoro. Today one of Djakarta's most elegant streets lined with the homes of government officials and foreign diplomats is named Diponegoro, and the girls' dormitory of Gajah Mada University in Jogjakarta is named after the prince's wife.

In the middle of the nineteenth century piracy was still rampant and the Dutch fought a war in Celebes against a Buginese queen who had ordered her ships to fly the Dutch flag upside-down. Fighting continued to flare up in Sumatra and Java. From 1846 to 1849 a series of expeditions were made to Bali where the Balinese, still independent, had gathered an army of thirty thousand with arms purchased in Singapore. The Dutch won several victories but were always forced to retreat, and in 1849 they agreed not to occupy Bali or interfere in its internal affairs in return for an acknowledgment by its rajahs of Dutch 'authority'. There was also a violent war in southeast Borneo, the 'Bandjarmasin War', in which the Dutch bested the sultan.

But the longest and most devastating of all the Dutch wars in Indonesia was the one with the Sumatran state of Atjeh, which had remained independent under British protection (Singapore and Atjeh had an active trade). In 1871, the Dutch negotiated a new treaty with the British in which England withdrew objections to a possible Dutch occupation of Atjeh. In 1872 Atjenese envoys began negotiations with the Italian and United States Consuls in Singapore, and the draft of an American-Atjenese treaty of friendship was sent to Washington. The Dutch forestalled further developments by declaring war on Atjeh in 1873. A Dutch army of seven thousand retreated when its commander was killed and a new expedition twice as large met with no more success. The war went on for thirty-five years, until 1908 when the last guerilla leaders surrendered.

Between 1900 and 1910 south-west Celebes was occupied by Dutch troops as part of a policy of 'pacification of the outer islands', and more than two hundred and fifty rulers throughout Indonesia were forced to sign over their rights to Batavia, including those of Bali, which the Dutch finally occupied in 1906. But by this time the first 'nationalist' movements, which were to lead to the Republic of Indonesia, had begun.

From the outside, especially from the colonizing vantage point of Europe, the East Indies were a tropical archipelago of warring tribes which could be subdued or seduced, if not easily, in the great games of trade and religion. To the self-conscious Indonesian of today, however, they are a back-projection of the modern nation.

Every evidence of organized resistance to the invader is proof of today's national spirit. Evidence of absorption is proof of today's national tolerance. Indonesian leaders refer to the 'once prosperous and vast empires' of Shrivajaya and Majapahit or, if they are Sumatran, probably to Malayu, as proof of the standing of Indonesians before they were reduced to penury by the Dutch. It is not surprising, Sukarno told the United Nations General Assembly in 1960 when explaining the traditions behind his ideas for modern Indonesia, that 'concepts of great strength and virility have risen in our nation during the two thousand years of civilization and during the centuries of strong nationhood before imperialism engulfed us in a moment of weakness'.

CHAPTER TWO

The Nation

The first stirrings of Indonesian nationalism are usually dated from the time, about the turn of the century, when the Dutch finally 'pacified' the entire archipelago. It is as if the invader, having laboriously established the outline of his territorial possessions in the East Indies, provided the people for the first time with a definite area by which to assert their rights to national independence. In the world outside, especially as shown in Asia by the nationalist developments in India and China and, in particular, Japan's military defeat of Russia in 1905, the time was ripening for the huge shifts of power against the Europe-centred world domination that are still in process today. In the East Indies themselves, various factors provided the groundwork for the slow and by no means confident nationalist movement of the next half century. Islam, as the professed belief of some ninety per cent of the population, became, in effect, a popular gesture of unity against the Christian overlord. The Malay tongue became a national language, having been elevated from the bazaars by the colonial authorities who used it in administration as a means of keeping Indonesians from acquiring the status symbol of Dutch. Improvements in transport and the development of press and radio made it possible for the idea of nationalism to be given an audience, as Sukarno quickly discovered.

There was also the incalculable quality of the Dutch themselves. The spectacle of European colonialism is astonishing in retrospect; the arrogance of the 1494 Treaty of Tordesillas with Portugal and Spain, two sides of a small European peninsula, seriously dividing the world into two spheres of interest, is only a little more unreal to contemplate in today's world than the thought of France's vast possessions or the far flung empire of Britain. But no conquest is more difficult to appreciate than that of the Dutch in tropical Asia. The virtues that made the Netherlands the most ardently-worked plot of land in Europe—thrift, care, cleanliness and attention to detail—were lost in the sprawling plenitude of the East Indies.

Holland is about one-quarter the size of Java, or half the size of Tasmania, and the flatness of its skyline, bringing suburbia within reach of everyone's bicycle, was hardly a preparation for pioneering one of the most mountainous and erratic landscapes in the world. To travel today in Indonesia is to be impressed with the administrative difficulty of running the archipelago from the island of Java. The Dutch eventually did it with sea power, for which they had to thank the industrial revolution and, after the Napoleonic wars, the connivance of the British. But on the land of the islands themselves, they were conspicuously out of place. The tall blond invader strode among the small brown people like someone from another world.

Dutch colonization of the East Indies followed the pattern of Africa rather than Asia, with settlers rather than absentee landlords. Before World War II there were about 250,000 Dutch living in Indonesia and although a probable majority were Eurasian the figure is still high by comparison with the experience of other Asian colonial territories. The number of Dutch in Java, for example, was almost the equivalent of all the British in India. Some Dutchmen and their families came to treat the colony as their homeland, with the unfortunate effect of denying the same emotions to the indigenes. At the apex of the power pyramid, with the Chinese interposed as economic middlemen, the Hollander ruled indirectly, through the traditional forms of village government. His prejudices were evident but he was not a fanatic, either religious or political. He showed no anxiety to divert the Indonesians from their mysterious spiritual sources nor to convert them from their pre-capitalist agricultural habits, with some regional exceptions. When the great naturalist Alfred Russel Wallace visited the Dutch East Indies in the 1870s he described Java as the 'richest, best cultivated and best governed tropical island in the world'.

But the love that bound the Dutch securely to the islands through three and a half centuries was that of money. It has been said that no colonial power developed its economy to rely on colonial possessions to the extent that the Dutch did in the case of the East Indies. At its pre-war trading peak the archipelago provided an income directly or indirectly to one in every seven Dutchmen, when Holland's population was about nine million. Before World War II the Indies were estimated to have supplied 90 per cent of the world's production of quinine, 86 per cent of the world's pepper, 75 per cent of its kapok, 37 per cent of its rubber, 28 per cent of its coconut-palm products, 19 per cent of its tea and 17 per cent of its tin as

well as sugar, coffee, oil and most of the world's cigar wrappers.
Holland's investment was about U.S.$1,422 million in 1940, earning
an annual $103 million in interest.

Psychologically, the Dutch dependence on the Indies was considerable. As Dr Herbert Feith makes the point: 'With the Indies,
Holland was the world's third or fourth colonial power; without
them it would be a cold little country on the North Sea'. Yet for all
their skill and perseverance, the Dutch impression on their rich and
varied possessions was oddly barren and unexciting. There is nothing
to compare with the romantic literature of imperialist England, and
accounts of the Dutch hegemony, though allowing credit for its remarkable pursuit of commerce, all tend to stress the humourless
propriety of the colonizers. Money-making aside, the Dutch in the
Indies seem to have been noted mostly for their consumption of food
and Dutch gin. Professor Clark writes:

> The Portuguese Catholics spoke of infinite merit: the Dutch
> Calvinists spoke of uncommonly large profit. There was something
> sensuous and elemental in their discussion of the uses to which
> they would put the spices from the Moluccas. They wanted pepper
> for food and for a physic, ginger because it made a man go easily
> to the stool . . . cloves because they strengthened the liver, the
> mouth and the heart, furthered digestion . . . preserved the sight,
> and four drams being drunk with milk, procured lust.

Some modern historians see the Dutch, with their Puritan attitude
to sex, as spiritual prisoners of the Indonesian women's insights.

The first Indonesian nationalist groups were organized around
education, reflecting a desire for social rather than political equality.
In 1902 Kartini, the daughter of a Javanese regent, founded a school
for daughters of Indonesian officials. In 1908 an organization called
Budi Utomo (High Endeavour) was formed; it sought to stimulate a
sense of national dignity through education. It received early support
from students at the Batavia Medical School; like women, physicians
had an unusual influence in the nationalist movement, probably
because they were independent and could move among the people,
and the number of medical doctors in responsible political posts today
is noticeable. Budi Utomo quickly gained members, but it was supported mainly by Javanese officials and aristocrats and looked to
India for philosophical guidance and for teachers. It never became a
mass movement.

A Eurasian founded the Indian Party in 1912 with the slogan
'The Indies for those who make their home here'. He was Eduard

F. E. Douwes Dekker, a great-nephew of the Dekker who in 1861 wrote *Max Havelaar,* a novel which exposed Dutch oppression in the Indies and is sometimes described as the *Uncle Tom's Cabin* of nineteenth-century Java. Douwes Dekker's grandparents were Dutch, French, German and Javanese, and the party was not surprisingly multi-racial. It opposed direct Dutch rule, advocating independence and racial equality. Its leaders were expelled from the country.

The first truly mass movement was Sarekat Islam (Islamic Association), which had its origins in a trading society formed in 1909 to protect Indonesians against Chinese dealers. In 1912 it began to expand under the chairmanship of Tjokroaminoto, a Surabaya businessman. Lenin noted the development of Islam in Indonesian nationalism at that time, which suggested to him links with the 1908 reformist Muslim revolt in Turkey and the emergence of an Indonesian capitalist intelligentsia. Sarekat Islam was soon to become the most significant of the early nationalist movements and although it proclaimed itself to be non-political for security reasons, it quickly attracted support well beyond its outward objectives. Also in 1912, the Mohammadijah, a modernist Islamic society devoted to education and social services, was founded.

In 1914 the Indies Social Democratic Association was created by Henrik Sneevliet, who had been a member of the Social Democratic Labour Party—later the Communist Party—in the Netherlands. This small Marxist group, which became the Indonesian Communist Party (Partai Kommunist Indonesia—PKI) penetrated the Sarekat Islam and influenced it towards a more revolutionary programme. A showdown came at the 1921 Sarekat Islam congress between the PKI faction led by Semaun and Tan Malaka—two names which recur in modern Indonesian history—and the moderates under Tjokroaminoto. The moderates included Agus Salim, another figure of lasting significance, who took the floor with the argument that Mohammed had preached socialism twelve centuries before Marx. The PKI faction lost and resigned en masse, setting up 'Red' Sarekat Islam branches in opposition.

The communists tried to establish revolutionary conditions along Marxist class lines and by the early 1920s had created unrest in the young trade union movement. Strikes were organized in urban businesses and in sugar factories, leading to revolts on Java in 1926 and among the Minangkabau of Sumatra in 1927. The Dutch suppressed the uprisings with considerable bloodshed and arrested some thirteen thousand Indonesians. Six thousand of them were imprisoned, detained as political prisoners, or deported.

The failure of the communists, coupled with the tough response of the administration, turned the nationalist movement momentarily away from political activity. The Taman Siswa (Garden of Pupils) movement, established in 1921, aimed at a school system based on a blend of Indonesian and western culture as Kartini's had been. Politics were forbidden, but the schools were responsible for the education of many who later joined the nationalists.

The Perhimpoenan Indonesia (Indonesian Union) was formed in 1922 by Indonesian students studying in Holland as a nationalist, leftist political group. Some of its members who had returned to Indonesia established the Partai Nasional Indonesia or Indonesian Nationalist Party (PNI) on 4 June 1927. The young Sukarno, who had not been to the Hague to study, was its chairman. The PNI became the most powerful nationalist organization in Indonesia and remains today one of the most influential parties in the country. In 1928 came the 'Vow of Youth', a declaration of support by the second Congress of Permuda Indonesia (Young Indonesia) for the red and white flag, the Indonesian language (Bahasa Indonesia, which is basically Malay) and the anthem 'Indonesia Raya' ('Greater Indonesia'), as the symbols of the nation.

The Dutch quickly recognized the threat in the PNI's growing strength and in 1930 Sukarno and three other PNI leaders went to jail for the first time. The PNI was outlawed and its membership split into factions. In 1932 two men who were to become famous Indonesian nationalists, Mohammed Hatta and Sutan Sjahrir, returned from university in Holland where Hatta had been president of the Indonesian Union. They joined Golongon Merdeka (Freedom Group)—the name was later changed to Pendidikan Nasional Indonesia (Indonesian National Education Club)—a small group devoted to building up an activist leadership. On his release, Sukarno joined Partai Indonesia (Partindo) which aimed at more of a mass following. In 1933 Sukarno was again arrested and exiled to Flores in the Lesser Sundas; the following year Hatta and Sjahrir were sent to Boven Digul concentration camp in New Guinea. None of the three leaders was freed until the Japanese invaded in 1942.

Sjahrir's book *Out of Exile* remains one of the best sources of this period not only because it is brilliantly readable but because, through the author's isolation, we have an insight into the feeling of some of the men who spent those long years in prison. Sjahrir was only twenty-five when he was arrested on the point of returning to his Dutch wife in Holland, and later sent to a camp for supposed violent revolutionaries. His subsequent career marked him as a moderate with a thoughtful and sensitive mind, and it is not surprising to find him wondering in a letter to his wife what exactly his offence is supposed to have been and where his sympathies lie. He was accused of 'spreading hate and endangering public tranquillity and order', but no precise charges were laid, a typical failing in precision which has not improved with the removal of the colonialists from Asia.

He is appalled at the spiritual disintegration of many of the prisoners at Boven Digul, some younger than himself. He wrote (in 1936 after he and Hatta had been moved to Banda Neira in the Moluccas where his mail was not censored) of an attempted suicide at Boven Digul. The man, a wealthy Christian from Menado in Celebes, had been at the camp for nine years. He was an early socialist and had been a member of Douwes Dekker's Indian Party. Sjahrir describes him as 'a fine and cultivated man with a real humanity in his character . . . I can still see him in my mind's eye, wearing his torn pajamas and digging in the intense heat of his garden'.

In one of the few flashes of bitterness in his book, Sjahrir turns on the Dutch officials at the camp, where he claims a majority of the inmates became mentally ill. It did not have the same degree of brutality as the concentration camps being established in Germany at the same time, but its terrible isolation in inland New Guinea and the social distance between the prisoners and their guards provided a different kind of torture. The Dutch had not 'the least idea of the mental suffering they are inflicting. The exiles are simply "trash, scum and criminal"; how could they possibly experience mental suffering? Such suffering is only for Europeans with their more highly developed souls and sensitivities!' At Digul also were the student and youth prisoners 'so completely idealistic, and the only thing with which they could be charged was making propaganda for their ideals'. Of the communists, who were sent to the camp after the uprisings in 1926-7, Sjahrir is surprised at their ordinariness, which he puts down to eight years of intellectual stagnation. 'It is a strange sort of Communism indeed, a mystical, Hinduistic-Javanese, Islamic-Minangkabau or Islamic-Bantam sort of Communism, with definite animistic tendencies. There are not many European Communists who would recognize anything of their Communism in this Indonesian variety!' Sjahrir himself was not unchanged by Boven Digul. 'I have acquired a certain hardness . . . the human being of Tolstoi and even of Gandhi, whom I had long held before my eyes, has left me. In reality, man is stupid, vulgar, cruel and brutal.'

With the arrest of its leadership the Indonesian nationalist movement developed a milder exterior and there was more of an effort to co-operate with the Dutch in the Volksraad or People's Council, a local assembly which had been set up in 1917 as an advisory influence on Dutch authority. But as the British diplomat-journalist Bruce Lockhart reported on a visit in 1936, there was an air of repressed nationalism throughout the Indies which contrasted with the amiable atmosphere in Malaya. He notes the heavy jollity of Dutch society in Batavia and the blandness of officialdom. He quotes the Dutch Governor-General, Jonkheer de Jonge, as telling him, 'I always preface my remarks to the nationalists with one sentence: "We Dutch have been here for three hundred years; we shall remain here for another three hundred. After that we can talk."' (Sjahrir quotes de Jonge as saying in a press interview, 'We have ruled here for three hundred years with the whip and the club, and we shall still be doing it in another three hundred years.', Lockhart records that on a visit to Makassar in Celebes to see the grave of Diponegoro, neither the Dutch Governor nor his Assistant Resident knew that the great Indonesian rebel leader was buried there, although the local Indonesians knew the exact spot with pride.

The reaction of the Dutch, accompanied by the international growth of fascism, caused the most articulate nationalist leaders, including Amir Sjarifuddin and Mohammed Yamin, to establish in 1937 a new party, Gerindo (Gerakan Rakyat Indonesia—Indonesian People's Movement). Gerindo was left-wing but like the Indian nationalist movement regarded its struggle as dependent on the outcome of the impending showdown with Germany and Japan. Its members tried to use the People's Council to gain self-government; in 1936 the council had called for a ten-year plan of orderly political development. But despite the efforts of a moderate, Mohammed Thamrin, who was mainly responsible for uniting eight of the major nationalist organizations including Gerindo in an effort to reach solidarity with the Dutch provided guarantees of self-determination were given, no sign of understanding came from the Hague. Right up to the war, and even after the Germans invaded Holland, the Indonesian nationalists were given no encouragement to believe that their co-operation was needed or their ultimate aims recognized. Nor was an effort made to increase their responsibility in governing the Indies as they were. In 1940 only 221 of the 3,039 top civil service positions in the administration were held by Indonesians.

The Japanese occupation of the Netherlands East Indies in 1942, following the quick Dutch collapse, was carried out at first to the accompaniment of local applause. The red and white bicolour was flown, Bahasa was spoken, 'Indonesia Raya' was sung; gestures of

Asian solidarity were made. Moreover, because all the Dutch administrators were interned, educated Indonesians were rapidly promoted. But it became clear after a few months that the Japanese were
not going to be any easier to get on with than the Dutch. Politically
they were more flexible, but partly because of the stress of war and
also, many Indonesians felt, because of their philosophy, they were
extremely cruel. Today the Japanese are welcome visitors to Indonesia, but the Indonesians still speak privately of the Japanese occupation with horror or contempt.

The nationalist leaders split their forces. Sukarno and Hatta, who
were the best known, worked above ground, collaborating with the
Japanese. Sjahrir led one underground group and Sukarni, who had
worked with the illegal PKI under Tan Malaka in the twenties, led
another. Among the members of Sukarni's group were Amir Sjarifuddin, who later declared his communist sympathies, and Chairul
Saleh, whose chequered career brought him finally to power as a
militant arm of the Sukarno régime. There was a third body of
younger men, often students, including Ruslan Abdulgani and Subandrio, both prominent in today's Indonesian politics, who kept in
touch with the underground groups. Sjahrir lived at his sister's house
in Tjipanas, among the mountains outside Batavia, supposedly because of ill-health; in fact the high altitude was good for radio
reception and it was from his secret receiver that the underground
was kept informed of the real state of the war. Sukarno, as chairman
of various Japanese-sponsored organizations to control Indonesian
manpower and enlist mass support for the war effort, and Hatta, in
charge of an advisory bureau on relations with the Indonesian
nationalists, lived in Djakarta.

The period of the Japanese occupation is immensely important in
the development of the nationalist movement, yet it is necessarily obscure and controversial. There is no doubt, however, that the movement gained strength. The Japanese, unlike the Dutch, sponsored
mass organizations, based on Islam and anti-western sentiment. Sukarno and Hatta were allowed to travel about addressing gatherings of
Indonesians and Sukarno in particular used the occasions to insinuate
nationalist propaganda into respectful addresses celebrating Hiro-
hito's birthday or a Japanese victory. In 1943 they were flown to
Tokyo to thank the Emperor for the creation of a consultative body,
with Sukarno as chairman, which made concessions to the nationalists. Professor George McTurnan Kahin, whose book *Nationalism
and Revolution in Indonesia* is the classic on this period, suggests
that the Japanese authorities on Java suspected at this time that Hatta

was not playing the game. They proposed that he should be detained in Japan and were greatly surprised when instead he was treated with Sukarno as an honoured guest and returned safely to Indonesia.

As the Imperial Army began to look to recruiting at the end of 1943, the Japanese in Indonesia formed the Volunteer Army of Defenders of the Fatherland, or Home Defence Corps (Soekarela Tentara Pembela Tanah Air, or Peta). Given their first opportunity to bear arms for their cause, Indonesians joined in large numbers. Sukarno and Hatta were allowed to address the recruits in the interests of the patriotic spirit and Peta soon became a hotbed of nationalism. In 1944 an armed revolt broke out at Blitar in east Java, and although it was bloodily suppressed by the Japanese a succession of smaller revolts followed. Anti-Japanese activity, especially by students, became more open.

In late 1944 and early 1945, as their military defeats continued, Japanese resistance to nationalist pressures weakened. The Indonesian leaders felt the change and from his Tjipanas hideout Sjahrir pressed the others for an uprising, an unconditional declaration of independence. Sukarno, however, believed that the Japanese might recover, and hesitated. But it was at this point (1 June 1945) that Sukarno made a speech announcing the *Pantja Sila,* the Five Principles. These principles (Faith in one God, Humanity, Nationalism, Representative Government and Social Justice) were the foundation on which Sukarno said an independent Indonesian nation was to be based. This remarkable speech angered the Japanese authorities. But it quickly became the blueprint of the nationalist movement and today still provides the ideological framework for the Indonesian State. It shows Sukarno at his best, as a formulator and expounder of ideas that are only vaguely in the minds of others. Professor Kahin comments, 'Probably in no other exposition of principle can one find a better example of the synthesis of Western democrat, Modernist Islamic, Marxist and indigenous-village democratic and communalistic ideas which form the several bases of the social thought of so large a part of the post-war Indonesian political élite'.

In introducing the *Pantja Sila* Sukarno did not define precisely the boundaries of the new Indonesia, and he brought into prominence problems of nationalism which his leadership throughout the years of independence failed to solve. He said,

> We will establish an Indonesian national state. . . . This is what we must all aim at: the setting up of one National State upon the unity of one Indonesian land from the tip of Sumatra right to Irian!

. . . the national state is only Indonesia in its entirety, which existed in the time of Shrivajaya and Majapahit, and which now, too, we must set up together . . . let us take as the first basis of our state: Indonesian Nationalism. Indonesian Nationalism in the fullest sense.

. . . But, but—undoubtedly there is a danger involved in this principle of nationalism. The danger is that men will possibly sharpen nationalism until it becomes chauvinism, and think of 'Indonesia über Alles'. This is the danger. We love one country, we feel ourselves one nation, we have one language. But our country, Indonesia, is only just a small part of the world.

. . . do not let us say that the Indonesian nation is the most perfect and the noblest whilst we belittle other people.

. . . We must proceed toward the unity of the world, the brotherhood of the world. We have not only to establish the state of Indonesia Merdeka, but we also have to proceed toward the familyhood of nations.

The *Pantja Sila* speech was made to a group of Indonesian leaders gathered by the Japanese to form a constitution for an independent Indonesia. Called the Body for Investigation of Indonesian Independence, or BPKI (Badan Penjelidik Kemerdekaan Indonesia), the group was at this time discussing the territorial boundaries to be claimed from the Japanese, who were still in control not only in the East Indies but throughout South-east Asia. After lengthy debate the sixty-six Indonesian members of the BPKI voted by secret ballot on the correct territorial definition of their proposed nation. There were three plans and the voting was as follows: 1. Former territories of the Netherlands East Indies and the territories of North Borneo, Brunei, Sarawak, Portuguese Timor, Malaya, New Guinea, and surrounding islands—39; 2. Former territory of the Netherlands East Indies—19; 3. Former territory of the Netherlands East Indies combined with Malaya and omitting New Guinea—6. (Two votes were informal.)

The debate as recorded by Mohammed Yamin, a close colleague of Sukarno's, in a book published in 1959 shows Sukarno as leader of the Greater Indonesia faction, while Hatta supported the second plan and was prepared even to drop New Guinea. Sukarno championed the cause of Pan Indonesia even to the extent of technically including the Philippines; he recognized, however, that as an already independent country it should have its sovereignty respected. Yamin felt that Indonesia's boundaries should be based on the German concept of culture and soil (*Kultur und Boden*) and defined the area by references to the old empires of Shrivajaya and Majapahit. Sukarno also showed special interest in Malaya, producing to one of the meetings some Malays who had come to offer allegiance. He argued that Indonesia could not be secure unless both sides of the Strait of Malacca were in her hands. In spite of the majority feeling of the meeting the Japanese seem to have influenced the nationalists to accept the second plan, but the discussions are important for the attitudes they reveal and for the glimpse of an historical point in time when 'nationalists' had to think precisely of the 'nation' they intended to liberate.

By August 1945 Tokyo was prepared to promise independence and Sukarno and Hatta went to Japanese regional command head-quarters in Dalat (South Vietnam) to receive the news. When they returned they found the underground movement determined not to wait but to rise against the Japanese. Sjahrir, with his radio tuned to outside reports of an armistice, urged a revolutionary declaration of independence, but Sukarno and Hatta still hoped for a peaceful transfer of power. In the early morning of 16 August a group of impatient students kidnapped Sukarno, his wife and children, and Hatta, and took them to a stronghold outside Djakarta. The two leaders learned that the Japanese had surrendered the day before and as mere agents of the Allies could not grant independence. After an all-night discussion on the text of a declaration a small group gathered at 10 a.m. on 17 August at Sukarno's house, 56 Pengang-saan Timur in Djakarta. The red and white flag was hoisted and the Republic of Indonesia was proclaimed.

Several versions of the 'kidnapping' episode exist. One creates the impression that Sukarno was more or less forced at pistol point to declare Indonesia's independence. The other, which was outlined by Aidit, the present PKI leader, in an interview with Arnold C. Brackman, American journalist and author of *Indonesian Com-munism*, is that a form of 'consultation' took place; Aidit also stresses the caution of Hatta rather than Sukarno. But common to all ver-sions is the conflict between the 'underground' and the 'collaborators'; traces of this conflict remained long after the issues they reflected had been resolved.

After Sjahrir had sounded out the feeling of the people and had become convinced of the genuine popular loyalty towards the Sukarno-Hatta leadership, the anti-Japanese underground groups swung their support behind the Republic. Sjahrir was its first prime minister, Sjarifuddin its second. The Republic had a constitution, a national committee of 135 men, which later became a legislative assembly, and a cabinet responsible to the president who was, of course, Sukarno. Hatta was vice-president.

For six weeks the Indonesian Republic, with a government of sixteen ministers formed on 31 August, sparred with the Japanese authorities. Intermittent fighting took place as rearguard nationalist army units tried to arm themselves from the Japanese, but when the first British troops landed at Djakarta on 20 September, the situation was calm, with the Republic's administration in effective control of most parts of the country.

The task of the British and Australian troops, who began arriving throughout the territories from October onwards, was barely practicable. They had to disarm the Japanese and return them to Japan. At the same time, they had to deal with the nationalists until the Dutch, still recovering from German occupation, could return to assert their 'lawful' sovereignty over their old territories.

It is sometimes said by Indonesians now that the fighting which followed would have been reduced if the British had not used the Japanese army to recapture towns, such as Bandung, held by the Indonesians. But the real confrontation, which was with the Dutch, would not have been materially altered. Heavy fighting broke out in Java, especially at Surabaya, which the British, with Indian troops, took after ten days of bitter resistance by armed Indonesian youth. There was also resistance in Bali and south Celebes, where the Dutch brought in Captain 'Turk' Westerling to restore order. The western military alliance against Indonesia, the brutality of Westerling and the heroism of the Indonesian civilians and guerillas who fought for the infant Republic in those days has become part of the folklore of Indonesian nationalism. This is the period of high endeavour, when the capital was transferred from the dubious safety of Djakarta to Jogjakarta, the cultural centre of Java, where the patriotic Sultan refused to co-operate with the Dutch; when Nasution, later to become the nation's first military leader, learned his lessons in guerilla warfare; when Sukarno was a knight in shining armour, rather than a skilful politician; and the people of Indonesia proved their worth. Today, there is a nostalgia for the 'Jogja Days', when the nation lived perilously and the national motto, 'Unity in Diversity' was an active slogan. Still today, an Indonesian, if he happened, say, to have been a member of the contingent of armed youth which marched from Jogjakarta to relieve Surabaya, can hold the floor at a party, by common consent. As he tells his story, it becomes evident that the episode is national property. His audience prompts him at well-known incidents and adds small, second-hand stories of its own.

For four years, until the Republic of the United States of Indonesia was recognized by the United Nations in 1949, a state of intermittent war and political bargaining continued. The nation existed for its parent nationalists, and for some friendly midwives, like Australia, the United States and India, but at times it seemed unlikely to survive. In the negotiations with the Dutch, Sjahrir led a cautiously pro-western government, opposed by the more violent leftists and nationalists. An abortive attempt by the national-communist Tan Malaka to stage a coup d'état—the so-called 'July 3rd affair'—took place in 1946.

In November 1946 the government negotiated the Linggadjati Agreement which Sukarno and Hatta approved a little ahead of Sjahrir, who was prepared to press for more concessions. The agreement achieved for the Republic de facto recognition in Java and Sumatra and proposed by 1949 a federal Indonesia within a form of union with the Netherlands. But both sides began to undermine the agreement, Indonesia by seeking diplomatic recognition for itself, the Dutch by technical quibbles. The first of the two Dutch 'police actions' followed in July 1947, representing the fact that the Dutch then had 150,000 soldiers in Indonesia. Sjahrir's government fell and the Renville Agreement recognized the advanced military position of the Dutch in Java and Sumatra.

It was a hard time for the nationalists. Hatta had taken over the prime ministership from Sjarifuddin and the communists, reacting against his moderate leadership and playing on the disorder and unemployment, staged a revolt in September 1948 at Madiun in east Java. Sukarno appealed by radio: 'I call on you . . . to choose between Musso [the communist leader] and his Communist Party, who will obstruct the attainment of an independent Indonesia, and Sukarno-Hatta, who, with the Almighty's help, will lead our Republic of Indonesia to become an independent Indonesia which is not subject to any country whatsoever'.

The effect of this stand may have been important in bringing western opinion into more open sympathy with Indonesian nationalism. Also the Dutch forced the issue by launching the second 'police action' in December 1948, when the Madiun revolt, a stab in the back to the nationalists, had barely been suppressed. The Republican capital of Jogjakarta fell and Sukarno, Hatta and the other top leaders were captured and exiled. The Dutch expected the Republic to collapse but it resisted vigorously with an effective scorched-earth policy. As world opinion swung strongly against the Netherlands and it became clear that the war against the Republic could not be won without a sustained campaign, Dutch policy changed.

The Netherlands apparently decided to sacrifice its political sovereignty in the hope of protecting Dutch investments in Indonesia, and this is the course negotiations took. The Round Table Conference at the Hague ended on 2 November 1949, with an agreement transferring sovereignty to Indonesia. Moscow called the 'Sukarno-Hatta clique' traitors. Sukarno returned to power in triumph.

It could not be said, however, that the nation was complete either in letter or in spirit. West Irian was missing. Moreover, the Republic of the United States of Indonesia (RUSI) as the sovereign state was called, was a federation of the former Republic and fifteen autonomous states created by the Dutch, mostly in the outer islands, between 1945 and 1949. These states would have numerical control of the proposed house of representatives and senate. In addition, special guarantees to Dutch investors were provided and RUSI undertook to consult with the Netherlands on aspects of financial policy affecting Dutch interests. The Republic balanced these losses by gaining effective control of the armed forces. The compromise did not succeed. Within seven months the Indonesian government, under nationalist pressure and suspicious of Dutch intentions, had violated the Round Table Agreement by dissolving the constitution. The new 1950 constitution, establishing a unitary state, was proclaimed to the ominous accompaniment of armed revolt in Makassar and Ambon.

By now the outside world had formally recognized the victory of Indonesian nationalism but the nationalists were themselves divided on the extent to which a victory had been won. The new constitution gave greater power to the centre, but less to its executive. The cabinet was no longer responsible to the president as in 1945, but to a parliament. Parties proliferated (reaching the number of forty-three) and political deals for cabinet seats increased the rate of government turnover. There were seventeen cabinets for the period 1945-58, an average of a change every ten months. After the Japanese occupation and the guerilla war against the Dutch, the economy was in need of immediate repair and national policies of development. Instead, the game of politics occupied everyone's attention. This is the period of Mochtar Lubis' depressing novel *Twilight in Djakarta* and of one of the major works of scholarship on Indonesia, Herbert Feith's *The Decline of Constitutional Democracy in Indonesia*, in which the gradual rise of the 'solidarity-makers' at the expense of the 'administrators' is traced.

The chief solidarity-maker was President Sukarno, who was determined not to be cut off from power by Parliament and who was sustained in that ambition by the Javanese masses, for whom he had become a father figure or, to use their mythology, a messianic 'just prince'. The President's tendency to interfere when cabinets decided on a policy he disliked, perhaps because it affected friends or political allies, helped to speed the deterioration of constitutional democracy, especially in parliamentary government control of the army. The government of Prime Minister Wilopo (April 1952-August 1953) collapsed over an issue on which the president opposed it—the eviction of squatters from the concession of a foreign tobacco company in east Sumatra, so that the acreage under production could be increased.

Frequently postponed elections helped to aggravate instability by prolonging the continuous election campaign, but when the elections were held in 1955 they did not provide conditions for a change. No party gained more than twenty-five per cent of the seats, and short-lived coalition governments continued. The elections did show, however, a dramatic decline in the fortunes of Sjahrir's Socialist Party (PSI), which captured only five seats (compared with the fourteen it had been given in the provisional parliament), while the Communists (PKI) jumped from seventeen to thirty-nine and the Nahdatul Ulama (Muslim Teachers' Party—NU), a traditional Muslim group strong in Java and little influenced by modern ideas, leapt from eight to forty-five. The Nationalists (PNI), regarded as Sukarno's party, topped the poll, gaining fifty-seven seats. The Masjumi, whose modern Islamic ideas on economics were close to the rational, pro-western socialism of the PSI, received fifty-seven seats but was surprised by the rise of the NU, a breakaway group. Partai Kristen Indonesia (Parkindo), the Protestant party, received eight seats and the Partai Katholik, the Catholic party, won six, and there were many smaller groups, like the League of Upholders of Indonesian Independence (IPKI) which had a following among army officers (four), and Partai Murba, the national-communist party (two). With a total of 257 seats, the scope for parliamentary manoeuvring was again limited more by the power situation outside Parliament than by the strength of the parties within.

By 21 February 1957, when President Sukarno proclaimed 'guided democracy' to bring 'liberal, Western-style democracy' to a close, the Indonesian leadership was in disarray and the new nation was in danger. Hatta had resigned from the vice-presidency on 1 December 1956, breaking the Sukarno-Hatta duumvirate which many non-

Javanese (especially Sumatrans) saw as a balance of the Sumatra-born, Muslim, West-leaning Hatta and Java-born, polytheistic, Soviet-leaning Sukarno. Regionalists, served in the field by several army commanders outside Java and with the moral support of the Masjumi and PSI, were critical of the merry-go-round of Djakarta politics, and the burden of inefficient and corrupt administration on the rich exporting areas of Sumatra and Sulawesi.

The regionalism which had been preserved by the Dutch was intensified at this stage by Java's declining share in the export trade. The foreign earnings of the other islands, which had the mineral deposits and the staple export crops, were used to import rice and consumer goods for Java's increasing population. As the effects of the Korean war boom wore off and Djakarta's discordant politics wore on, regional feeling grew stronger. Army commanders organized smuggling of copra and rubber on a large scale, and in a series of bloodless coups between December 1956 and March 1957, they took over from several Djakarta-appointed civilian governors in Sumatra and Sulawesi.

After protracted negotiations failed, the regionalist group declared itself (on 15 February 1958) as the Revolutionary Government of the Republic of Indonesia (Pemerintah Revolusioner Republik Indonesia, or PRRI) in Padang, central Sumatra. The north Sulawesi arm of the revolution called itself Permesta (Overall Struggle). It was a revolution of economists and colonels—a significant comment on the weaknesses of the Djakarta régime. Its prime minister was Sjafruddin Prawiranegara, a Sundanese member of the Masjumi who, while minister for economics, had taken over as prime minister of the Republic in 1948 when the Dutch in their second 'police action' captured the leadership at Jogjakarta. His speciality was taxation and he had been governor of the Bank of Indonesia, urging harder work and government economies. With him in revolt were Dr Sumitro Djojohadikusomo (PSI), generally regarded as a brilliant, frustrated finance minister, and two former prime ministers, Mohammed Natsir and Burhanuddin Harahap, both Masjumi. Among the dissident colonels were some of the most promising in the Indonesian army.

Although it has been described as an unnaturally civil war, it was in its early stages a threat to the unity of the nation, especially as the rebels received supplies from outside, airdropped and smuggled from Singapore and Manila. It ended with the return of the defeated rebels to 'the fold of the Republic' on mild amnesty terms. But in the three years of the rebellion the shape of domestic politics had been radically altered. In 1960, the Masjumi and the PSI were banned and some of the old nationalists were discredited. (Sjahrir and others were placed under arrest in 1962.) The army, led by General Nasution who had proved his loyalty to the Sukarno régime by taking up the fight against the rebels, many of them his personal friends, had gained administrative authority throughout the country because of the war emergency regulations. The communists had strengthened their position and were helped by the rebellion to erase the memory of Madiun.

Most important, Sukarno had transformed the machinery of government and was now able to exercise almost unchecked legal power. In 1959 he abolished the 1950 constitution and ordered a return to the Republican constitution of 1945. It was a return not only to a presidential cabinet secure from parliamentary control, but to the '1945 spirit', sometimes called the 'Rails of the Revolution', before the nationalist movement was forced to 'compromise'. In March 1960, the elected parliament was dissolved by presidential decree, to be replaced shortly afterwards by a parliament of 281 members appointed by the president as follows: 130 representatives of 10 political parties (the others being dissolved) and 151 representatives of 'functional groups'—the armed forces, peasants, labour, women's organizations and so on. It had no authority over the president and enacted laws subject to his agreement. The task of electing the president and vice-president (the latter post unfilled since Hatta's resignation) was taken over by the Provisional People's Consultative Congress (Madjelis Permusjawaratan Rakyat Sementara—MPRS) which was required to meet once in five years to determine the broad outlines of policy. Called the highest authority in the state, as an embodiment of all the people, it was composed of the entire parliament plus 94 regional delegates and 241 representatives of functional groups, a total of 616 members.

Much of the former authority of the cabinet passed to the Supreme Advisory Council, a body of 45 members including the president, who appointed the others. Its proposals did not bind the government but it became the chief policy-making body, submitting proposals to be discussed by the parliament and carried out by the cabinet. The cabinet, or Council of Ministers (called *kabinet kerdja,* or work cabinet to signify its non-party nature) comprised the president as prime minister, a first minister, two vice-first ministers, and eight deputy first ministers in charge of sectors, as well as numerous ministers in charge of departments. After the death of First Minister Dr Djuanda in November 1963, three vice-first ministers were appointed—Dr Leimena, Dr Subandrio and Chairul Saleh. The authority of the supreme court was vague. The National Front was installed in September 1960. A mass organization intended to 'mobilize the revolutionary forces of the people' it had a seventy-member central executive board, presided over by the president. It became a useful adjunct to government in organizing 'demonstrations' such as sacking embassies.

The changes were intended to give the President real power. As he said: 'What is the use of being called President, Supreme Commander of the Armed Forces, Prime Minister, Chairman of the Supreme Advisory Council and even the Great Leader of the Indonesian Revolution, if my commands are ignored?' To mesh this apparently unwieldy machinery with the concept of guided democracy, Sukarno abolished the western parliamentary form of voting (called 'fifty per cent plus one democracy') and introduced the traditional Indonesian techniques of *gotong royong* (common, voluntary effort by the community, whether for its own benefit or that of some member), *musjawarah* (deliberation among elders) and *mufakat* (decision by unanimity, a form of veto).

Under its new-style leadership, the Indonesian nation turned toward the completion of its territorial boundaries. The issue of West Irian had never been allowed to rest. In 1957 the Dutch estates had been confiscated and in 1960 diplomatic relations were severed. With the negotiation in 1960 of an arms agreement with the Soviet Union costing about U.S.$1,000 million, Indonesia began a diplomatic and military 'confrontation' of the Dutch position in its sole remaining territory. An agreement was finally reached on 15 August 1962 under the auspices of the United Nations, by which administration of the territory passed to Indonesia on 1 May 1963.

Now the nation was complete from 'Sabang to Merauke' for the first time, although the requirement that the Papuans in West Irian be given the opportunity by 1969 to decide if they wanted to remain with Indonesia or become independent was criticized by some extremist elements. Sukarno stood by the agreement, however, and called his 17 August (Independence Day) speech in 1962 'A Year of Triumph'. The civil war was over; West Irian had been 'regained'. Now the third task of the revolution—*sandang pangan*, or food and clothing for the people—could be fulfilled. But, before the year was out, Indonesia had begun to embark on another test of her national strength, the confrontation of the new nation of Malaysia on her northern boundaries, and fresh sacrifices were being asked of the Indonesian people.

CHAPTER THREE

The Leader

As early as 7 a.m., when the tropical air was still cool enough for them to wear scarves and sweaters, crowds of people were making their way to an open field, the equivalent in Indonesia of the town square. It was Heroes' Day in Jogjakarta and Sukarno was to speak. The people came, astride hundreds, probably thousands, of bicycles; in *betjaks*, the brightly painted, three-wheeled pedicabs; on foot. The car-loads of important persons would come later. They laughed and chattered as if they expected to enjoy themselves. They did not give the impression of having been forced to come, although for those interested in political advancement there would be no advantage in ostentatiously staying away. Rather this was a great show, like the *wayang*; a public holiday. Seeing and hearing Bung (Brother) Karno has become one of the folk traditions of the new Indonesia.

A Colombo Plan conference was in progress and the city was decked out with flags and streamers, slogans stretched across the streets. The flags of all the Colombo Plan countries were flown, but the red and white bicolour of Indonesia, represented in hundreds of thousands of miniature paper flags, created the dominant effect. Jogjakarta is a university city and many of the early morning bicyclists were students. Some of them sang as they pedalled abreast in small groups. They were western-dressed in casual fashion and they seemed, of all students I had seen in Asia, to be the most relaxed and carefree.

In essentials, this scene could have been anywhere in Indonesia on any of Sukarno's speech days. In nearly two decades as president, and before that as a nationalist leader noted for his oratory, Sukarno has been billed at least once in all the major cities of the archipelago. But since the Asian Games, in August 1962, the President has spoken on big occasions in Djakarta in the main stadium, which seats one hundred thousand and is the equal of the best in the world. Some of the atmosphere of the open-air gathering is lost. The President does not face the crowd directly, as he does from an open-field platform, but, speaking from one side of the stadium (the side sheltered from the sun), he half confronts, and is half-surrounded by, his audience. The stadium is also noisier. The murmuring of the audience rises to fill the huge saucer; the roars of the crowd boom and rebound. The top of the stadium is spaced with flags; the tiered balconies are hung with slogans and the groups, identified by placards (national front, youth organizations, and so on), are organized like cheer-leaders. They sing and stamp at appropriate moments. A helicopter drops leaflets, an electric board announces messages, sirens wail, guns salute, balloons are released. There is the air, in the great structure of steel and concrete (especially if the armed services are on display in the arena), of a modern, military nation on show. For a westerner, the link with the European dictatorships is easily made, emotionally, as the President steps to the rostrum.

But Sukarno is not a violent orator, in the tradition of the great European mob-rousers. His style is friendly, coaxing and confidential. He begins quietly and slowly. 'Sisters and Brothers . . .' His voice, a slightly throaty baritone, plays with each word, sometimes skipping quickly over two or three, sometimes repeating a word or a phrase three or four times with a rising sharpness; but generally the tone is low. Dressed smartly, either in a sparkling white uniform, with ribbons, swagger stick and *kopiah* (black velvet cap) or in a modest grey uniform (but always in uniform) he moves quickly into his speech. He stands lightly, leaning slightly forward, using the microphone discreetly, like a nightclub entertainer rather than an orator. His figure is the trim indication of a younger man. Occasionally he punches the air, languidly, as if exercising a tired shoulder.

'Do you and you and you and you . . . do you consider yourself as Bearers of the Message of the People's Sufferings? Are you really aware that you are Bearers of the Message of the People's Sufferings, do you really feel to the marrow of your bones that you are Bearers of the Message of the People's Sufferings?' No answer from the crowd, which is quiet and attentive. 'It is this social consciousness of the Indonesian people which is the basic element of the Message of the Sufferings of the Indonesian People. The Message of the Sufferings of the Indonesian People is thus part of the social consciousness of mankind.' In rising tempo:

Thus the Message of the Sufferings of the Indonesian People is part of the Message of the Sufferings of the whole of mankind! Thus our Message of the Sufferings of the People is not just a national idea or a national ideal. Our Message of the People's Sufferings is interlocked with the Message of the Sufferings of

Mankind, the Message of the Sufferings of Mankind is interlocked with our Message of the Sufferings of the People. The
Indonesian Revolution is interlocked with the Revolution of Mankind, the Revolution of Mankind is interlocked with the Indonesian Revolution.

The speech, repetitive and emotional, usually takes on great occasions at least two hours to deliver. People who know the language
well say he handles it adroitly, sometimes brilliantly, occasionally
beautifully. The English translation loses the flexible use of Indonesian words and the startling bursts of foreign languages—Dutch,
English, French or German—with which Sukarno spatters his
speeches. 'It is an entity of social consciousness like a burning fire'—
'like a burning fire' will be spoken in English, for no apparent
reason. Some think the President likes to show off his languages,
using frequently phrases like 'l'exploitation de l'homme par l'homme,
de nation par nation' or 'socialisme à la Indonésie' not because the
phrases have an exact meaning which Bahasa is not able to convey,
but because they suggest to the people an image of Sukarno's intellectual familiarity with the world. Others say he just likes the
sound of the words.

> Oh yes! I know that I am often ridiculed by people who do not
> like me for being a 'man of feeling'—a 'gevoelsmens'—and that
> in politics I have too much of the character of a 'man of the arts'—
> that I am too much the *artist*. How happy I am with these derisive
> remarks! I express thanks to the Almighty that I was born with
> traits of sentiment and artistry, and I am proud that the Indonesian
> Nation is also a 'Nation of Feeling'—a 'gevoelsvolk'—and a 'Nation
> of Artists'—an 'artistenvolk'.

Sukarno stresses in his speeches the non-material, lofty aims of the
Indonesian revolution. He often claims that it is bigger and more
complex than the French, American and Russian revolutions because
it embraces all aspects—social, political, economic as well as spiritual
—of Indonesian life. It is 'many revolutions in one generation', a
phrase which he uses in its English form. It will create a New Indonesian Man. A man of feeling like himself, demanding justice,
humanity and dignity as his due. His speeches are full of reassu-
rances. The Indonesian people have taken the right step on the right
path. Because their ideals are noble, they have God's blessing, all
mankind's blessing—especially that of the 'new emerging forces', a
concept which has lately become dominant. 'The Social Consciousness of Man prays for our Victory.'

Therefore, all you people of Indonesia, keep your heads high! Do not retreat, do not stop, put your feet firmly on the ground! If there are times that you feel confused, if there are times that you almost despair, if there are times that you do not quite understand the course of our Revolution which indeed sometimes resembles a vessel at sea tossed in a raging storm—return to the source of our Message of the Sufferings of the People which is congruent with the Social Conscience of Man.

The intimacy and mysticism of Sukarno's approach has grown more noticeable with the years. He has described each 17 August as a 'dialogue . . . a two-way conversation between myself and the People, between my Ego and my Alter-Ego. A two-way conversation between Sukarno-the-man and Sukarno-the-people, a two-way conversation between comrade-in-arms and comrade-in-arms. A two-way conversation between two comrades who in reality are One!'

I become like a person possessed. Everything that is non-material in my body overflows! Thoughts overflow, feelings overflow, nerves overflow, emotions overflow. Everything that belongs to the spirit that is in my body is as though quivering and blazing and raging, and then for me it is as though fire is not hot enough, as though ocean is not deep enough, as though the stars in the heavens are not high enough!

He also uses these occasions to affirm his determination to serve his country, however great the demands may be, 'until the Almighty calls me home to my source'. Sukarno has made the pilgrimage to Mecca several times, and lately his public references show a tendency to connect his political activities with the will of God. He claims that the Trikora (a three-fold plan to take West Irian issued by him in December 1961) was a 'vision' from God. References to his increasing age and decreasing strength, to humility in the face of the great responsibility which he carries as Great Leader of the Revolution, Mouthpiece of the Indonesian People, Main Bearer of the Message of the Sufferings of the Indonesian People—as well, of course, as being President, Prime Minister and Supreme Commander of the Armed Forces—have become increasingly frequent. Sukarno, who has become psychiatrist to a whole nation, increasingly shows concern with his own health.

Yet his speeches continue in the romantic, hopeful mould of his youth. There is always something new around the corner, even if it is as unpoetic as 'self-propelling growth'. Usually, the imagery is more conventionally mesmeric—the Dawn, the Rising Sun, the New

World are awaiting. The triumph, however, is elusive and Sukarno's object, in his long, rambling discourse, is to prepare the Indonesian people to struggle for it. He appears unhappy about the present, except as a vehicle of change. For a 'fighting nation' there is no journey's end. 'I am one of the people who is in love with the Romanticism of Revolution; I am inspired by it, I am fascinated by it.'

> If, for example, at this moment, an angel were to descend from the heavens and say to me: 'Hi, Sukarno, I shall grant you a miracle, to give the Indonesian people a just and prosperous society as a gift, as a present', then I would reply: 'I don't want to be granted such a miracle, I want the just and prosperous society to be the result of the struggle of the Indonesian people!'

When he says, 'Hi, Sukarno', there is a ripple of laughter. Indonesians enjoy cockiness. Angels descending from heaven are part of the Javanese mythology (one of the restaurants at the Hotel Indonesia in Djakarta is almost exclusively decorated with the story of such a visitation) and Sukarno enjoys the role of gamin in the play. His humour is generally deflationary, appealing to ordinary people; it is not sophisticated or elaborate. He uses it to overcome a political difficulty.

For example, on the troublesome question of a Nasakom cabinet —Nasakom is an abbreviation of Nas (nationalist), A (*agama*, or religion) and Kom (communist) to indicate the three political streams supporting Sukarno's government:

> There are still persons who suffer from the communist-phobia. Because they have the communist-phobia, they have the Nasakom-phobia! Whilst I have explained hundreds and hundreds of times that revolutionary national *gotong royong* ways cannot possibly be effected without Nasakom at its hub—Nas-A-Kom —the three objective groupings into which the Indonesian People's political consciousness falls, I have also often explained that to be anti-Nasakom is the same as being anti the 1945 constitution, the same as being anti *Pantja Sila,* the same as being anti the concentration of forces . . . the same as being . . . soft in the head!

The crowd murmured a laugh, but they were no wiser on the issue of whether communists would be included in the cabinet.

Or, taking account of the difficulties Indonesia has found in getting development in West Irian under way:

> **In West Irian, for example, a whispering campaign is being spread**

that 'under the Republic the situation is deteriorating as compared with what it was under the red-white-blue flag.' Deteriorating? Deteriorating in what things? If we ask such a concrete
question—'deteriorating in what things?'—then it turns out that
the problem is: *there is not enough canned beer in West Irian
now!* . . . Sisters and brothers in West Irian! You there, sisters
and brothers in West Irian! Sisters and brothers in Kotabaru, in
Sorong, in Merauke—sisters and brothers on the slopes of the
Trikora Mountain, the Sukarno Mountain, the Sudirman Mountain, the Yamin Mountain!—the Republic has never indeed promised canned beer to the people in West Irian! The Republic has
promised and is building schools, the Republic has promised and
has brought independence, the Republic has promised and is
bringing Clear Rays and Brightness.

Sukarno's speeches are not wholly tendentious. Often, he takes a
point of some complicated matter of principle or policy and produces
a masterly summary. His ideas on economics are often so human and
simple that they are misleading. But perhaps no crowd could possibly
survive a sincere and expert analysis of Indonesia's economic problems, if a leader could be found to deliver it. When Sukarno says
that his ideas on the 'economic question' boil down to this: 'If
nations who live in a dry and barren desert can solve the problems
of their economy then why can't we', he is posing the problem in
essentially realistic terms, although he may not like the answer some
observers would give.

On great occasions he is a stickler for correct procedure, as it
affects the prestige of the President of the Republic of Indonesia.
He keeps his correct distance ahead of others. His face is held in a
severe and disdainful pose. When he tries to be militant, raising his
voice or making strong gestures, he runs the risk of looking foolish.
Sometimes he plays the clown. While waiting for the delayed arrival
of Mr Khrushchev at Djakarta's airport in 1960, Sukarno sat on a
rolled-up red carpet, a lopsided umbrella shielding him from the
rain, grinning broadly. He still held his swagger stick under his
arm, but his cap was slightly askew. He looked like an actor who
had been called in to play a head of state.

As President, Sukarno's performance has often been criticized
privately by Indonesians, however careful people may be not to reflect on the dignity of the position of head of the Indonesian State.
Sometimes the criticism is public. In August 1963 a teacher in the
east Indonesian island of Flores was given fifteen months' gaol for
having said that the President was 'a good orator' but had 'an empty

head'. The sentence—indeed the judgment—seems harsh until it is thought what it might have been in the England of Elizabeth I or Henry VIII. Most heads of state, including those of advanced countries today, are overweight with solemnly accepted virtues which do not exist. As an orator, however, Sukarno is among the masters, and his speeches provide a continuing reality in Indonesian politics: they represent his hold over the Indonesian people, which no other leader can hope to break, and they represent his capacity, sometimes exhibited under strain, for playing with ideas and concepts. Sukarno takes this role seriously and he tries, sometimes with great success, to make the occasion of his ceremonial speeches an inspiration to his people. The people may well have ceased to expect clear-cut advantages from Sukarno's speeches—if they ever did expect such practical results. But they do expect to be moved emotionally and to be assured that, whatever hardship lies ahead, they are on the right side in the old struggle between the forces of darkness and the forces of light. Sukarno's talent as a political manipulator of the Indonesian domestic power constellation has been widely recognized. It is probably not sufficiently appreciated that to the Indonesian people he also offers salvation, not from economic distress, but from the belief that the inevitable suffering of their lives has no meaning. To all those who labour and are heavy laden he offers, not rest, but revolution.

*	*	*

Sukarno was born outside Surabaya in east Java on 6 June 1901. His mother was a Hindu Balinese and his father, who was a schoolteacher and a member of the Theosophical Society, was a Muslim Javanese. His zodiacal sign of Gemini convinced Sukarno, he once said, that he was to serve as a meeting point of all the world's philosophies. His father's profession and the support of several prominent friends, including the father of Ruslan Abdulgani, a long-time political associate of Sukarno's (now minister for information, and leading official ideologue since the death of Professor Mohammed Yamin), helped young Sukarno to get the kind of education reserved for Indonesians privileged under the Dutch. He spent some of his early youth with his grandparents at Tulungagung (east Java) and, according to his official biography, was spoiled. At school he was good at languages, but did not shine in class. As a lively youngster he earned the nickname 'rooster'. He could climb higher on trees than his friends and he stage-managed their games.

At fourteen Sukarno went to Surabaya High School. During his five years at high school, he lived with the family of the founder of the Sarekat Islam, Tjokroaminoto, a Surabaya businessman, at whose house he met early nationalists like Agus Salim, Alimin, Musso and Semaun. He joined the youth organization Young Java where his liking for oratory first showed, and he contributed editorials (signed 'Bima'—the strong-willed prince in the *wayang*) to Tjokroaminoto's newspaper *Utusan Hindia* (the *Indies Messenger*). In 1920 he went to the Bandung Technical Institute to study civil engineering. The official biography notes that after two months he broke off study to earn money for the family of Tjokroaminoto, who had been arrested. Sukarno worked in the state railways. He is also said at this time to have become a member of Sarekat Islam, but while studying he developed 'a more definite and concrete system of political ideas of his own'.

The Dutch claim that Sukarno failed twice in 'Theory of Structures' and never graduated. The official version is that he graduated in 1925 with a thesis about harbour construction, earning a civil engineering degree and the title Ir (*Ingénieur*), although his particular study was architecture. He set up as an architect in Bandung and became known for a modernized style of hut design. He also helped to design a mosque. He had previously married and divorced a daughter of Tjokroaminoto. While in Bandung he married Ibu Inggit, a widow from a well-off Javanese family.

Sukarno, who was already known to the Dutch authorities as a fiery speaker, became chairman of the Bandung Study Club, the members of which formed in 1927 the Persarikatan Nasional Indonesia (Indonesian Nationalist Organization) which became in 1928 the Partai Nasional Indonesia (Indonesian Nationalist Party— PNI). The party's aim was complete independence for Indonesia and it urged non-co-operation with the Dutch authorities as the means of achievement. Sukarno was active at this time in developing a philosophy which he called *Marhaenism*. He used the word *marhaen* ('proletariat') to describe not only the peasantry and proletariat but a kind of pauperized mass of 'little people', small wage-earners and small farmers, and developed from this theories of a kind of socialism particularly suited to Indonesia. It was useless waiting for 'an aeroplane from Moscow or a caliph from Istanbul', he said in speeches at this time, urging self-reliance and unity of the nationalist movement.

In December 1928 a step toward unity was taken when, on PNI initiative, six groups came together in a federation, Permuakatan Partai-partai Politik Indonesia (Federation of National Political Parties, or PPPI) and elected Sukarno as chairman. By 1929, the PNI

had over ten thousand members and the Dutch were becoming concerned at its growing influence. In December, the authorities arrested
Sukarno and three others for allegedly planning a rebellion. After
eight months detention they were brought to trial at Bandung. The
trial lasted four months and enabled Sukarno to make a now famous
defence plea, 'Indonesia accuses', in which he spoke of the poverty
of the *marhaen*. He received the longest sentence—four years, later
reduced to two.

While Sukarno was in jail, the PNI was split by differences over
strategy, and two new groups were formed: the Partai Indonesia
(Partindo), a party aiming at a mass following, led by Sartono, who
became speaker of Parliament, Ali Sastroamidjojo, who became a
prime minister, Mohammed Yamin, later minister for information,
and Iskaq Tjokroadisurjo, former secretary of the PNI; and the
Pendidikan Nasional Indonesia (Indonesian National Education
Club) led by Sjahrir and Hatta. The latter group was a small cadre
organization, which aimed at slow, long-term persuasion of a growing
circle of Indonesian élite. Sukarno, released in December 1931,
sought to unite the two organizations. Having failed, he joined Partindo in July 1932, and was elected chairman. Under his leadership
the party grew rapidly. By mid-1933 it had twenty thousand registered
members.

Before the end of 1933, Sukarno, Hatta and Sjahrir had all been
arrested and were not released until the arrival of the Japanese in
1942, so their differences on tactics became an academic matter.
But, without the opportunity to put their ideas into practice, except
in the peculiar circumstances of the Japanese occupation, the differences were still untested when the three men were called on to
supply national leadership in 1945. In one way or another they
combined to provide this leadership for a decade, although they were
often at loggerheads, but the rise to power of Sukarno at the expense
of his two former colleagues has been a feature of recent years. Hatta
resigned as vice-president in 1956, and has not returned to the government. Sjahrir, after a long period as self-appointed critic of the
Sukarno régime, was placed under arrest in 1962.

Sukarno's long exile began, with his wife, mother-in-law and
adopted daughter, on the island of Flores. Unlike many Asian and
African nationalists who continued their political writing during
imprisonment and later wrote about their time in detention, Sukarno
has been reticent about his years of enforced isolation and it is a
difficult period to document. But after four years on Flores his health
broke down and he was transferred to Bencoolen, in south Sumatra.

During this time he wrote several pamphlets on Islamic law and theology. As the Japanese advanced, the Dutch moved him to Padang, in central Sumatra, reportedly with the intention of taking him to Australia. He assisted in the evacuation of Dutch civilians and, perhaps fearing Japanese reprisals for pamphlets he had written attacking their ambitions in the Pacific, he 'managed to escape', as the official biography phrases it, 'appearing' later at Bukittingi. According to Sjahrir, Sukarno was treated 'rather roughly' by the Japanese and he regarded them as 'pure fascists'. He worked for them in Sumatra as a translator, then, on the initiative of Hatta and Sjahrir, who some months earlier had decided on tactics to be pursued under the Japanese, he was taken to Batavia, under the assumed name 'Abdul Rachman'.

Sukarno's reputation as a 'collaborator' with the Japanese was utilized by Dutch propaganda after World War II, when the Netherlands was anxious to show that the Republic was a Japanese creation rather than a product of genuine nationalism. The criticism was picked up by the communists in the early post-war years. The leader of the 1948 Madiun revolt, Musso, attacked Sukarno as a 'romusha dealer', a reference to the romushas (slave labourers) conscripted by the Japanese, most of whom perished. (Sukarno was chairman of the People's Manpower Centre—Pusat Tenaga Rakyat or Putera—created by the Japanese in March 1943.) Yet in reality Sukarno seems to have behaved no differently from many Asian nationalists who were forced suddenly to cope with the unknown Japanese after the colonial power had retreated. With Hatta, his role was pre-arranged, and whether he was 'actively pro-Japanese' or 'anti-British and American' as has been claimed, is beside the point, which is that he tirelessly used his position under the Japanese authorities to strengthen Indonesian nationalist sentiment.

Explanations of his tactics will vary from time to time and country to country. It is noticeable now, for example, that Indonesian communists make the claim that Hatta was willingly pro-Japanese, while Sukarno was a genuine nationalist, which is a different story from 1948, when Moscow Radio called Sukarno 'a Japanese quisling'. The fact is that the Japanese occupation provided the nationalists with a fresh set of conditions for independence, of which they took advantage. It may have been that Sukarno was more impressed with the Japanese than were some of his colleagues, who had been educated abroad and had seen the civilization of Europe. Sukarno at this stage had never left Indonesia except to visit Japan and the Japanese headquarters in Vietnam, and his chief source of comparison with the Japanese was the Dutch, against whom his prejudices were natural enough. His caution about declaring independence, dealt with earlier, seems to have been mistaken, though understandable in the confusion of the period, and it provides an early glimpse of a capacity for self-preservation which has proved remarkable.

In 1943 Sukarno's second marriage, which had been childless, ended in divorce. Toward the end of the Japanese occupation he married Fatmawati, a village girl in her late teens. They had four children. Fatmawati proved herself a popular first lady after Sukarno became president, and there was criticism in 1954 when Sukarno took another (fourth) wife, Hartini, the former wife of a minor Shell Oil Company official, by whom she had had five children. Some wives of leading Indonesians refused to recognize Hartini, and still do not.

But Sukarno's reputation in the early years of the infant Republic was high. His actual power was limited by constitutional practices, but the quick achievements of Indonesian nationalism and the international sympathy shown for the new nation helped to create an atmosphere which he could probably have used to justify strong action. In fact, he allowed the natural play of the political parties to come into force and he concentrated on gaining recognition for Indonesia in the world and for himself abroad. He travelled to India, Pakistan and Burma in 1950 and to the Philippines the following year, beginning the run of world tours that reached a peak in the years 1959-63, when he spent 319 days abroad. In 1955 Sukarno was host to the foreign heads of state and government who came to Bandung for the Afro-Asian conference. In 1956 he visited the United States, Canada, West Germany, Italy, the Vatican, Switzerland, the Soviet Union, Yugoslavia, Austria, Czechoslovakia, Outer Mongolia and communist China. He was greatly impressed with progress in China and the USSR, and in February 1957 he announced his conception of 'guided democracy' which brought western-style constitutional democracy in Indonesia to an end. He had always been critical of the largely ineffective parliamentary system which Indonesia had chosen, but the turn-over of governments and the constant unrest had kept him occupied. He was also required to pay respectful attention to the views of men like Hatta and Sjahrir, who were inclined now to concentrate on administrative policies rather than nationalist fervor. His visits abroad, however, especially to communist countries, gave him first-hand evidence that alternatives existed and that support would be available to Indonesia from countries outside the West. He called the period of constitutional democracy 'listening to the voice of the Dutch'.

The 1958-61 rebellion in Sumatra and Sulawesi strengthened Sukarno's position by discrediting his opponents at home and by proving his authority to nations abroad, where there were doubts of his ability to survive. But the years of the rebellion also brought increased authority and enlarged practical power to the army. This was a period of greatly increased symbol-making, such as Manipol-Usdek, Manipol standing for 'political manifesto' and Usdek being an acronym of the five points of the manifesto—the 1945 constitution (*undang-undang dasar* 1945), Indonesian socialism (*sosialisme*), guided democracy (*demokrasi*), guided economy (*ekonomi*) and Indonesian identity (*kepribadian*).

Sukarno developed a mass of new slogans with prompt appeal to the communist bloc. He advocated a return to the revolution, turning his back on the long and difficult process of legitimizing government. When the elected constitutional assembly failed to support him, he dissolved it, and, ruling by decree, abolished the 1950 constitution, replacing it with the 1945 constitution, with its revolutionary allowance of presidential power which continues today. As he has never been elected and as his promulgation of the 1945 constitution by decree has no lawful basis, it could be claimed that his present authority is illegal. But opposition has been largely formal. In 1960, during one of his trips abroad, opposition showed in the formation of the League of Democracy, which claimed the right to speak as loyal critics. Sukarno banned the Masjumi and the Socialist Party (PSI), which were supporting the League, and its activities lapsed.

As if to retain his balance above the power forces of Indonesian politics, Sukarno, in 1960, formulated for the first time a conception which has steadily grown in emphasis—'the new emerging forces' versus 'the old established forces'. In his speeches at the Bandung conference in 1955, the Indonesian president had faithfully preached the precepts of non-alignment: 'The peoples of Asia and Africa . . . cannot indulge in power politics. Diplomacy for us is not a matter of the big stick. What can we do? We can do much. We can inject the voice of reason into world affairs . . . We can demonstrate to the minority of the world that lives on the other continents that we, the majority, are for peace, not for war . . .' This idea of the neutralist position as a rational brake on the power-maddened nuclear rivalries of the two world blocs is a continuous theme in early Indonesian statements about the world and remains operative today. But from

1960 Sukarno has adapted this 'three world' theory into a 'two world'
theory, in which the Afro-Asian nations are part of 'three-quarters
of mankind'—the new emerging forces—engaged in a deathly struggle
with 'one quarter'—the old established forces. The first mention of
this theme occurs in a speech to the United Nations General Assembly in 1960, entitled 'To Build the World Anew'. It was developed in September 1961, at the Belgrade conference of non-aligned
nations. Being non-aligned did not mean being a buffer state between two giant blocs, Sukarno said; non-alignment should be based
on a new approach that would 'startle mankind with its freshness'.
In Karachi in 1963, he welcomed Pakistan as a member of the new
emerging forces in a speech that made no reference to Pakistan's
membership of Seato. During the visit to Indonesia in 1963 of
Liu Shao Chi, communist China's head of state, Sukarno embraced
China as a new emerging force. In his 17 August (Independence
Day) speech in 1963, Sukarno defined the forces in more detail and
answered some criticisms.

> The New Emerging Forces is composed of the Asian nations, the
> African nations, the Latin American nations, the nations of the
> Socialist [meaning Communist] countries, the progressive groups
> in the capitalist countries . . . at least two thousand million
> people on the earth! Is this not a mighty power, as long as it is
> effectively organized and built up? . . . There are persons who say,
> why bother about the Old Established Order . . . live and let live!
> Stupid such a person is! . . . The safety of the world is always
> threatened by the Old Established Order . . . the safety of his
> own nation is always threatened by the Old Established Order.

The old established forces (or order) has never been defined
except by elimination. But it represents, apparently, the western
world, except for those 'progressive groups' which presumably means
those elements in sympathy with the destruction of the old established order. For, central to the theory, is the idea of conflict, which
because 'one cannot escape history' will lead to the destruction of
the 'old' and the establishment of a 'new' society. In the meantime
the conflict, expressed as a confrontation of the 'old' by the 'new',
is continuous. 'A Revolution is a long chain going from one confrontation to another. When one confrontation is finished, another one
appears! In fact, sometimes these confrontations even appear simul-
taneously, appear together, attacking from all directions . . .'
    With this emerging ideology, there has been emphasis under
Sukarno's recent leadership on status-symbols of the new Indonesian identity—a national monument supposed to last one thousand

years, a mosque designed to be the biggest in the world—and on freeing Indonesia from its tainted western colonial heritage by a mixed-bag ban on the Rosicrucians, Moral Rearmament, cha-cha and the twist. A more aggressive attitude on foreign affairs has also become characteristic of Sukarno's increased authority.

*   *   *

In the *wayang*, of which President Sukarno is an avid and intelligent follower, one of the stock characters is Gatutkacha. He stands for courage—as compared, say, with Puntadewa, who stands for integrity and modesty, and Bima (Gatutkacha's father) who stands for a strong will. He can also fly, is very popular, and cannot bear injustice. Gatutkacha is Sukarno's favourite, and it may be that the Indonesian president has modelled himself on his hero.

There is something of the effortless charisma of great leadership in Sukarno's life. The short list of candidates for leadership of Indonesia was by no means insignificant. Both Hatta and Sjahrir were men of sterling capacities, and there were several others who, if fortune had smiled the other way, might have been preferred to Sukarno. But he always managed to create in the minds of those around him —whether Indonesian, Dutch or Japanese—an impression of having been chosen to lead the Indonesian nation in its first entry into the world. His ability was largely inspirational. Unlike many revolutionary leaders, he is not an organizer and, unlike some revolutionary leaders, he seemed unable to settle down, after acquiring power, to the detail of its application. Like many romantics who enjoy pleasure, Sukarno developed essentially withdrawn and protective attitudes to his leadership role. In recent years he has rarely been seen informally among the people, except when he tours Java or one of the islands, when he is able to keep up, for astonishingly long periods of the day and night, a running social contact. He does not play games, as many other Asian leaders do, enabling them to mix casually on the golf course or the tennis court. He is informal at parties, but in a proprietorial way, more a matter of style than of sentiment. On these occasions he treats the services of diplomats—including their ability to sing their native songs, like 'Home on the Range' or 'Waltzing Matilda'—as his private property, behaviour reflected in his attitude to paintings or pretty ankles that catch his eye. In Djakarta he lives in his heavily guarded palace, one of five he inherited from the Dutch governor, flying by helicopter to the palace at Bogor or, when forced to travel about the city, moving in a motorcade of great noise and size—eight motorcyclists, eight jeeps, with several staff cars following the President's own black limousine; all with sirens wailing.

Part of his seclusion is, of course, inevitable. An Indonesian friend who accompanied me to the President's palace at Merdeka Utara in Djakarta said, as we approached the gate sentry: 'It is better to take off your sun-glasses. The guards like to see your eyes.' This mysterious message was translated later: the guards had orders to shoot first and ask questions afterwards. A trick of would-be assassins is to conceal the tell-tale emotional flicker of the eyes seconds before the act, with sun-glasses. Perhaps my friend was an unusually cautious man, or perhaps he had something to hide; but as five attempts had been made on Sukarno's life it is not surprising that the crack regiments that guard his palaces are sensitive to strangers. His escapes from assassination may have confirmed his right to leadership in the people's eyes, as proof that the magico-historic royal quality of imperviousness to weapons is his.

Like all political leaders, Sukarno in private has moments of relaxed charm which surprise a visitor. The image of inhuman self-possession which the cabled reports of Sukarno's official activities necessarily create is upset by the spectacle of a balding man in shirt-sleeves, with a battery of vitamin pills and other stimulants on the breakfast table. But Sukarno is not warmly regarded by his close associates, although they may respect him. One of his colleagues expressed his feelings about the President in oblique fashion: 'Sukarno has strong personal views which, as head of state, he must be prepared to defend and justify'. A head of state with strong personal views is not a person to be easily trusted; personal matters can be elevated into affairs of state.

Nor has Sukarno managed to create in the minds of most Indonesians a great awe or fear. Many Indonesians will react against personal criticism of him, especially if it is made by foreigners, but they do not walk in his constant presence, even to the extent that Indians have done since independence with Nehru. Sukarno is a very human leader and is so regarded by his people. Earlier, Sukarno's name was often mentioned with extreme distaste by anti-communist intellectuals (especially non-Javanese). Visiting foreigners would be regaled with gruesome accounts of his latest sexual exploits, his irreligious flirtation with Marxism, his personal saturation of flattery and deceit and his insensitivity to economic conditions. But recently he has become more generally accepted. It is as if the Indonesians have changed their view of him for the third time—first, the revolutionary, nationalist leader; second, the controversial nationalist leader; and now, the controversial head of state. Now one finds that the same Indonesians will question whether Sukarno's faults are not in some way attuned to the deeper sympathies of his country. They pay respect to his ability to survive and to keep in touch with the 'people's emotions'. They may not believe that Sukarno is positively good for Indonesia, but, if he is not permitted to do irreparable damage, they seem happy to accept his rule as an interregnum. When he is gone the real life and death battle for Indonesia will begin, they say.

No other Asian leader has so keenly offended the puritan values of the West. Abstinence, monogamy, balanced budgets and other virtues believed to justify the pleasures of success are conspicuously under-valued by the Indonesian President. By claiming to be a believer in God and a Marxist, Sukarno added insult to injury, confusing his foreign friends and confounding his enemies. Within Indonesia, these human failings amounted to little. Especially among the Javanese, the ability to hold apparently contradictory beliefs at the same time is considered merely as evidence that the soul is marvellously flexible. Of all the qualities required in an Indonesian leader, many of them possessed by Sukarno and none of them accountable to puritan values in personal life, Sukarno's notorious liking for women is, on the whole, an advantage for him in Indonesia. The defiance of recognized rules because of magic power, possessed so strongly that it cannot be controlled, is an ancient Javanese mark of leadership, springing from animist beliefs. One day Sukarno appeared at a press conference attired correctly except that he was not wearing shoes. Curious correspondents asked why. He explained that an electric storm was brewing and he had been told by his *dukun* (medicine man, although sometimes used to mean a masseuse), that he was so full of vitality that he would attract lightning (and presumably without shoes an electric charge would be conducted away). Western correspondents found this episode unearthly evidence of Sukarno's lack of rationality, but Indonesians expressed no surprise. Sukarno's tremendous energy, whether in dancing all night, or in political *musjawarah* that lasts perhaps ten hours, is a badge of leadership. He is not expected to be a good family man, faithful to his wife in the tradition of western politics. The siren of his outrider escort, which speeds him through the town, is popularly called, without malice, his 'mating call'. The women who objected when Sukarno took Hartini were not complaining about his being unfaithful to Fatmawati. They complained at Fatmawati's loss of social position, by being excluded from the palace and the functions as first lady. They would not have objected to Hartini becoming a mistress, which is a common enough pattern in Indonesia, as in most Asian—and some western—countries.

The history of modern Indonesia shows how Sukarno, irresolute compared with the decisive Sjahrir or seeming flippant beside the serious patriotism of Hatta, retained his position while they faltered. A Minangkabau born in 1909, Sjahrir's intellectual ability and honesty stand out in post-war Indonesia, but he never managed to bring his great talents into the forum of peacetime politics. It was said that the Partai Socialis Indonesia (PSI) which he founded in 1945 was only Sjahrir; this is not true, but it is true that the men who gathered around were, generally speaking, intellectuals without a mass following. Sjahrir became the voice of the non-communist left in Indonesia and was admired abroad, except of course in the communist bloc. His difficulty as a politician was that he lacked rapport with the 'Indonesian people'. Nor did he trust Sukarno politically; he regarded him not as a true revolutionary but as a vain man who wished to be admired and indulged, like a sultan. Sjahrir was probably a brilliant teacher rather than a man who understood power, and he and the PSI lost influence long before they were formally rejected by Sukarno.

Hatta (also a Minangkabau, born in 1902) is another great figure of the revolutionary days who has been forced into premature retirement. He is still respected; Sukarno made a public demonstration of this in 1963 when he visited his old colleague in hospital. But since 1956 Hatta has not taken an active part in the government of the country he loves so well, and his suburban villa in Djalan Diponegoro in Djakarta has become a sad landmark for politically curious tourists. Like Sjahrir, Hatta was educated in Holland, which provided a rational basis to his thinking. As an economist, he was particularly attracted to slow and careful national development, based on hard work and thriftiness. For this reason, perhaps, he was regarded as a moderate, and pro-western, although he is a Muslim and —reflecting European teaching of the twenties—has been influenced by Marxism. Sjahrir respected Hatta, although he seems to have considered him politically naïve. Less impatient than Sjahrir, Hatta's attitude to Sukarno is summed up in an article he wrote in 1960 when he decided to support the League of Democracy, which for a brief while challenged the President's ideas of guided democracy.

It cannot be denied that Sukarno is a patriot who seeks to achieve a just and prosperous Indonesia as quickly as possible. Due to his nature and aptitude, however, he sees only the broad lines of his conceptions, without bothering about details which may be decisive in their implementation. Consequently, he often achieves the reverse of what he seeks. His aims are always good, but his measures lead him far afield; the dictatorship he has created in the name of guided democracy will bring him to a situation contrary to his ideals.

Sukarno's achievements have retained substantial advantages for Indonesia. His influence was important in the establishment of a secular, rather than an Islamic, state; the advantages of this are probably more apparent to a non-Muslim than to a Muslim, but it does seem generally true that the removal of religious tests from the operation of government improves stability. He has promoted national unity. It is arguable whether a unitary state is more suited than a federation to Indonesia's peculiarly varied needs, but Sukarno has proclaimed the unity of the people of Indonesia 'from Sabang to Merauke', with such persistence that a national awareness has become the badge of modern Indonesia. Sukarno has also striven to awake in his people a sense of pride in their own achievements, after centuries of being regarded by the Dutch as hopelessly second-class and improbable human beings. Guided democracy, which most of the outside world has regarded as a technique to gain power, is for Sukarno a product of a glorious past. *Pantja Sila* is 'the essence of two thousand years of our civilization'.

This is not an unusual kind of declaration for nationalist leaders to make—Nehru has made similar reference to ancient India—but it can be contrasted with the following statement of Sjahrir's in 1935, not as a comparison (which would be unfair in time to Sjahrir) but as an indication of where the roots of Sukarno's particular nationalism lie:

In our country there has been no spiritual or cultural life and no intellectual progress for centuries. There are the much-praised art forms, but what are these except bare rudiments from a feudal culture that cannot possibly provide a dynamic fulcrum for people of the twentieth century? What can the puppet and other simple and mystical symbols offer us in a broad and intellectual sense? They are only parallels of the out-dated allegories and wisdom of medieval Europe. Our spiritual needs are needs of the twentieth century. Our inclination is no longer towards the mystical but towards reality, clarity and objectivity.

In substance, we can never accept the essential difference between the East and the West, because for our spiritual needs we are in general dependent on the West, not only scientifically but culturally.

We intellectuals here are much closer to Europe or America than we are to the Borobudur or Mahabharata or to the primitive Islamic culture of Java and Sumatra. Which is our basis; the West, or the rudiments of feudal culture that are still to be found in our Eastern Society?

It can be shown that much of Sukarno's flamboyance and apparent radicalism is camouflage for an essentially hesitant man, who is also an expert politician. He is effusive about communism, which gives him the support of both Moscow and Peking and therefore of the Indonesian communist party, but he kept communists out of the inner cabinet because of the army's attitude and the position taken by the United States that economic aid would be affected. His 'new emerging forces' do not accord with any international reality, as presumably the forces so defined do not propose to let Indonesia take over the leadership of their three-quarters of the world. This does not mean, however, that to Sukarno the concept is not real and useful. If standards based on international realities were imposed on Indonesia, the nation would splinter. Sukarno has created his own reality, which accords with his domestic political situation—namely that the communists are strong and western interests and values are either unrepresented or tend to be discredited.

The vociferous, revolutionary quality of Sukarno's nationalism can also be explained by the theory of compensation; as the economic and social structure of Indonesia has been so little altered by the great revolution, its national character must be emphasized. In the same way, stressing that the revolution is continuous is a useful explanation of the fact that so little has been achieved. Suffering, even martyrdom, for the privilege of being right, usefully includes that suffering which is caused by being stupid or mistaken.

These are the threads of the President of Indonesia's intricate web of authority. He is not a dictator in the sense that he has a party behind him to force in the name of its leader or an ideology actions which cannot be taken in the name of the state. He dictates through persuasion of conflicting forces, and his rule has been relatively free of the brutality and bloodshed of conventional dictatorships.

This analysis of Sukarno's power, which is common among observers of Indonesian politics, explains otherwise curious facets of his career, especially in his careful role as captive anti-hero of the armed forces. It is worthwhile, also, in drawing attention to the environment in which Sukarno must act and decide. In the long run, it is undeniably more fruitful in foreign relations to try to understand why nations and their leaders behave as they do than to concentrate on how best to punish them for doing it. In the case of Sukarno, however, as with all powerful men, one cannot neglect the self-imposed policies and the self-justified strategies. While, as leader of the tribe, he may be required to extract unanimous agreement from the council of elders, it is up to him whether what he extracts is the lowest common denominator or the highest common multiple of their positions—whether, in other words, it is unassailable on the grounds of its caution or its belligerency. As he grows older and has trouble with his health, the mind of Sukarno becomes an important element in a political situation where the constitutional restraints on power have been removed. Intellectually, he has always been a radical, however conservative his personal politics may be.

He cannot look forward at his age to a period of building, with its slow and unspectacular processes. He has no time—as, say, the prime minister of Malaysia, Tunku Abdul Rahman, has, at about the same age—to establish his niche in history as the leader who achieved not only independence but security and prosperity as well. His niche is assured, however, as a revolutionary, and his purpose recently seems to have been devoted to enshrining it.

Sukarno was called a Japanese quisling and a western puppet by communist commentators in the early days of Indonesian independence. More recently he has been called a communist by western commentators preoccupied with anti-communism. He is, of course, neither, but to say that he is a genuine Indonesian nationalist does not mean that he does not offer a challenge and perhaps even a threat to his neighbourhood. Sukarno believes passionately in his destiny and Indonesia's. He believes, as do the communist leaders in Peking, that Asia was humiliated by western colonialism and has still not equalized the score. He has led Indonesia into a position that is generally critical of western ideas and values and, because Indonesia is surrounded by western military influences, of western power. His speeches, which are sensitive to the lessons of history, see the present world balance, whether expressed in the membership of the United Nations Security Council or in military and economic power, as 'unfair'—a legacy of that unhappy time when Indonesia was 'a nation of coolies and a coolie amongst nations'. Now, Indonesia is not a 'beancake nation', but the flower of centuries of civilization and, by population, the fifth country in the world. It wants 'recognition', as the psychologists say. Yet it may be asked what recognition of Indonesia's 'rights' can be given, on the terms which Sukarno has unveiled in speech after speech, short of dominant leadership in the region.

CHAPTER FOUR

The Communists

The Indonesian Communist Party or PKI (Partai Kommunist Indonesia) is the oldest communist party in Asia and the biggest outside the Soviet Union and China. It claimed a membership of two and a half million in 1963, which may not be an exaggeration. It has penetrated the apparatus of government in great detail, except for the inner cabinet. It controls the biggest trade union organization, the Central All-Indonesian Workers' Organization or Sobsi (Sentral Organisasi Buruh Seluru Indonesia) and the largest peasants' group, the Indonesian Peasant Front or BTI (Barisan Tani Indonesia), and has influence in the major mass organization, the National Front. Its leadership is young, gifted and experienced. Dipa Nusantara Aidit, the secretary-general of the party for the last ten years, was born in 1922. First deputy secretary-general M. H. Lukman is four years older. Njoto, second deputy secretary-general, is a year younger than Aidit. In other words, they are men of the generation of Nasution, Chairul Saleh and Subandrio, the nation's second-rung leadership. They have waited already a long time for power, but they still have time to spare, even if we assume that they view the attainment of power in a sufficiently personal way to desire it for themselves. They are pleasant to meet and, in the obscure operation of Indonesia's domestic politics, their propaganda is more understandable internationally than most. They know what is going on in the country, and although they are extremely careful not to be critical of the President, who is touchy about criticism of his performance, they are not backward in pointing out the shortcomings of his government. In the shadow-play world of Djakarta politics, direct criticism is like a shaft of natural light.

As they have never been in government, the years of corruption, mismanagement and slow economic deterioration have not tainted them. Their reputation for spartan living, their apparent dedication and concern for the public welfare, appeal more than ever as the rift between the living standards of the governing élite and the mass of people widens, especially in urban areas. In the 1955 general elections (the last to be held in Indonesia) the PKI was the fourth biggest party, polling 6,176,914 votes, or 16·4 per cent of the total. In the local elections in Java two years later, they did better. They came second in Djakarta, first in central Java, and second in both east and west Java. In seaports and inland cities like Cheribon, Madura, Malang, Magelang, Semarang, Surabaya and Solo, the party registered absolute majorities. If anything, the PKI has improved its position since then. It has increasingly won the ear of the President on foreign affairs and it has earned popular respect for its critical attitude toward the government's failure to provide *sandang pangan*: food and clothing for the people. If an election were held now, the PKI would poll better than in 1955. It could easily become the biggest single party, although in President Sukarno's 'guided democracy' this would not mean as much as it might have before 1957, when the forms of parliamentary democracy prevailed. But it would be extremely difficult for the President not to allow PKI representation in the cabinet under those circumstances.

It is in fact surprising that the PKI is not already better represented in the government. The arguments against it outside Indonesia are not persuasive inside the country. It may be said by influential western governments such as the United States that if communists are admitted to the cabinet, aid will have to be reconsidered, or friendly attitudes re-examined. Indonesians are right to suspect this. The United States is providing aid to Yugoslavia, which has a communist government, and to Poland. A closer parallel exists in Laos: the United States signed the agreement which established the idea of a neutral Laos, based on a composite government including the communist faction. Aid has continued. Moreover, the Indonesian government has reason to believe that whatever Australia and the United States may themselves want for Indonesia, they would accept a neutralist Indonesia, with communist support, in preference to a violently communist Indonesia brought in on the wave of revolution.

The reason the PKI is not already in the inner cabinet is not simply because Indonesia is frightened that it will lose western aid. It is rather that President Sukarno is aware that influential nationalist opinion in Indonesia—especially in the army—has not fully accepted the communists, despite the President's efforts, as genuine and trustworthy Indonesian nationalists. To understand this it is necessary to trace a little of the history of communism in Indonesia.

The PKI was formed in the Dutch East Indies against a background of militant international communism. The Russian revolution was three years old. The Communist International (Comintern) was understandably too engrossed in the great events of the northern hemisphere to concern itself with the details of the Indonesian situation. Indonesia seemed a long way away to the new rulers in the Kremlin, especially when, after Lenin's death in 1924, they began a new struggle for power among themselves. South-east Asia was a 'region' and it is symptomatic of the remoteness of their approach that at the fourth Comintern congress in 1922, Tan Malaka, a young Sumatran, was appointed Comintern agent for something called Aslia, namely, South-east Asia and Australia.

In its early days, the PKI had its main contact with the world through the Netherlands communist party and the Comintern's far eastern office in Shanghai, headed by Sneevliet, the founder of the Indies Social Democratic Association from which the PKI sprang. The PKI had infiltrated the Sarekat Islam thoroughly, and in 1921 made a bid for open control—the main contenders for power being Tan Malaka and Semaun. They were blocked and repulsed by Agus Salim, later to become one of the Republic's early foreign ministers and an elder statesman of the Masjumi party. Their precipitous action placed them in opposition to the most powerful religious influence in the country. It also exposed the leadership. Tan Malaka was exiled by the Dutch in 1922. His successor as chairman of the party, Semaun, was banished in 1923. Decapitated, the party began to spin to the left. Stalin, who was developing his theme of 'socialism in one country', with the corollary that communists should build up a solid base of power and popular support before attempting to change the world, said in August 1925, 'the Communists in Java, who recently erroneously put forward the slogan of a Soviet government for the country, suffer, it seems, from a [leftist] deviation . . . which threatens to isolate the Communist party from the masses and transform it into a sect'. Undeterred, the PKI proceeded with a general strike, which was a failure, and Darsono, a founder-member and deputy chairman, was arrested and exiled. Other leaders like Alimin, Musso and Sardjono, fled to Singapore. In the confusion that followed, an interesting piece of duplicity occurred. Tan Malaka, who was in Manila, opposed any further adventures and presented Alimin in Singapore with a memorandum to that effect. Alimin and Musso were convinced, however, that a rebellion would succeed, and Tan Malaka's memorandum was suppressed. Tan Malaka got word of his opposition through to Java, and confusion deepened. Alimin, uncovered by the British in Singapore, was sent to China. Still plans for the revolution proceeded. Semaun, now in the Netherlands, signed a pact with the students' union, led by Hatta and Sjahrir, to bring the nationalists on side. (The pact was dissolved a year later.)

On 13 November 1926 the great rebellion took place. In the middle of the night, two hundred armed men seized the telephone and telegraph building in Batavia. At Bantam, on the west coast of Java, the barricades went up at the same time. At half a dozen other towns in west and central Java, takeovers of various kinds were effected, some accompanied by murder and violence. But within a week the revolution had been crushed by the Dutch; the mass of the Indonesian people had not moved. Dutch punishment was thorough. Nine were hanged and thousands interned: 823 were sent to Boven Digul in New Guinea. The PKI was thoroughly beaten. It did not surface again until 1935, and not until the end of the Japanese occupation and the beginning of the nationalist defence of independence did it become effective again.

In 1935 Musso returned to Indonesia (one of the curious by-products of being an Indonesian communist seems to be an ability to travel: to this day Indonesian communist leaders are peripatetic) and established the so-called 'illegal PKI', whose job was primarily to work with the nationalist movement and the Dutch to prepare a common anti-Japanese front. This clear-sighted analysis of Japanese intentions in the Pacific was offset by other developments. In the Netherlands, the communist party decided to abandon, as its contribution to the Popular Front fashion sweeping Europe, immediate independence for Indonesia. This had the effect of disillusioning Indonesian nationalists about communist motives, and although many Indonesians who studied at the Hague returned to their country with a strong Marxist approach, shown especially by their interest in economics, they were pure Marxists as it were, who distrusted the practical politics of the Soviet Union and the organized communist movement.

In Indonesia, the Popular Front revived the PKI, which became a moving force in Gerindo (Gerakan Rakyat Indonesia—Indonesian People's Movement)—the left-wing party under the leadership of Amir Sjarifuddin, Sartono and Mohammed Yamin. When the Japanese arrived, they were able to operate underground, partly with money provided by the Dutch, before they left, to Sjarifuddin, who was believed to be a nationalist at the time but later claimed that he had been a communist since 1938. Other underground groups operated in conjunction with Sjahrir and were especially successful in infiltrating Peta (Soekarela Tentara Pembela Tanah

Air—Volunteer Army of Defenders of the Fatherland) set up by the Japanese for Indonesian self-defence. Sardjono, who had been in Boven Digul, was released with some six hundred other prisoners and sent to Australia. (These prisoners included the parents of Lukman, now deputy secretary-general of the PKI, whose mother died in Australia and who visited her grave there in 1963.) Sardjono and his group were used for intelligence and propagandist work against the Japanese, operating first from Brisbane and later from Morotai, in the Moluccas.

In September 1944 Tokyo instructed the military administration, which was based in Saigon, to cease 'haughty and arrogant behaviour', abandon the 'idea of colonial subjugation', encourage 'nationalistic activities', promote 'racial consciousness' among the people and impart 'political training' to the Indonesians. Tan Malaka, who appears to have returned mysteriously to Indonesia in 1942 and worked during the war as a collaborator on Japanese propaganda, became the key figure in an extraordinary sequence of events that today have still not been successfully explained. The head of Japanese naval intelligence in the East Indies (Vice-Admiral Mayeda) seems to have enlisted the help of Tan Malaka and other pro-Japanese communists like Subardjo, who later became foreign minister, in an effort to put 'nationalist' communists other than Stalinists in the saddle of an independent Indonesia. Mayeda established 'schools', which Sukarno, Hatta and other leaders addressed, proclaiming social justice for the world in terms of the overthrow of imperialism and capitalism—a view not popular in Moscow just then, which was not anxious to upset its capitalist allies until fascism was thoroughly beaten. The schools turned out several hundred graduates, including Aidit, now PKI secretary-general. They were encouraged to join ostensibly nationalist underground movements; many of them joined Tan Malaka. The illegal PKI, suspicious of Tan Malaka, who had established his own party called Pari (Partai Republik Indonesia—Indonesian Republic Party) at Bangkok in 1927 and had been for a long time sympathetic toward Japan's ambitions in Asia, counter-infiltrated and eventually gained control of the schools. The Japanese intention in the manoeuvre has puzzled historians. Its effect, however, was to open the conflict between 'nationalist' and 'soviet' communists. This conflict is part of the Indonesian political scene today.

It was, of course, the non-communist Indonesian nationalists Sukarno and Hatta who proclaimed independence, and from that moment one of the chief concerns of the PKI was to determine its attitude to the new 'bourgeois' republic. For a while the party equivocated, but when the leadership was taken over by Alimin and Sardjono, the PKI fell into line with Moscow, even sometimes when it appeared to run contrary to its own political interests. In 1947, for example, the PKI rejected concessions which Sjahrir's government had made to the Dutch, thus causing the fall of the government and the prospect of a coalition more favourable domestically to the PKI. Word came from Moscow that the 'international situation' required that the concession to the Dutch should be made, and the PKI reversed its stand.

PKI confusion reached its peak in 1948, as in 1926, with an abortive revolt. In January, the left-leaning government, headed by Amir Sjarifuddin, had been replaced by one under Hatta, whose attitude to communism was well known. In addition, Hatta, as vice-president, was personally responsible to the President, rather than to Parliament, which was at that time under the influence of the Sajap Kiri, the left-wing coalition group. The Sajap Kiri withdrew its support for the government and underwent a reorganization, emerging as the Front Demokrasi Rakyat (People's Democratic Front). On two issues Hatta's government showed itself to be increasingly out of touch with Moscow's plans. The USSR suddenly announced that it had signed an agreement for an exchange of consular representatives with Indonesia. The Indonesian government did not respond— although the agreement had been initialled by the Indonesian representative in Prague, Suripno, a communist, who had been sent there the year before. The second issue concerned the rationalization of the armed forces, which the PKI opposed, fearing rightly that this would mean the demobilization of those guerilla units under communist control.

In August 1948, Suripno arrived surprisingly by air (the *deus ex machina* appearances of communists is another facet of Indonesian history) at Bukittingi, Sumatra, with a 'secretary' who turned out to be Musso, returning after an absence of twelve years. Musso was clearly an emissary from Moscow, and quickly established his authority and the 'New Road for the Republic of Indonesia'. His solution, perhaps reflecting the Soviet's disenchantment with the post-war turn of events in Europe, was for a communist-dominated national front—a tough line. He may have hoped for a peaceful solution in the long run, but he gave no indication that Hatta would receive quarter. He advised the armed groups to defy rationalization and began to prepare to consolidate communist power. This was the beginning of a period of violence and unrest all over Asia, with communist rebellions in the vanguard. Rebellions began in 1948 in Malaya, Burma and the Philippines. 1949 was the year of communist triumph on the Chinese mainland. 1950 brought Tibet and Korea. It was not until the death of Stalin in 1953 and the era of co-existence ushered in by Khrushchev that the communists in Asia began looking seriously again at the prospect of co-operation with the bourgeois-nationalist governments.

Musso, then fifty years old and an experienced communist, may have planned his course carefully, but events took over, as they have a habit of doing in Indonesia. Local communist army commanders took the initiative on 18 September 1948, and seized power in Madiun, a town in central Java. The PKI leaders, including Musso, were on a speaking tour and were taken by surprise, but they were caught in their own propaganda and hurried to Madiun to support the rebellion. Musso over the radio launched his attack on Sukarno and Hatta, and declared that they should die as 'Japanese and American' traitors. Radio Moscow announced that a 'people's government' had been formed in Madiun following 'a popular uprising against the government of the fascist Japanese quislings, Sukarno and Hatta'.

Within three months, after guerilla fighting in which the communists had little chance, the insurrection was at an end, broken by the now famous Siliwangi division (named after an ancient Sundanese king), formed two years earlier by Sjahrir to deal with Tan Malaka. Almost the entire communist leadership had been liquidated —either dead like Musso, killed in a skirmish, or Amir Sjarifuddin, executed, or, like Sardjono, imprisoned. Perhaps more critical from the PKI's point of view was that the Madiun revolt was regarded by the Indonesian people as an act of treachery. The Republic was at that time undergoing a blockade on the eve of the second Dutch 'police action'; the communist 'stab in the back' is remembered to this day. The communists have twisted the history of Madiun, describing it as a 'provocation', but they have acknowledged that it was a disastrous mistake.

The Dutch action saved the day for Moscow, which could argue that colonialism was still Indonesia's primary enemy. But in Indonesia the PKI was too beaten to take immediate advantage. Its old competitor, Tan Malaka, who had formed the Partai Murba (Proletarian Party), under the slogan of 'nationalist-communism', now took over the leadership of the Left. He set up in opposition not only to the Sukarno-Hatta duumvirate, but to the PKI, the Dutch, the Americans and the Russians. His guerilla exploits were not, however, as convincing as his propaganda, and his troops were eventually disarmed by the regular army, and, in April 1949, Tan Malaka was arrested and executed. One of his lieutenants, Chairul Saleh, who had been in the group of students which kidnapped Sukarno and Hatta to force the proclamation of independence in 1945, continued the struggle against the 'weak' Sukarno-Hatta leadership, and began terrorizing the countryside. Saleh was arrested in 1950 and virtually exiled by Prime Minister Wilopo's government; after a stay in Holland he was exiled by the Dutch government and spent his time studying in Berlin and Bonn until his return to Indonesia in 1956. In general the left wing, whether Partai Murba or PKI, gradually gave up the armed struggle and adopted a soft, flexible line toward the bourgeois nationalists in control of the country's government. The PKI began its long compromise with Marxist-Leninist doctrine which continues today. Domestic capitalism is all right, because it is oppressed by foreign capitalism. Non-alignment is all right, because it is directed against encircling imperialism. A belief in God is all right, provided it is accompanied by tolerance of non-belief.

With the party's reputation in tatters and Korea in the limelight, Alimin, who took over the PKI leadership, did little more than hold the fort for Aidit, who became secretary-general in 1954. As no party would co-operate with the PKI, the old tactics of a united front from above had to be replaced by a united front from below, broadening the base of its recruitment. The party also swung into a more nationalist position. In 1952, on the thirty-second anniversary of the PKI's founding, the new strategy was announced; Aidit called for a national front and pledged PKI non-interference in the affairs of other parties. Alimin voiced the new slogan: 'Long live Sukarno! Long live the PKI!' According to one observer, Arnold C. Brackman of the *Christian Science Monitor*, whose book *Indonesian Communism* is the best documentation of its subject, the audience gasped, but the slogan was repeated with Aidit's visible encouragement and applause broke through. The transition to the new line went smoothly, although it was not easy for the PKI to be patriotic when Indonesia's government was a composition of all its old enemies—the Wilopo cabinet being a combination of Masjumi, PSI and PNI. There were some odd incidents, such as the occasion at Solo when police removed a portrait of Musso from the dais at a PKI gathering, causing the delegates to shout defiantly, 'Long live Musso!' when they should have been calling for Sukarno's longevity.

Within the general strategy since then, only tactics have changed. When the Wilopo government fell in 1953 the PKI, relieved to see

its enemies Masjumi and the PSI out of the way, gave active parliamentary support to Ali Sastroamidjojo's basically PNI government.
The PKI's success in the 1955 general elections and the 1957 local
election in Java showed how well it had recovered from the stigma of
Madiun. Membership grew steadily from the 7,910 recorded for
1952, 1,500,000 in 1959 and 2,000,000 in 1961, to the current figure
of 2,500,000. The party was immensely helped to recover its prestige
by the rebellion of 1957, which dealt a corresponding blow to the
Masjumi and PSI, and by the constancy of its propagation of the
West Irian issue. For a while, the PKI was uncertain about President
Sukarno's guided democracy, fearing perhaps that it was in Bung
Karno's best tradition of looking north and hitting south—an elaborate attempt to curb the new electoral strength of the PKI by restrict-
ing the power of the political parties. But, caught up in the competition for the President's favours, it has no prospect, except the
twice-failed course of open revolt, other than ardent support. One
might quote here a popular Indonesian song (popular in the sense of
a folk-song rather than in the sense of the national culture one hears
on the radio or reads in the press) which may have arisen at the
time of the depression or the Dutch wars, or another time of national
emergency, but has a topical application, especially to critics of the
present régime.

> We have lived to see a time without order
> In which everyone is confused in his mind
> One cannot bear to join in the madness
> But if he does not do so
> He will not share in the spoils
> And will starve as a result.

To the PKI the political mixture of Djakarta must seem sometimes
like madness, but although the party has not 'joined in' completely,
it has not been for want of trying. A Nasakom cabinet, which
would extend the idea of communist participation in government to
the inner cabinet, is the theme of almost every major speech. The
reason is not only to gain more policy-making power. It is debatable
whether in the new set-up, where the cabinet is responsible to the
president and does not initiate policy, the PKI would have noticeably better opportunities to influence policy-making than in its present position, where it is represented in the national planning council,
etc. But the PKI's power over the 'spoils' would be increased and its
prestige enhanced by control of a senior ministry such as finance.
PKI leaders still react sharply to the suggestion that the interests of

the party would be better served by keeping out of government and allowing the country to reach economic rock-bottom, when a complete takeover on classical communist terms would become possible.

The PKI is still trying to broaden the base of its support as much as possible. When I visited party headquarters in Raya Kramat, Djakarta, on the last occasion in August 1963, it was a hive of industry, reflecting a building programme based on an extension of the present office and the construction of a five-story 'people's university' in the grounds. Both Karel Supit, who is in charge of foreign affairs, and Lukman (Aidit was away on one of his frequent tours) were concerned to point out that the party was part of the apparatus of respectable government in Indonesia. They launched on a strong argument for a Nasakom cabinet, asking why it caused such concern in the West. 'If you are democratic in Australia, you will support it', Lukman said. He added frankly: 'President Sukarno would like a Nasakom cabinet. We are convinced that it will come—and it will come sooner if people like the Australians and the Americans do not oppose it'.

This interview with Lukman was singularly lacking in the kind of tension that often occurs when communist leaders are cross-examined by western correspondents. Lukman had not long returned from his short visit to Australia (where he found Sydney 'very large'). He joked about his visit. Four times he had been refused a visa; then one was granted. Was it because he was now deputy speaker of Parliament, with the rank of minister and an official passport? 'You see the advantage of Nasakom', he said. I questioned him on his early life and that of the party. 'I have been a communist from birth, because of the economic conditions.' (His parents were exiled to Boven Digul in New Guinea and he, as a small child, with them.) He repeated the stock responses to the historical questions. Madiun was a 'national tragedy' provoked by anti-communists. The party had corrected its early mistakes and was now finally on the Marxist-Leninist rails. It was a 'slander' to suggest that the party would benefit from worsening economic conditions in Indonesia. 'We need better living conditions in Indonesia so as to fight imperialism better.' That was why the PKI criticized 'bad management and corruption in the government'. 'We must be patriotic, as long as so many ministers in the government are not patriotic.' Equally, the party was not in two minds (unlike communists in Australia, he pointed out) over the Moscow-Peking split. 'The only effect of the disagreement of opinion is the fact that by this members of the PKI are being urged to study more intensively Marxist-Leninist literature, including documents and writings issued by both the Communist Party of the Soviet Union and the Communist Party of China and other parties as well,' he said, as recorded in the PKI's official version of the interview. The PKI was supported on the question by 'the entire party, from top to bottom'. He laughed off a question enquiring into the truth of suggestions that Aidit was pro-Moscow, while Lukman leaned to Peking. 'We are both pro-Indonesian.' Did not this raise difficulties when Indonesia's interests clashed with those either of Moscow or Peking—as, for example, when the Indonesian government banned foreign (Chinese) traders in the rural areas? Lukman observed that that 'problem' had been 'resolved'. What about the border conflict between China and India? India was a non-aligned nation, with which Indonesia might be supposed to have some sympathy. Did the PKI support Peking or Moscow, which was continuing to give aid to India, including military equipment? Lukman was quick to answer. 'What the government of the Soviet Union is doing is not in accordance with a policy of Marxism-Leninism.' I wondered, as I took down his answer, what might have been the reply if I had been questioning Aidit.

It is a little unfair to select these points from a long interview, most of which was taken up with a detailed and comprehensible dissertation by Lukman on the parlous state of the Indonesian economy and the efforts of the United States to 'blackmail' Indonesia into implementing the May 1963 economic reforms (which were strongly opposed by the PKI as American-inspired). Lukman was also definite and straightforward on Malaysia, which was an attempt, as the PKI saw it, to encircle Indonesia and draw it into the western orbit. 'We believe Indonesia belongs to the new emerging forces, which, as President Sukarno has said, include the communist countries, and that we must confront Malaysia, which represents the old established forces.'

The impression one gains of Lukman, as of Aidit, is of competence and accessibility. They are probably devout communists, but their fanaticism is sophisticated. They are cheerful and busy, giving the impression that they are 'in' rather than 'out' in present Indonesian political élite society. They are apparently relaxed in other respects. Aidit occasionally attends Muslim prayers at a mosque or in the fields. Jusuf Adjitorop, a member of the central committee of the PKI, goes occasionally to a Protestant church in Djakarta.

As communists, the PKI leaders keep their eyes on the big game—United States imperialism and its inexhaustible evils—but as Indonesian politicians, they are watchful of practical checks on their power. They expect these checks from the extremist Muslims; and especially from the army, usually defined as 'capitalist-bureaucrat' in the thick Marxist jargon of PKI pamphlets. The army does not have an ethic which is part of the establishment of the state, as Islam does. So it can be opposed openly, except, of course—and significantly—as the country's defence. When General Nasution negotiated the huge arms deal with the Soviet Union in 1960, as part of mobilization for the West Irian campaign, the PKI rejoiced that Indonesia was becoming more closely tied militarily to the Soviet bloc, while wondering what the army would do with its new strength and prestige when the West Irian campaign was over. The answer was the PKI's successful campaign for an end (in May 1963) to the emergency regulations which enabled the army to act almost as a second arm of government in maintaining security. Hence Aidit, in February 1963, at the opening of the first plenum of the central committee of the PKI, in the peculiar language of Indonesian politics that is sometimes beyond the comprehension of the foreign observer:

> The masses will not only complete the struggle to liberate West Irian and re-establish security, but will rush on to crush all obstacles in the way of the people's revolutionary movement, such as the War Emergency status, the capitalist-bureaucrats, compradores and landlords, in short, everything against the Manipol and national gotong royong on the basis of Nasakom.

In an obvious reference to Nasution's plan for civic action, by which army manpower would be retained for part-time civilian work after the regulations were lifted, Aidit went on, 'The capitalist-bureaucrats and other reactionaries are doing their utmost . . . to take away the democracy which the people would get by the abolition of the state of emergency . . . [by] the formation of organizations to meddle in the task of the existing civilian authorities and thus disturb the public order.'

President Sukarno is a trusted ally on these occasions.

> It is quite obvious that Bung Karno's ideas show no similarity at all to the ideas of Hitler and Mussolini and their disciples in Indonesia, i.e., establishing one bourgeois reactionary party and suppressing the party of the labour class . . . It is therefore not taboo to have more than one party; in fact there are now ten parties in our country. Which one of them will become the leading party is for the people to decide . . .

The army is an identifiable enemy. Islam, on the other hand, cannot be opposed; it must be skirted, with appropriate genuflections.

Aidit's speeches are full of careful references, in the spirit of Bung
Karno's early reference to Nasakom: 'It is not our purpose to ask
the Marxists and Islamists to become nationalists; what we hope for
is intimacy, unity of these three groups.' In the same way, Njoto, a
more aggressive speaker, on 6 February 1963, on the occasion of the
twelfth anniversary of *Harian Rakyat (People's Daily)*, stressed the
tolerance of the *Pantja Sila* and attacked the concept, advanced by
some Muslims, that the 'backbone' of the *Pantja Sila* is the 'principle
of an Almighty God'. 'Bung Karno did not speak of a backbone, or
any other bone', Njoto declared, but said that in the final analysis
gotong royong was the essence of the *Pantja Sila*. It will be noticed
that *gotong royong* is a hard-worked phrase with all Indonesian pro-
pagandists. Its usefulness is obvious; it sets up 'co-operation' as the
highest standard and overrides competitive tests that would exclude
one group or another.

The PKI needs President Sukarno to keep the army from its
throat. It also realizes that he is as tolerant a non-communist dictator
as any communist party is likely to get. While the President is
moderately accessible to them at present and allows them to provide
the party with a base for action in the future, it would be suicidal to
contemplate revolution. Aidit, who has close contact with Moscow,
must appreciate that while Sukarno remains in power in Indonesia
and Khrushchev in the Soviet Union, any PKI attempt to unseat
Sukarno would be jumped on.

The party therefore lives in a much less dramatic atmosphere than
in its early days. It has become constructive, which is dangerous for
a revolutionary party. But Indonesian communists have learned that
the textbooks of revolutionary tactics have to be adapted to local
conditions. Their strength at present is mainly in Java and if they
were to try to take power, even legitimately, as the result of an election, they would find themselves in the midst of a civil war. Java
cannot feed itself. It would be encircled by anti-communist neighbours, like Australia, Malaysia and the Philippines, perhaps only too
anxious to support breakaway governments in Sumatra, Sulawesi, the
Moluccas and West Irian. On this reckoning, it is more profitable for
the PKI to expand its influence slowly and unobtrusively through the
accepted channels of present government leadership. At the same
time, it can go on, given legitimacy by the President, building its
power in the country at large. Arnold Brackman interestingly notes
recent PKI efforts to build its following among the fishermen in an
effort 'to secure a hospitable coastline, an escape hatch . . . a reliable
line of communications and supplies . . . an "active sanctuary" . . .

in the event of a voluntary or involuntary showdown with the army with Sukarno's passing . . . '

The PKI's nightmare is the split between Peking and Moscow, which again could bring the party's international allegiances into prominence. This would strengthen the Tan Malaka legacy, 'nationalism-communism' as represented by the Partai Murba, which already has influence in both the administration of government and the officer corps of the army. (In March 1963, on representation by Murba, President Sukarno agreed to recognize Tan Malaka as a national revolutionary hero.) PKI leaders stress their impartiality in the dispute and have shown some independence of both Peking and Moscow, but throughout 1963 there were indications that the party leadership was more inclined—at least in propaganda—to follow its Chinese comrades. Red Flag, the theoretical journal of the Chinese communists, applauded the PKI warmly in an editorial on 20 May 1963 for its 'correct line' and 'unremitting struggle against modern revisionism'. The PKI has been critical of the Indian communist party's support of the Nehru government in its border conflict with Peking, although it would have difficulty not supporting Sukarno in similar circumstances, as it discovered during the trouble over Chinese nationals in Indonesia during 1958-60. The Chinese racial element in the PKI is one reason why it might be expected to support Peking. At the same time, this makes the party vulnerable to outbursts of anti-Chinese feeling, such as took place in several places in Java during May 1963 when Chinese houses were smashed, partly, it is believed, as a reaction to the excessively friendly reception given President Liu Shao Chi and partly as a protest against difficult living conditions.

There are racial and regional reasons why, in the long run, China should try to exercise a greater influence than the Soviet Union over the course of Indonesian communism, but at the moment these are offset by Moscow's readier purse and the fact that Sukarno's recent foreign policies have been radical enough not to need stimulation from Peking.

CHAPTER FIVE

The Military

The role of the armed forces, especially the army, in Indonesia, is widely accepted as crucial. They have been seen, particularly in the United States and Australia, as a counter to the influence of communism under the Sukarno régime and an effective deterrent to a communist takeover in the future. From this has been drawn the conclusion, sometimes unavoidable in the abbreviations of journalism, that the army is 'pro-western'. These assumptions are misleading. From time to time they provide the correct answer, and in the long run they may turn out to be right. But they are based on insubstantial evidence at the moment.

The political importance of the military in the new countries of Asia, as in the Middle East and Latin America, arises in its simplest form from the failures of the political leadership. Because the military is the guardian of the new nation's security, it is able to stand aside from civilian society, establishing its own standards and forming its own judgments. Generally speaking, its officer corps come from families which do not belong to the traditional political interest groups —land-ownership, commerce or officialdom. With this 'lower middle class' background, they tend to be radical, with puritan prejudices enforced by discipline. They respect education and technology as aids to efficiency, and distrust journalism and politics as temptations to licence. Although not part of the traditional society, they are sympathetic to tradition, because of their role in preserving and securing the state and because of their trained respect for authority.

In central and eastern Asia (aside from communist countries, where the military has a clearly defined role as an arm of government), armies have gained a strong political position in Burma, Indonesia, Laos, nationalist China, Pakistan, South Korea, South Vietnam and Thailand. In India, Malaysia and the Philippines, countries with an established political continuity, they have not. In the cases of nationalist China, South Korea and South Vietnam, there are special, external reasons for the military's authority. Laos is still at a stage of war-lordism. Burma, Indonesia, Pakistan and Thailand are all instances, however, of army government or, as in Indonesia's case, army politics, directly associated with the failure of the political leadership. It is perhaps worth noting that two countries are Muslim, two Buddhist, which helps to correct the picture, gained from the Middle East, that there is a special connection between Islam and military rule.

Because the alternative to an army coup d'état has been thought in most cases to be a communist revolution, military régimes in Asia have been considered favourably in the West. But to assume they are 'pro-western' is to take another step, unjustified by the experience in Burma or in Pakistan. In the case of Indonesia, the armed forces have been modernized with weapons and equipment from the communist bloc and, in the West Irian and Malaysia crises, have taken up political positions at odds with what might be called the western interest. For a variety of reasons the Indonesian armed forces, while they remain under the direction of General Nasution, may be anti-communist, but they are too implicated in the Sukarno régime for this to be regarded automatically as a western asset. The influence of the military in Indonesia has so far been negative and dispersed rather than direct and positive. Part of the reason lies in its own disorganized beginnings.

Before the Japanese occupation, Indonesians had little chance of military service as a career. Soldiers, especially from Christian areas like Minahasa and Ambon, served with the Royal Netherlands Indies Army (KNIL), but there were few Indonesian officers, some noted exceptions being the nation's premier soldier, General Abdul Haris Nasution, who is minister of defence and chief of staff of the armed forces, Major-General (now retired) T. B. Simatupang, and Air-Marshal Suryadarma, formerly air force chief of staff. By far the greatest number of senior officers now serving with the Indonesian army received their first training under the Japanese. The first army chief of staff, the late General Sudirman, and the present chief of staff, Major-General Achmad Jani, were officers of Peta, the self-defence corps established by the Japanese in 1943. By the end of 1944 there were sixty-six Peta battalions (about five hundred men in each) in Java. The Japanese also recruited Indonesians to an auxiliary army and labour corps called *Hei Ho*.

A third group of officers came from the so-called *laskar* battalions (Laskar Rakyat or People's Army), independent guerilla units which sprang up during the struggle for independence from 1945 to 1949. Armed sometimes only with spears, these groups roved throughout western and central Java, some of them hard to distinguish from

Java's traditional armed bandits and marauders. They included political extremists of all kinds, and were the most difficult to bring under the single command of the official army, Tentara Nasional Indonesia (Indonesian National Army or TNI), when it was formed on 3 June 1947 (existing before that time as the People's Security Association, later changed to People's Safety Army and later still to Tentara Republik Indonesia or Army of the Republic of Indonesia, called TRI).

The army, in other words, did not appear on the scene, when the nation won its independence, as a unified and disciplined body. Guy J. Pauker makes the point in his chapter on Indonesia in *The Role of the Military in Underdeveloped Countries* that had the army been well-organized it might have intervened in public affairs 'only at crucial moments, decisively and purposefully'. Instead, riven by factions, it began a piecemeal involvement with politics, acquiring the habit of 'settling for small gains, individual rewards or, at best, tactical objectives'. There was a good deal of distrust among army units in general toward the political leadership. Seen from the field, the diplomatic agreements which the Republic's government negotiated with the Dutch compromised the nationalists' military position. The official *History of the Armed Forces of the Republic of Indonesia* describes the Renville Agreement, 1948, as 'a very detrimental step'. Republican troops were withdrawn from areas which they had under control and the Dutch were given greater scope to launch their later attacks. 'Every member' of the armed forces was 'deeply hurt' by the humiliation, the history recites. It goes on to complain generally: 'We had to sacrifice repeatedly our military position for the sake of diplomatic interest; however diplomacy had repeatedly experienced failures.'

As early as 1946, the army had become involved in politics by giving sectional support to Tan Malaka's 'no compromise' campaign against Sjahrir, who was then prime minister. Tan Malaka, ordered to be arrested, was released by General Sudirman, and Sjahrir was himself kidnapped one night at Solo by regular army troops. Sjahrir was later released by another army unit, while other troops tried to kidnap the minister for defence (Amir Sjarifuddin), who was believed to be plotting against Sjahrir. Eventually the army leadership withdrew support from the Tan Malaka 'national-communists', but according to Sjarifuddin, as quoted by Professor Kahin, the left-wing People's Democratic Front in July 1948 controlled about 35 per cent of the armed forces. The figure may be high. The Madiun rebellion at the end of 1948 did not show army support to anything like this degree for the communists. But it is clear that in the years before the Republic was internationally recognized in 1949, the army was militant politically and was inclined to trust its own fighting spirit rather than the devious techniques of diplomacy. The armed forces' history comments:

> Basically it was the armed forces and militant government officials, the Indonesian youth and the people in the villages which formed the last bulwark of the Republic of Indonesia. If this last bulwark fell, the political position of the Republic of Indonesia in the occupied cities as well as at the sessions of the Security Council and later also at the negotiations... would have been entirely lost.

In 1948, Hatta began the rationalization programme of the armed forces which was a political issue for years and has still not been carried out. The main instrument of the reorganization—and initially one of its victims—was Nasution, then a colonel, who had been to the Round Table conference at the Hague in 1949 to assist in the final negotiations with the Dutch, and returned as army chief of staff and deputy chief of staff of the armed forces. Almost immediately he was attacked in Parliament for urging Indonesia to enter the Korean war on the side of the United Nations. He was criticized both inside and outside the armed services for supporting the presence of a Dutch military mission in Indonesia, which he declared was necessary for expert military training of the rough and ready Indonesian forces. Also, he favoured the dissolution of the scores of roving armed bands. This latter issue, although presented as a military argument in favour of professionalism, was also an attempt to disarm the partisans, like Tan Malaka's army, who were politically leftist.

Moreover, the reorganization of the army under the new defence minister (the Sultan of Jogjakarta), the chief of staff of the armed forces, Major-General Simatupang, and Nasution affected the interests of many who had built up a living out of the years of turmoil. There were, for a start, some 80,000 of the older men of the estimated army strength of 200,000 who were to be gradually retired, a prospect that did not appeal by this time, when the effects of the Korean war boom were wearing off. There were the regional war-lords, local leaders who had been given high rank during the revolution to bring their units into the official army. Japanese-trained officers were placed at a disadvantage by the military techniques taught by the Dutch experts. President Sukarno resented the decisions to close down a military academy conducting a political indoctrination course at

Bandung, where some of his friends, men of the Peta group, were in senior positions. A distant relative of the President's, Colonel Bambang Supeno, began to agitate for Nasution's removal.

The defence committee of the parliament, encouraged by party political rivalries, sought to publicize the grievances of some of the officers against the army high command. The high command, including Nasution, is believed to have seriously considered at this stage a coup d'état which would break Parliament's authority and establish either Sukarno or Hatta as the head of a military dictatorship. Details of this are naturally scarce, but it is widely believed that the coup might have occurred had not Sukarno and Nasution disagreed over the list of left-wing politicians to be arrested.

On 17 October 1952, demonstrators, numbering about 5,000 and bearing slogans like 'Dissolve Parliament' and 'Parliament Isn't a Coffee Shop', broke into and damaged the parliament building in Djakarta. They then marched, swollen to some 30,000, to the President's palace, where they were supported by army tanks, armoured cars and cannon, which entered the grounds of the presidency and trained their guns on the building. Sukarno came to the steps and in a masterly display of oratory, in which he both scolded and soothed them, dispersed the demonstrators. Immediately afterwards seventeen army officers, including Nasution, had an hour and a half discussion with the President. They urged that Parliament be dissolved, although there is still disagreement over the precise terms in which the demand was made. In any event, the President refused, and although for a few days Djakarta was tense, with soldiers swarming the streets and the army command making several arrests, the expected army revolt did not take place.

The meaning of the 'October 17th affair' has been difficult to isolate from the variety of intentions which brought it about, especially as many of the participants are still too engaged in politics to want their motives to be clarified. Some officers seem to have been prepared for Sukarno to take dictatorial power, while Nasution argued for—and Simatupang against—a military junta. Herbert Feith, in describing the incident in detail, writes of the 'independent initiative' of army elements in the affair; most divisional commanders did not know the demonstration was to take place. 'Even at the palace there were contrasts in the behaviour of different members of the officer group. Some were defiant, others had tears in their eyes as they spoke.'

The immediate effect, however, was that Nasution and several of his supporters were suspended and Colonel Bambang Sugeng, a former Peta officer, took Nasution's place. The official history notes that this 'solution of the October 17th affair' did not 'yield results'. To overcome the growing split in the army, 270 senior officers, including pro- and anti-October 17th factions, met in Jogjakarta in February 1955, and declared the army to be 'one and indivisible'—the 'Jogja charter'. They visited the grave of General Sudirman and read a statement: 'We are not yet able to offer you incense in the form of a free, secure, prosperous and calm Indonesia'. The conference also declared that the October 17th affair was 'wiped out' and it showed, in the wording of several resolutions, that it was determined to close army ranks against political interference.

A few months later the charter was successfully tested in the 'July 27th affair'. The cabinet decided to replace Bambang Sugeng, who had resigned, with Colonel Bambang Utojo, a junior and 'anti-October 17th' officer. The 'Jogja charter' committee urged that the appointment be made on the basis of seniority and ability, which pointed to the eligibility of Colonels Simbolon, Nasution, Gatot Subroto, and Zulkifli Lubis. The boycott of the formal installation, organized by Lubis, as acting chief of staff, was so effective that no military band could be found for the national anthem, and Bambang Utojo was sworn in to the strains of a fire brigade band. Pressure was brought on the Ali Sastroamidjojo cabinet in Parliament, and the minister for defence (Iwa Kusumasumantri) resigned. But the army officers remained firm, and eventually the cabinet itself fell. The new government reappointed Nasution as chief of staff.

The 'July 27th affair' points to a refreshed appraisal by the army of its role of guardian of the Republic. By 1955 disillusionment had set in and if it had not been for the elections in that year, which promised, but in fact did not bring, a solution, it seems likely that the army, or a section of it, would have acted to stop the succession of parliamentary governments by imposing a military régime. In that event, they would have anticipated Sukarno, who was equally dissatisfied with constitutional democracy, which he brought to an end in 1957 with 'guided democracy'. As it was, the army was itself moving toward greater disunity—the rebellion of 1958-61.

The colonels—Kawilarang, Simbolon, Husein, Warouw, Samual and Z. Lubis—who led the regionalist revolts in Sumatra and Sulawesi during those years were a mixed group, some Muslim, others Christian, with pro- and anti-October 17th affair factions both represented. Their competence and energy, coupled with sophistication in world affairs and military science, had marked them out as men of unusual capacity and likely attainment. At the beginning, their personal qualities were probably enough to gain them support. They were united in blaming 'Djakarta' for the nation's troubles, and later came to focus their political discontent on Sukarno's tolerance of communism, but their actions seemed born of frustration and desperation rather than practical political planning. Some were probably motivated by private ambitions, too, but they maintained an idealistic attitude. Their difficulty was that, although they had a clear emotional view of what they did not like about Indonesian politics, they were undecided what they wanted in its place. They stood against the 'Javanese-aristocratic' pole of Indonesian politics, but they were too much of a Muslim-Christian alliance to represent the other pole, 'Islamic-entrepreneurial'. 'Regional autonomy' was not the kind of rallying cry that would send men happily to meet their Maker, but it was, in the last analysis, all they had to offer. When they returned to 'the fold of the Republic' in 1961—in a remarkably peaceful ending to a costly civil war—they were acknowledging that their cause was not only lost, but essentially trivial.

The army proper gained from the rebellion, once Nasution and his senior officers had demonstrated their loyalty to the government and their superiority over the rebels in the field. In July 1959 Nasution entered the inner cabinet as minister for defence and security—the first military appointment to the post. He was able to arrange the amnesty terms for the rebels, which were an unexpected gain for army unity. Except for Warouw, who was killed in Sulawesi in 1960, the colonels are all now back in Java and, although they are politically quarantined and unable to rejoin the army, they have not been persecuted, despite PKI and PNI protests that they were being treated too leniently.

Using the war emergency regulations, the army reached into the administrative life of the country. It banned strikes, broke up demonstrations, controlled the use of slogans, closed down newspaper printing offices, ran the former Dutch estates. In July-August 1960, it moved against the PKI, banned the party newspaper *Harian Rakyat* and interrogated the leaders (Aidit for eight consecutive days) to the extent of 190 typed pages of questions and answers. It cancelled the PKI's sixth congress. When Aidit challenged Nasution, declaring the congress would go ahead as scheduled, President Sukarno intervened and the result was one of his compromises. The congress was not cancelled; it was postponed. When it was held, army stenographers, like police, sat in and took a record of the proceedings.

The army's use as an instrument of authoritarian government was not, however, confined to the communists. It was generally tough on civil liberties during this period. In an effort to root out corruption it investigated thousands of charges, many trifling, without any noticeable result except that corruption appeared to spread to the army. With the responsibility of supervising import-export trade, rice supplies, government services, all forms of transport, to mention only some of its functions, the army began to develop as a duplicate administrative élite. An army signature was necessary in many daily transactions, and the citizenry began to complain about military interference. Foreign visitors were affected, being checked by the army on arrival and before leaving. In February 1959 two correspondents and I were trying to reach Bali from Djakarta in time to catch the Soviet Premier, Mr Khrushchev, who was doing the usual grand tour for important guests. All planes were full. But we eventually got such a high army signature to our request that a capacity-load of tourists, block-booked from New York months before, was dislodged from an aircraft. We flew in lonely splendour to Denpasar airfield in Bali. Not only the PKI, but the foreign ministry and the tourist agencies began to complain about the army.

Since the end of the rebellion and especially since May 1963, when the emergency regulations were rescinded, the army's detailed supervision of Indonesian life has receded. But its prestige and political authority have increased. It has grown in size (from 200,000 before 1958 to 300,000 now) and has become better trained and equipped. Indonesia's armed forces now total about 500,000 men (if the 100,000 state police, of which a quarter are militarized, are included) and, with modern bombers (TU-16) and fighters (MIG-21), a cruiser, submarines and missiles, Indonesia is now qualified, at least on paper, as a second-class military power. Her armed forces have become, in fact, a status symbol of the ideological leadership which President Sukarno is offering the world, or that 75 per cent of it which comprise his 'new emerging forces'. Nasution has supported the President in projecting this image abroad of a powerful and dynamic nation, not afraid of military consequences; over Malaysia, it sometimes seemed that Nasution was leading the way.

The army has gained in unity. The officers' feuds seem to have been exhausted by the rebellion, and the 'confrontation' campaigns over West Irian and Malaysia have channelled loyalties and energy under Nasution's widely respected leadership. In addition, Nasution has tackled the army's old problem of demobilization with vigour. His 'civic mission' is intended to absorb the army in building bridges, roads and schools as well as in production and distribution at village level. Although the military element of the budget was reported to have been slashed from more than 80 per cent to 29 per cent, the figures are misleading. In 1962, the routine budget for the armed services (excluding the special allocation for West Irian) was 53 per cent. In 1963-4, it has been scheduled at 44·9 per cent, including 'civic mission' and other developmental expenses. Nasution hopes, in effect, to prevent demobilization, allowing only for a wasting away of army personnel, mostly of older officers and poorly educated men. At the same time the army will be able to keep an eye on communist field work and establish links with (or also keep an eye on) provincial government. According to reliable reports, communist infiltration of the army officer corps has been arrested. Nasution has himself admitted to a figure of 10 per cent, with special concentrations in central Java, central Sulawesi and west Kalimantan, although some observers put the figure higher.

The effect of the Indonesian military's symbiotic relationship with President Sukarno has probably blunted whatever political drive may have come from its unity under Nasution's leadership. It has lost its reforming zeal, probably partly because of its experience of the difficulties of administering Indonesia, and more of its leaders, now past middle-age, are prepared to settle for the small comforts that life as part of the Establishment brings. Like the PKI, it must join in the 'madness' to gain the 'spoils'. It has certainly made no move to check the President, being apparently content, at this stage, to build up its own strength, and keep that of the PKI at bay, for the post-Sukarno power struggle.

*   *   *

One day, in the course of a discussion with General Nasution at his house in Djakarta, I threw in a question, for no real reason except that we were talking of leadership qualities in relation to army recruiting. The question was, 'Who do you think is the greatest man in history?' I had in mind Alexander or Napoleon, or perhaps one of the great Indonesian military leaders like Diponegoro. His response was quick: 'Mohammed'. 'Why?' 'Because he was not only a prophet but a man of action as well—a soldier and a statesman in one.'

This statement by Nasution is, I believe, the key to his political ambitions. He is emotionally a soldier and a patriotic Indonesian and, with Mohammed as a guide, neither of these disqualify him from the great responsibility of head of state. In the last ten years, he has had several opportunities to depose Sukarno and establish a military dictatorship. The fact that he has not done so has caused some commentators to conclude that he has not the real qualities of leadership, that perhaps he is not tough and ruthless enough for the job. There is a difference, however, between overthrowing President Sukarno, with the danger of splitting the army and causing another civil war in Indonesia, and following him after he has been honourably removed by death or disablement. General Nasution is a generation younger than the President. He is also a genuine nationalist, by which I mean that he is a loyal and ardent lover of his country and people. He may personally disagree with much that Sukarno has done, but he regards the President as a true leader of the nation and would not feel morally justified in trying to remove him.

It is quite possible that after Sukarno's death, Nasution would be prepared to support a leader from outside the government, such as the Sultan of Jogjakarta. But he gives every impression of thinking of himself as a man with the cares of state to manage. His associates say that since he entered the cabinet in 1959 he has grown increasingly political. One close colleague and friend said: 'Nasution's weakness is that he won't not think of himself as President', making the point that Nasution should devote himself to building Indonesia militarily and let the political future wait on events.

What kind of a man is he? Again the labels are too neat—'anti-communist' and 'pro-western' do not describe the values by which Nasution's actions appear to have been governed. As a Muslim, his devotion to Islam, though not fanatical, is serious and long-sustained; whether this disposes him for or against the Christian 'west' or for or against the communist 'east' is a matter for argument. He has never given any indication, in his various pronouncements on political affairs, that he believes in the private enterprise system of capitalism, which is regarded by some as an essential element in the western position. He is more a socialist, in the Indonesian sense of believing that everything belongs to the nation and should be worked and distributed as communal property. In foreign affairs and defence, he has followed a strongly nationalist line which has not been cut to a pro-western pattern. He negotiated the Moscow arms deal in 1960 and has been belligerent on the Malaysia issue. In an interview he gave me in August 1963, shortly after Sukarno and Subandrio had returned from the 'Maphilindo' meeting in Manila, Nasution argued strongly for the removal of British and American military authority from the region of South-east Asia. While bases like Singapore and Clark Field (the American air base in the Philippines) remain under western control, he said, Indonesia's security was threatened. Britain and the United States were major powers which Indonesia could not expect to control; it must therefore regard them—with the example of aid to the outer-island rebels in 1958-9 on record—as a danger. There is now some recognition that Nasution is not the simple, uncomplicated man that some of his western supporters believed him to be.

Abdul Haris Nasution was born in Kotanopang, Tapanuli, north Sumatra, on 3 December 1918. His parents were Batak, educated but not rich. He went to a Dutch-operated secondary school in Sumatra and later to the Jogjakarta High School. For a year he was a school-teacher, but he was selected to attend the Royal Netherlands Military Academy in Bandung in 1940, and was commissioned as a subaltern in the Royal Netherlands Indies Army the following year. Captured by the Japanese in 1942 and imprisoned for a few months, he later worked for them, becoming leader of the Bandung division of the youth military organization Barisan Pelopor (Pioneer Legion), which the Japanese sponsored. Immediately the war ended, Nasution became involved in the struggle of the infant Republic to survive. In 1945 he organized a security and defence force in Bandung, and as a major and later lieutenant-colonel was chief of commando operations in the Bandung residency. A year later, at the age of twenty-eight, he was a major-general and commander of the third (Siliwangi) division. His task was complicated militarily and politically—he had to fight the Dutch but at the same time watch the guerilla bands. Some of the bitterness of this confused period, shown in the official history of the armed forces, is reflected also in Nasution's later writings, when he complains that Indonesia's political leaders surrendered too easily in negotiations with the Dutch. Reduced to the rank of lieutenant-colonel as a result of Hatta's reorganization of the army in 1948, Nasution was appointed deputy to the ailing commander-in-chief, General Sudirman.

Then came Madiun, when the communists seized power, an event that has probably remained more fixed in Nasution's memory, as a military man, than it has in the minds of the more ideological of the nationalist leaders. Nasution was chief of staff of operations at nearby Jogjakarta when Madiun was seized by troops of the fourth (Senopati) division, commanded by a communist sympathizer, Lieutenant-Colonel Suadi. Nasution acted immediately, sending a brigade of the Siliwangi division which, within twelve days, had recaptured Madiun. The back of the rebellion was broken and within three months it was over. But by then the second Dutch military action had begun. Sudirman was so ill that he had to be carried in a sedan

chair to inspect his troops, and Nasution was made commander of all
the forces in Java. His military reputation, which had already grown
quickly, reached fresh heights at this time, when he led his troops
in a famous 'long march' from east to west Java, executing a scorched
earth policy behind the Dutch lines.

His career from the Round Table Conference in 1949 to the
'October 17th affair' of 1952 has already been noted. After his sus-
pension, Nasution was for three years 'non-active', as the brief lines
of his official biography put it. They were years of reflection, during
which he helped to organize the League of Upholders of Indonesian
Independence or IPKI, and wrote three books which have now
become standard works of reference. The best-known, *Fundamentals
of Guerilla Warfare,* has been translated into several foreign languages, including English, and is required reading for foreign military experts on Indonesia.

This book reveals Nasution as a shrewd military strategist, with
some knowledge of military history outside his own time and country. Compared with the communist classics on guerilla warfare, like
those of Mao Tse Tung or the Vietnamese soldier, Vo Nguyen Giap,
Nasution's book lacks an explicit ideology, but there is no doubt of
the importance he gives to ideology. 'The people adhere to certain
ideas, nurture certain desires and needs and look forward to obtaining certain ideals. They will be able to discriminate which side can
better provide these needs, and it is the side which can furnish them
that will finally be supported. . . . A guerilla war is in principle
merely an ideological war.' Nor is there any doubt of Nasution's
position on the issue of the military in politics. 'The soldier . . . must
not be isolated from politics. He must have both feet in the middle
of politics. The education of an army must include that of political
ideology as well as military technique. The awareness of a political
ideology is his conscience and his strength.'

Nasution's support of Sukarno follows logically his return from
the wilderness. He has always spoken warmly of the 'spirit of 1945',
partly to keep ahead of the PKI and the 'youth' or '1945 generation'
in the competition for Sukarno's favours, but also because of a belief,
which shows so clearly in his writings, that the noble, revolutionary
spirit of that time had been despoiled by the politicians. He was also
aware of the army's difficulties competing in a democracy with a
popular movement like the PKI. In supporting Sukarno's return to
the revolutionary spirit of 1945 and the enforcement of guided democracy, Nasution was in effect putting a stopper on the kind of
constitutional democracy that may in the long run have given the

PKI real political power, with the army forced to serve as its instrument.

He has become more subtle and more confident with his experience of power since 1959. In the interview already mentioned, he spoke frankly of several meetings he had had with A. M. Azahari, leader of the Brunei rebels, and of defence discussions with his 'counterparts' in Malaysia and the Philippines. In earlier interviews, Nasution had tended to be nervous and cautious on political questions. In form of address and in public pronouncements, Nasution has also shown recently a greater ability to pontificate and draw attention to his authority.

He does not cultivate an authoritative style, however, in dress or habits, and contents himself with looking neat and pleasant and behaving in a businesslike, courteous manner. He is not fluent and quick-witted like Subandrio, or sharp and amusing like Chairul Saleh. He is reserved, with a cheerful, direct smile. He lives quietly with his Eurasian wife and two daughters in an unpretentious villa in Djakarta. They do not take part in the social round. Nasution plays tennis at competition standard and has lately taken up golf. His personality is not powerful, and he gives the impression that he would willingly serve another Sukarno, brilliant and dynamic enough to capture his imagination, provided Indonesia was also given a genuinely nationalist ideology.

But he has also shown that he regards himself and the armed forces as watchdogs of the honour and dignity of the Indonesian State, and it is likely that he would take the great step upward to the presidency himself before he would allow it to be taken by someone he could not trust. The next few years may test his judgment sorely.

CHAPTER SIX

The Economy

In 1945, when Sukarno enunciated the *Pantja Sila,* he spoke emotionally of one of the principles, Social Justice. 'Do we want an independent Indonesia whose capitalists do their unscrupulous will, or where the entire people prosper, where every man has enough to eat, enough to wear, lives in comfort, feels cherished by his Motherland which gives him sufficient *sandang pangan,* the basic necessities?' *Sandang pangan* was for Indonesians older than capitalism. It is a traditional central Javanese expression, meaning a time of economic welfare, a peculiar economic category which Javanese call *tjukupan,* to 'have enough'. For most Indonesians Sukarno's words had the same connotation as the 'decent living' promised by western politicians during the Depression to do away with the indignities of the employment queues and the dole. In his Independence Day speech of 17 August 1963 Sukarno apologized for not keeping his promise. 'Go ahead, be angry with me; go ahead, point your finger at me; go ahead, pour your wrath upon me—and I will accept it all with a calm heart . . . I say: Be patient a while longer, be patient.'

They had already been patient, if at times restless, for eighteen years. When independence was declared in 1945, those Indonesians who heard of it expected economic welfare to follow. Instead, intermittent war followed; with the Japanese and British, with the Dutch, with the communists, with extremist Muslim groups. It is not surprising that in the early years many village people began to ask, as recorded by Selosoemardjan in his book *Social Changes in Jogjakarta,* 'When will independence come to an end?' Independence, by which they meant the hardship of revolution, has still not come to an end.

There is no doubt that in some respects the average Indonesian is today better off materially than before the revolution. Selosoemardjan, a native of Jogjakarta, tells how he stood on the side of a road near a village outside the city at 7 a.m. and counted 170 bicycles in five minutes going toward the city. The bicycle is to the Javanese peasant as the small car is to the average Australian family. It has increased his mobility, enabling him to bring his goods more quickly to market and to commute daily to town during off-seasons for an additional job. Selosoemardjan points out that the cow and the buffalo are no longer status symbols for the peasant; a bicycle and education for his children are taking their place. The peasant or farmer is better off now than pre-World War II, Selosoemardjan argued (in 1958).

The average peasant of 1938 had a bamboo house, usually no more than one suit of clothing, no furniture in his home except his bamboo bed, and almost no cash in hand. In 1958, in part because of his growing awareness of his human dignity and his dignity as a citizen of the state and also because of the means that he has at his disposal, more and more brick houses are replacing the old bamboo shacks, while thatched roofs are rapidly giving way to earthen roof tiles. Chairs, tables, and other pieces of furniture are now to be found in many village homes. In general, both men and women have three suits of clothing. They no longer need to wait naked when their clothes are being dried in the sun after washing.

On the other hand, greater mobility, education, newspaper reading and other aspects of life as part of the revolution have raised the level of most Indonesians' material requirements. Not only rice and fish are now demanded, but bicycles, pens and propelling pencils, cameras and radios, even automobiles. And if the peasants' rice income has not been affected basically by inflation between 1938 and 1958, Selosoemardjan estimates that of the wage labourer to have dropped by one-half and the civil servant's income to be one-thirtieth of its pre-war value. He notes also that the average government official could live for only eighteen days on his monthly salary, which opened up excellent prospects for corruption. Since 1958, foodstuffs and textiles have increased in price nearly ten times on an average in villages in Java and Madura, with slightly less increase in the outer islands. The civil servants' salary has been increased only about 50 per cent, which means that corruption (to a spectacular degree) takes up the slack.

Before 1958-9, the Indonesian economy was primarily in the hands of the Dutch and the Chinese. After the Dutch estates were nationalized and various attempts made, with limited success, to loosen the grip of the Chinese middleman, Indonesian leaders began to run short of reasons for their failure to provide *sandang pangan*. Smuggling can be blamed, as can international fluctuations in the prices of commodities; both are true enough but difficult to turn to local effect. The remarkable ends to which the threat of the foreigner can still be put, however, were shown on 30 July 1963, when the Djakarta police chief (Brigadier-General Suhud) said that the operations of pickpockets in the city were 'engineered by foreign subversive elements' in order to 'disrupt and undermine the struggle of the new emerging forces'. The politics of a declining economy prefer the 'solidarity makers' to the 'administrators'.

For some of the Indonesian people, the attacks on foreigners, now focused on the British and Malaysians, keep alive the hope that their poverty is not lasting, that it can still be removed at the stroke of the Leader's hand, once the right combination of magic symbols is found. For those who do not find this satisfying, no alternative is at present offering.

* * *

When a western diplomat called on President Sukarno early in 1963, he found the President preoccupied with economic problems. 'Everyone tells me there's inflation and something must be done about it. I don't think there's too much inflation, do you?' he asked. The diplomat, being experienced, managed to avoid giving an answer, although he was aware that money in circulation was twice the volume of the year before, that the budget deficit was about 47,000 million rupiahs (or more than 50 per cent of revenue) and that the free-market value of the rupiah had fallen to 1250. (The exchange rate of the rupiah is classified in so many different ways that it is difficult to establish its relative values. In Djakarta during 1963, the unofficial (black market) rate ranged between 900-1300 rupiahs to the U.S. dollar. The official rate was 45. But the tourist rate was 180 and for export-import transactions the rate ranged from 315 to 810, depending on the type of goods. At the Hotel Indonesia, a special rate of 1000 operated.)

Inflation, in fact, was rampant. But behind the President's naïve observation was the confidence of experience. The collapse of the economy had seemed imminent for years, and Sukarno had had fun with the predictions of the western experts. It may, of course, already have taken place, if collapse is defined in terms stockholders would understand. Production was down, exports were down, per capita income was down, foreign exchange in the sense of reserves was non-existent, depending as it did on the state of trading month by month. But somehow the economy went on, with sufficient, ramshackle strength to maintain a population of 100 million. For

Sukarno, population is the key statistic. 'We are a nation of 100 million people, the fifth largest nation in the world', he said in a speech to the National Front in Djakarta in February 1963. 'When I recall my aunt, who has 23 children of her own, I am sure that before long our Indonesian nation will number 250 million people.'

One factor in this stability is nature. The islands are rich in food, and although Java needs to import rice, which carries its own insult to the ingenuity of the originators of the marvellously reticulated padi-fields, the land is generous. Water is available and bananas are never far from hand. When, in an exceptionally dry period toward the end of 1961, famine occurred in Lombok Island and some parts of Java and people were reported to have died of starvation, the surprise expressed showed the essential difference between the traditions of the tropics and the arid regions of the world. In the Indian subcontinent, China and the Middle East, famine takes its toll almost as a matter of course. In Indonesia, food is taken for granted and clothing, in a tropical climate, is not demanding. About 70 per cent of the Indonesian economy is rural subsistence. When things are bad, as measured by foreign exchange reserves, exports-imports and other indices of the monetary system, the people retreat, as they do in western countries in a minor way under emergency rationing such as in wartime, into the old, well-trodden ways of the barter economy.

Another factor is foreign aid. Beginning in 1950, United States aid to Indonesia reached a total of U.S.$710 million by the end of 1962. (This figure includes grants and loans and sales of surplus agricultural commodities.) Soviet bloc aid did not begin substantially until 1956, although the first communist aid, an East German loan of $9·2 million, occurred the year before. The total by the end of 1962 was U.S.$643·7 million for non-military aid, with an estimated U.S.$1,000 million for the arms and military equipment bought from the Soviet bloc since 1960. In addition, Indonesia has received assistance from communist China, Yugoslavia, various United Nations' agencies and Japan, which agreed in 1958 to pay war reparations of U.S.$223 million and advance U.S.$400 million in loans over a twelve-year period. Several western countries, West Germany, France, Italy and Britain among them, have advanced credit to Indonesia. Australia has added its support through the Colombo Plan. Altogether, the total aid given to Indonesia since it became independent until the end of 1963 is probably in the region of U.S.$3,000 million—an average of about U.S.$200 million a year, which is now just about what Indonesia needs each year to service its debts—to pay back the interest in other words. In 1963 this amount was estimated to be U.S.$225 million, with the Soviet Union (U.S.$80 million) the largest creditor. One way of estimating the importance of aid to Indonesia is to compare it with the value of exports—U.S.$840 million in 1960, less in succeeding years.

The Dutch left the Indonesians with what is often described as a 'dual' economy, one part geared closely to the great markets of the world and one part to the traditional requirements of peasant village life. It was clear to some leaders in the early days of independence—Hatta seems to have been among the most clear-sighted of them—that the economy would need to be basically restructured for its role as support of a nation in the twentieth century. But, like the Russian general who didn't like war because it destroyed discipline in the army, Indonesian leadership has tended to treat serious economic reform as if its purpose were to destroy the harmony of the people's poverty. From time to time, as the economic situation has got out of hand or as politics have dictated, drastic remedies have been tried. Whether draconian measures like those of August 1959, when almost half the currency in circulation was withdrawn by cutting the value of large denomination notes by 90 per cent and freezing bank accounts above a certain amount, or dramatic gestures of foreign policy, like the nationalizing of the Dutch estates in 1957-8, they have, however, affected only the symptoms. Surveying the decade of the fifties, a report of the United Nations Economic Commission for Asia and the Far East (Ecafe) described Indonesia's economy as giving an impression of 'long-term stagnation and decline'. In the sixties, it has worsened.

At the end of 1962—the Year of Triumph—all the indices were down. Not only had very little been done in the way of developmental work; existing productive capacity was slowing to a halt in some fields. A shortage of weaving yarn had reduced the weaving industry in north Sumatra and west Java to under half its operating capacity, according to spokesmen in October 1962. During the debate in Parliament on the supplementary budget in December, a speaker, quoting a parliamentary investigation, said that an average of only 50 per cent of all buses and trucks in Java were on the roads, because of a shortage of spare parts. At the end of the year, the late Dr Djuanda announced in the press that the production in the non-agricultural sector of the economy was generally only between 25 and 35 per cent of capacity.

It was obvious that after years of disturbance and mismanagement, the Indonesian economy would be more quickly placed on a firm basis with the help of foreign aid; the questions were how much and for what purposes. In August 1961, a United States team under Professor D. D. Humphrey, of Tufts University, visited Indonesia and produced a report for the American President in June 1962. The Humphrey Report recommended an expanded programme of U.S. aid, to be placed on a permanent basis. It introduced some cautious criticism, suggesting that Indonesia should be told that American aid would be placed on this footing only if Indonesia made serious attempts to balance its budget. But its general tone was optimistic and it stated its belief that Indonesia had a strong desire to maintain its independence and had the potential to realize, over a period, a strong and self-supporting economy. The report proposed aid between U.S.$325 million and $390 million over a five-year period, with $125-155 million raised multi-nationally and $200-235 million given directly by the United States. It recommended that early efforts should concentrate on rehabilitating the economy, noting that Indonesia at the moment had a limited capacity to absorb aid for new capital projects, especially if they were not accompanied by training and management assistance. American officials in Djakarta were confident that the Humphrey Report would become the basis for a fresh U.S. approach in Indonesia. Their confidence seemed well-judged early in 1963 when Indonesia set out seriously to meet the conditions imposed by the International Monetary Fund for a new loan.

In March 1963 the Indonesian government produced an Economic Declaration (Dekon) which was in some respects a serious effort at reform. It contained many of the usual themes, but it also outlined an economic strategy for Indonesia involving two stages, the national-democratic and the socialist, and made plain its opinion that Indonesia was as yet only in the first of these. Its emphasis was on increasing production, stressing the need for production incentives, administrative decentralization and, most surprisingly in view of the revolutionary economics of the past, for economic laws and principles to be heeded. The Dekon, pronounced by Sukarno, was in fact the product of his advisers, especially, it is believed, of Djuanda and Subandrio, who themselves sought advice outside.

It was generally well received. But in May, regulations designed to put the Dekon into effect ran into solid opposition. Part of the unpopular reaction might have been expected. The regulations were essentially deflationary, and involved an attack on some of the privileges enjoyed by the *marhaen*. The government cut down on com-

Dr Johannes Leimena
Vice-First Minister and Co-ordinating
Minister for Distribution

Dr Subandrio
Vice-First Minister and Co-ordinating
Minister for External Affairs and Foreign
Economic Relations

Mr Chairul Saleh
Vice-First Minister, Co-ordinating Minister
for Development, Minister for Basic
Industry and Mining, and Chairman of
the Provisional People's Consultative
Congress (MPRS)

General A. H. Nasution
Co-ordinating Minister for Defence
and Security, and Chief of Staff
of the Armed Forces

Mr D. N. Aidit
Secretary-General of the Indonesian
Communist Party (PKI), and
Vice-Chairman of the Provisional
People's Consultative Congress (MPRS)

Mr Ruslan Abdulgani
Co-ordinating Minister for Public
Relations, Minister for Information,
and Vice-President of Supreme
Advisory Council

modities distributed at subsidized prices (the rations of rice purchased from American surpluses were distributed often at fractions of the prevailing prices) and increased the cost of various public services. These services, mostly of transport and communication, were formerly operated as part of government departments; now they were turned into 'State enterprises' and told to strive for a self-financing situation. Rail fares were increased 300 per cent; rail freight 500 per cent. Bus fares were doubled and air fares increased 500 per cent. Electricity, water rates and postal-telegraph-telephone charges all went up 400 per cent.

But a sharper political criticism, led by the PKI, with the PNI joining in, was that the regulations were nothing more than monetary juggling to qualify for American aid. It was argued that the proposed balanced budget for 1963 (272,000 million rupiahs) and 1964 (391,000 million rupiahs) required such enormous increases in revenue over 1962 (74,000 million with expenditure 122,000 million) that they were unrealistic. The means by which the government proposed to meet the outlay of money in 1963 and 1964 did, in fact, show the dilemma of Indonesian finances. Direct taxation has never brought in state revenue to any extent. The head and land taxes imposed by the Dutch were replaced in 1951 by income tax, but it is light and is conscientiously avoided. (It has been estimated that in the rural areas of Jogjakarta there were fewer taxpayers in 1958 than there had been twenty years earlier. According to a senior tax official in Djakarta in February 1963, some 200,000 persons of high income in the capital avoided paying taxes.) About 60 per cent of the state's finances depend on duties and licences of various kinds on imports and exports. So while Indonesia needs, as an underdeveloped country, to build up its own industries and manufactures, its government needs a high flow of imports to provide it with revenue. The short-term problem was that to get these imports, Indonesia needed foreign exchange—not on the basis of permanence envisioned by the Humphrey Report, but quickly, to get the reforms moving.

It became evident during 1963 that, unless Indonesia restrained its opposition to Malaysia, American aid would be difficult to find. In March, a committee under General Lucius D. Clay delivered its report to the White House on economic and military measures 'to strengthen the security of the free world'. It was a tough-minded document, reflecting America's concern for its falling gold reserves and a growing impatience with other western countries, especially in Europe, which were not pulling their weight. It criticized 'gifts to prove our esteem for foreign heads of state, hastily-devised projects to prevent Soviet aid, gambles to maintain existing governments in power, leverages for political support . . . ' In particular, it had some thoughts on Indonesia. 'We do not see how external assistance can be granted to this nation by free world countries unless it puts its internal house in order, provides fair treatment to foreign creditors and enterprises and refrains from international adventures.'

After Indonesia's decision to 'confront' Malaysia, the United States Congress, both the house of representatives and the senate—voted to stop American aid to Indonesia unless expressly provided by the President. Britain, facing the military costs of Indonesian-based subversion on the Malaysian borders, pressed Washington to stop aid, and Malaysia and Australia, both well-regarded in Washington, made their representations. Japan and West Germany, with trading interest in Indonesia, were at times reported to be interested in helping Djakarta, but the amounts needed—estimated by the Americans to be between U.S.$300 and 350 million—were too large. The USSR had agreed to a rescheduling of repayments on its loans to Indonesia—in other words, time to pay—but it was not expected to finance a balance of payments deficit. The Soviet Union supplies credits readily enough for arms or for factories or for developmental purposes but it does not look favourably on general-purpose loans. In this case it could hardly be expected to do so, as the PKI was so opposed to the reforms. So it seemed that what might have been a genuinely stabilizing measure—which would have increased Indonesia's international standing and justified her claim that, after security was restored and West Irian regained, economic reform would be tackled—was doomed.

The worst had happened. Indonesia had done what its severest critics claimed it always would do under Sukarno's leadership—divert attention from its troubles at home by engaging in adventures abroad. The relationship between the ailing economy and the political sacrifice was shown by the interaction of the Dekon and Malaysia events to be intricately shaped. Sukarno's frequent diversionary technique is not a simple Machiavellian device manipulated at the top. The prospect is, rather, that Sukarno's régime is so heavily committed to a status quo which will not disturb the balance of forces supporting it, that economic reform—of almost any kind—is out of the question. The bureaucracy, the national businessmen, the large Muslim landholders and the rival voices of the ideologues are all intent on seeing that the economy is not reformed except in their favour.

For this reason Indonesian 'socialism' is propagated in the vaguest economic terms and with the loftiest symbols, typified by the National Over-All Development Plan, otherwise known as the Eight-Year Plan. The plan was described enthusiastically by the President as 'rich in fantasy'. It was produced by twelve 'expert committees' and three 'special committees' (on population, national income and socialism) working 'day and night for almost a year' (as the process was officially described), with some 270 Indonesian experts making contributions. The chairman of the project was the late Professor Mohammed Yamin, an old revolutionary poet, historian and ideologue. The result, presented to the President on 13 August 1960, was a massive creation of 5,100 pages, consisting of 17 volumes in 8 parts with 1,945 paragraphs to symbolize the date of the Proclamation of Independence on 17 August 1945.

The plan retains the Indonesian emphasis on consumption. It is based on the assumption of increases in national income which barely cover the population growth rate. It is not the kind of plan that calls on people to tighten their belts and knuckle down to work for later benefits, but as described officially, it is 'the first stage toward the ideal society'. It is divided into Projects A and Projects B—the first designed to improve living standards and the second intended to finance the first. The total investment planned over the eight years is 240,000 million rupiahs. Education, with emphasis on scientific and technical training, rather than the humanities (nautical schools are planned at Medan, Makassar and Ambon), and culture, mainly in providing institutions like a National Museum and a National Art Gallery, accounts for 7·4 per cent of the budget. Research is allotted 1·1 per cent. People's Welfare (2·5 per cent) emphasis is on new hospitals. In Government (1·51 per cent) the co-operative movement is stressed. Transmigration from Java to the outer islands is to continue but at a more modest rate. Special Development is allotted 12·5 per cent, which is largely concentrated on national security. Finance (4·7 per cent) includes tourism. Distribution has 25·1 per cent, including transport and communication, and emphasizes Indonesia's dependence on international and inter-island traffic of one kind or another. Production is given 45 per cent, divided into four sections: industry, foodstuffs, clothing and pharmaceuticals. Spinning mills, a steel mill, a fertilizer plant, power stations and cement factories are planned.

The B Projects required to finance the A Projects are expected to raise in foreign currency half the plan's intended cost. More than two-thirds of this will be provided by the foreign-owned oil companies and another ten per cent by rubber. The planners could not quite find the required U.S.$2,700 million foreign currency for the B Projects. The gap of U.S.$237·5 million would be 'eliminated', they said, by adding more projects or improving exports in the existing projects. The other half of the plan (estimated 120,000 million rupiahs) would be financed locally, although it is not clear how this will be done. There is to be no interference with the routine government budget, and no increased tax is proposed. The planners were 'mindful of the fact that the living standard of Indonesians at present is so low that it is not possible to burden them further with the need to pay large sums'. Pressure for capital expenditure on the normal budget would, however, be reduced, it was claimed in 1961, because the cost of development was transferred to the Eight-Year Plan. (In fact, budget expenditure increased 2·5 and 3 times in 1963 and 1964.)

About one thing the government seemed quite definite: no foreign capital investment. Loans and credits by all means, but not foreign capital, unless on the basis of production-sharing, the joint-enterprise scheme with which Indonesia has tried, so far without much success, to attract foreign investment. (Production-sharing invites foreign capital to finance companies and help to manage them, for a share of profits but no ultimate ownership.) Local private enterprise is welcome provided it recognizes that its function is 'community prosperity' and not 'individual profit'.

Foreign, especially western, observers, have reacted critically on the whole to Indonesia's Eight-Year Plan. It does not inspire confidence among the shrewd men who manage international business. While nearby Malaysia and Australia offer sound economies and attractive conditions for foreign investment, Indonesia's attitude, coming on top of years of economic trouble, is certain to promote caution. Only the riches of the country and its immense possibilities, which have beckoned outsiders for hundreds of years, are on the side of the Indonesian government. The trading prospects in Indonesia are considerable and, in order to trade, it may be necessary to invest on the terms Indonesia's economic nationalism demands. In order to assist private trade with Indonesia, some western governments—France, West Germany, Italy and the United Kingdom—have insured private credits offered by their exporters up to a value of 75 per cent.

Whatever may be thought of the mechanics of the plan, its spirit offers some idea of what Indonesian socialism means, or is meant to mean. Socialism based on the 'Indonesian identity' will see that social justice is done to 'the stupid and the handicapped, as well as to the clever and privileged, to the poor and the weak, as well as to the rich and the powerful'. The centuries of suffering by the Indonesian people under colonialism require reparation. The Indonesian revolution carries out this Mandate of the People's Suffering and Indonesian socialism is the offered balm. 'Close, warm human relations' are ranked highly in its scale of values.

At a more practical level, Indonesian socialism cannot be defined easily, but some elements can be extracted. It is, of course, strongly nationalist rather than internationalist. It offers a helping hand to struggling humanity and certainly to those still under colonialism, but it is not internationalist as are capitalism or communism. It is based on the family system, as a training ground for combining the 'two ideas of serving a group and, at the same time, of exercising authority as an equal member of that group'. It is based also on *kerakjatan*, a democratic principle which 'stresses the ideal of the entire people in action in society, rather than the mechanism of the ballot box'. Decisions are reached through *musjawarah* (deliberation) and *mufakat* (unanimity). *Gotong royong* (mutual cooperation) is also frequently described as basic to Indonesian socialism. These terms do not convey much to an economist, although they have been common terms in Indonesia for centuries. More precisely, Indonesian socialism lays down that 'only those enterprises which do not affect the lives of most people may be in the hands of individuals'. The rights of private enterprise are not derived from natural law, but are defined by the Indonesian government. Ownership of home and land is permitted, but the 'earth and water and natural riches contained therein' (such as minerals and oil, for example) are the State's property and should be used 'for the greatest possible prosperity for the people'.

All this is stated with a variety of possible interpretations. The vagueness is admitted, even emphasized: Indonesian socialism is not a ready-made system which can be introduced or imposed, it is said, but a guide to action. Using the constitution and the *Pantja Sila* as a 'fundamental rule', the Indonesian people are expected to create Indonesian socialism as they go along. As President Sukarno has said, 'each day must give birth to inspiration; every day must produce concepts; every day must give birth to *ideas* that are better than yesterday's as a continuation of the result of yesterday's work'.

No one can refute the Message of the People's Suffering. The PKI, the armed forces, the bureaucrats and little capitalists in the PNI or the Christian parties, the radicals in Partai Murba and the conservative Muslims in the Nahdatul Ulama are all supporters of Indonesian socialism. They can be so because Indonesian socialism is, like the *Pantja Sila,* based on *gotong royong.* Or as the official version puts it: 'No single principle represents an absolute, for each sets certain bounds and limitations upon the others, giving each its specially Indonesian colouring'. Whatever it is, it has not worked satisfactorily.

CHAPTER SEVEN

The Culture

More than one hundred million people live in Indonesia, making it the fifth most populous country in the world. The 1961 census established a population of ninety-seven million, putting Indonesia ahead of Japan and Pakistan and behind mainland China, India, the Soviet Union and the United States, with a growth rate of 2·3 per cent a year. The land these people live in comprises three thousand islands—and many more too small to be counted—stretching some three thousand miles from the western tip of Sumatra to the border of West Irian and Australian New Guinea. This land is an astonishing natural phenomenon. It is rich in resources and in beauty. Its region is one of the most volcanic in the world. The surface of the earth seems still to be in formation and the Seismographic Institute of Djakarta usually registers two or three earthquakes a day. Whether you fly into Djakarta westward along Java or from Singapore over southern Sumatra and the Sunda Straits, you will see the great cones through the clouds. On Java alone there are forty-four volcanic cones between 6,000 and 10,000 feet, and fourteen even higher. Mount Agung, on Bali, just off the eastern tip of Java, erupted in 1963 with great loss of life and property. Like the explosion of Krakatoa, in the Sunda Straits, in 1883, it was a reminder of the natural dangers in whose shadows the Indonesians live. The speeches of President Sukarno are studded with references to the active Javanese volcano, Merapi, whose fiery outbursts from the depths of apparent slumber are symbolic, Sukarno avers, of the spirit of Indonesian nationalism, and a warning to nations who take her peaceful appearance for granted. On Java the volcanic soil is so rich, and land so thickly populated, that the farmers press within a few miles of the treacherous crater. Their fields and houses are often destroyed, but they return with a prayer on their lips and a wooden hoe and mattock in their hands. It is not hard to imagine that this sporadic violence has been an incentive to the animist belief in the spirits of earth, air and water which was the earliest Indonesian religion. Bogor, in central Java, has more

93

thunderstorms than any other place in the world. Parts of Sumatra, Kalimantan and West Irian have over two hundred inches of rain a year. Padang Tingi botanical gardens, a few miles east of Padang, has perhaps the heaviest rainfall in the world—up to 400 inches annually. The mountains, jungles and rushing rivers on the larger islands, which separated the early people, allowing the development of distinctive cultures, are also an impressive reminder of natural forces.

Most Indonesians believe in spirits. Clifford Geertz, the American sociologist, records in *The Religion of Java* the matter-of-fact presence of spirits in people's lives. 'I don't know how it is in America', he was told, 'but here they are always upsetting one'. People mentioned the danger of 'bumping into' spirits when out walking. Beneath the formal religious observances, whether they are Muslim, Christian or Hindu-Buddhist, there is in Indonesia an awareness of things that go bump in the night. Among the educated younger generation there is less of this 'spiritualism', but there is not in modern education the great counter to the folk beliefs that there was in western education during the hey-day of rationalism. Science, having opened the atom and found that the mystery continues, is less likely to scoff at the idea of 'spirits' in stones and trees than it was when mechanical explanations seemed enough. The chief counter is religion. Islam is a rational faith, in the sense that it invokes conscience, but Geertz's book shows how much even the *santris* (devout Muslims) are affected by traditional beliefs. It is not surprising. In any country where tradition is strong and elaborate, the invading religion, whatever it is, will seem 'foreign'. It may be accepted, because it is backed by power, because to belong to it confers prestige or facilitates wealth, or even because it is rationally convincing, but the local customs, with their racial or tribal memories, do not easily release their hold on the imagination. In Indonesia, this hold remains strong. There is an Indonesian saying common in Sumatra and Borneo: 'Religion (*agama*) comes in from the sea, but custom (*adat*) comes down from the mountains'.

Adat has been a powerful unifying factor. The pattern of *adat* is similar throughout the islands in its approach to the essentials of life, especially social stability. It became so entrenched that none of the many changes of rulers and kingdoms altered it significantly. Perhaps the long Dutch rule might have done so, but except for an unsuccessful period of 'unified law' between 1904 and 1927, Holland generally accepted *adat* as the separate law of the *Inlanders* or 'natives'.

Adat was based on the needs of the village community, and especially in the areas such as Java, Bali and parts of Sumatra, where padi or *sawah* (wet rice) was grown, the demands of planting, irrigating and harvesting made mutual co-operation, or *gotong royong,* a necessity. Originally all the land belonged to the whole group, but gradually limited ownership developed into full ownership, or all land became the property of the hereditary ruler of the region. (The Dutch disturbed this by choosing to regard village land as communally owned, to facilitate their 'culture system' of forced cultivation.) The village chiefs were not elected, but were chosen through the mutual agreement of the villagers, and were considered not so much leaders as 'first among equals' who decided important questions through mutual discussion or *musjawarah,* resulting in a consensus, or unanimous agreement, *mufakat.* The principle of election by vote was first introduced to Indonesia by the Japanese during their war-time occupation of the islands, and to most Indonesians, the idea of '50 per cent plus one' does not seem at all democratic, as it does not take into consideration the disagreeing 49 per cent. The 'tyranny of the majority' would be understood by *adat*-oriented villagers, and President Sukarno, in introducing his *gotong royong* cabinet was exchanging a western for an Indonesian concept of democracy, as he stated on numerous occasions, for instance in a speech at Hasanuddin University in Makassar on 31 October 1958.

> How was democracy of former times in Indonesia? It still is practised in the villages in Java, Minangkabau, Sulawesi, Lombok, Bali and other places . . . But do they in these village meetings apply the practice of voting? Of free-fight liberalism where half plus one is always right? No, my friends . . . Everybody says something different until at one time a compromise is achieved out of all these different opinions, without voting . . . There is no dictatorship in *musjawarah* and *mufakat.* That is why democracy with leadership is a true, original Indonesian democracy . . . not American democracy, Dutch, French, British, German, or Soviet or anybody else's democracy.

There is a Javanese word, *tjotjog,* which means to agree or to fit, as, according to Geertz, 'a key in a lock, good medicine does a disease, a solution does an arithmetic problem, a man does with his wife (if not, they get divorced),' and the successful use of *musjawarah* results in a harmonious *tjotjog* of various elements, leading to *mufakat.* This idea was expressed to Geertz by a *dalang* or puppeteer of the ancient and highly popular *wayang kulit,* or shadow plays, which usually tell stories from the Indian epics the *Ramayana* and *Mahabharata,* or of the Indonesian kingdoms of Mataram and Majapahit. He said that the *wayang* has meaning for today too. 'The thing one has to do is talk and talk; and slowly the people come to agree (*tjotjog*) and then there is peace. Otherwise, if the talk breaks off, there is war.' It is interesting in this connection that the traditional five senses, to the Javanese, are seeing, hearing, feeling, smelling and talking.

Gotong royong, or mutual help, is based on the ideal concept of a family, extending to a community, in which the leader, or father, is expected to lead his people or family through their love and affection for him, supporting him by freely stating their opinions to help him make up his mind, and sharing in the group's goals of happiness and prosperity. In village *gotong royong* people co-operate as families, not as individuals, and in village councils only the heads of families have the right to express their opinions, in line with the traditional view that the family is the smallest village unit. This concept is so firmly fixed that often when they are married, both bride and groom drop their former names and take on a new name to show that they are now a 'family' with a new social position and role. *Gotong royong,* which was a mainstay of village life, had not existed as a national concept under Dutch rule or during the Japanese occupation, but after independence was proclaimed it became an administrative ideal in many parts of Indonesia, with the administrative head being referred to as the *bapak,* or father. Under this system, which came to be known as *Bapakism,* superiors no longer issued orders until the question at issue had been discussed with their subordinates and their agreement in principle obtained. The extreme enthusiasm of Indonesians for the official approval of such an extended *gotong royong* system, which was taken from the administration into the Republic's guerilla units during the post-war fighting against the Dutch, sometimes resulted in loyalty to the *bapak* which superseded loyalty to the higher command, and in the administrative system made it very difficult for the government to transfer a *bapak* to another post. President Sukarno, though he is known as *bung,* or brother, is the nation's ultimate *bapak.*

There are many other ways in which *adat* principles affect Indonesian life, which on the village level in particular is a naturally co-operative endeavour. The women of a village help each other with the transplanting of each family's rice seedlings, men join together to build a neighbour's house, and in many communities there are group collections of the plates, cups and other things which are needed to give a party or the traditional religious feasts at such times as childbirth, circumcision or marriage. In the post-war period, financial co-operatives were sometimes organized to buy these festive necessities, which are then shared around the group as they are needed. With the development of a money economy came the custom of a financial gift to your host at a party or feast to help cover his costs in food, the amounts and methods of presentation being fixed by a well-known *adat*.

Another unifying factor is nationalism. The variety of people and the scattered geography of Indonesia give real meaning to the national motto 'Unity in Diversity' (*Bhinneka Tunggal Ika*). It is not unusual for a nation to have to weld together peoples of different and competitive histories—the United Kingdom is an unlikely union of Scots, Welsh, Irish and English, not to take the diversity too far, and the USSR ranges from Europe to Asia. But at this stage of her history, Indonesia's diversity is a potent force, regarded with both fear and pride. Regionalism, as was shown in the 1950 revolt in south Moluccas, the 1953 rebellion in Atjeh and the 1958-61 rebellion in Sumatra and Sulawesi, is a threat to national unity. On the other hand, the diversity of peoples was a useful argument against the view that West Irian was ethnically separate from the rest of the archipelago; what was more 'different' about the Papuans than the wandering negrito-type tribes of Sumatra or the primitive inland Dyaks of Kalimantan? Compared with the Javanese aristocrat, they were all like people from another world. The backwardness of the Papuans, or anyone else, is also in itself a contributor to nationalism, for it was the Dutch who made them that way. President Sukarno gave the order that 400,000 (or nearly half) of the Papuans—those living in the jungle without outside contact—were to be drawn from the wilds ('at bayonet point if necessary', the then ambassador to Malaya, Lieutenant-General Djatikusomo, is reported to have suggested enthusiastically), and their level of life raised to that of 'us all' in five years. In October 1962 Dr Subandrio made an emotional address to a group of West Irianese visiting Djakarta, in which he told them he had wept in New York when he had seen the film *The Sky Above and the Mud Below*. He felt ashamed that his 'own brothers' were being 'put on show to the whole world as though they were half animals and half humans'. (After seeing the film, he resolved 'willy-nilly to liberate West Irian'.)

Many times during the long West Irian crisis, Indonesians privately expressed the view to me that the Papuans were their 'brothers' and whether or not Indonesia could afford to look after them as well as the Dutch, the Australians, or some international agency might do, it was 'better' for the Papuans to be part of their own family. The same sentiments are now expressed, although less confidently, about the people of northern Borneo (Sarawak and Sabah) who have joined Malaysia. Provided the view is taken that Malaysia is 'neo-colonialist' and therefore not part of the family, the Dyaks, Dusuns and others may be said to be artificially separated from their Indonesian 'brothers'. This is not the official view, at least as it is publicly expressed, but, at the emotional level at which the Indonesian people necessarily consider their relationship with others, it is easy to define 'diversity' very loosely and 'unity' very broadly, so that the concept of the Indonesian 'family' and its moral, indefinable ties, becomes a force for nationalism.

For the sake of statistics, Indonesia is regarded as 90 per cent Muslim. Islam is also regarded as a useful link with newly independent countries of Africa and the Middle East, and Pakistan. It is sometimes called upon to justify the 'brotherhood' of Indonesians and Malayans (now Malaysians), although the argument of common racial stock which then includes the Christian Philippines, is more widely used. The truth is that Indonesian Islam, like Indonesian Hinduism, Buddhism and Christianity, is a soft and pliable plant.

The Javanese have a genealogy of the creation in which Nabi (Prophet) Adam married Babu Kawa (Eve) and had two sons, Nabi Sis and Sajang Sis (the *wayang* clown-figure Semar). Nabi Sis gave birth to all the Prophets, such as Nabi Ibrahim (Abraham), Nabi Nure (Noah), Nabi Muhammad and Nabi Isa (Jesus). The various western peoples descended from their Nabis (the Arabs from Mohammed, the Dutch from Jesus, etc.) and Sajang Sis, or Semar, gave birth to the Hindus and the Javanese. Thus, all people and all religions are the same.

One day, in the middle of the Muslim fasting month, I had a lunch appointment with a minister of the Indonesian government. As food is prohibited between sunrise and sunset (or between the times when you can tell the difference between a black and a white cotton thread held at arm's length), I wondered what my host would eat while his infidel guest enjoyed—I hoped—a good assortment of satay sticks, curry and other Javanese delicacies. In fact, we ate at a Chinese restaurant and my host consumed as much as I did. So did two of his officials, who shared the meal. After three hours of food and talk, when we were all amiably at the point of collapsing into sleep, I managed to ask one of the officials, out of the minister's hearing, whether this was the normal behaviour for Indonesian government officials during the Muslim fasting month. 'It depends', he replied, 'on the guest.' This was not meant to reflect on the appetite of Australian visitors, although in the best Javanese circles hearty eating is associated with a thick head and rapid physical decay. It was a simple example of the flexibility of Indonesian standards.

Many westerners feel they cannot 'trust' Indonesians. What an Indonesian may regard as flexibility and common sense, or a proper deference, a westerner may find dishonest or indefinite. The Indonesian will almost certainly say the westerner's principles are harsh and arrogant. 'Westerners are too nervy', an Indonesian told me. 'You need to relax more, remove some of the tension.' Apparent lack of tension in Indonesia, which should not be confused with an absence of violence, is not only a matter of climate. It is supported by a complex philosophical system, developed on Java by the upper classes in their courtly societies, which has now seeped down to the people and is 'good form' at all respectable levels of Indonesian life. Javanese life, which sets the pattern in Indonesia, especially in official circles, is disciplined by a set of ideals and stylized behaviour patterns which are as sophisticated as any of the great aristocratic fashions of western civilization.

As developed over centuries, the central aim of the upper class, known as *priyayi* (a Javanese word meaning 'official'), was absolute self-control, leading to spiritual enlightenment. Only when the two forms of self-control—the ordering of one's inner nature and of one's relationships with others—were perfected, could one achieve the mystic understanding which resolves earthly ambiguity. External self-control was the first aim, as it was easier to achieve than internal control, and its perfection was meant to lead to a state of calm in one's relationships which, in avoiding emotional extremes, such as feelings of being startled or disappointed, left one free to concentrate on creating internal control. The ideal emotional state, a kind of unshakeable evenness of feeling, is expressed in the negative maxim, 'happy now, unhappy later'; one tries to get beyond happiness and unhappiness, as other mystics attempt to escape good and evil.

This approach to life has resulted in the two concepts, *alus*, the desired external attributes, including what is pure, refined, polished, polite, exquisite, ethereal, subtle, civilized and smooth, and *kasar*, the disapproved opposites, which also include such things as 'badly-played music, a stupid joke or a cheap piece of cloth', to quote Clifford Geertz. Passion is fit only for children, animals, peasants and foreigners, and the *alus* attitudes which lead to a placid stability have been codified into patterns of behaviour which, although quite logical when viewed in context, may be irritatingly illogical when seen through western eyes. It is, for instance, not only regarded as usual, but as a positive virtue, not to say what one really means, or to express one's true feelings. This is partly a matter of *priyayi* etiquette, as it is good manners to hide one's own wishes in deference to the other person—a perpetual and subtle 'after you, Alphonse; no, after you, Gaston'. It is also because negative feelings toward another must never be shown, and positive ones only in situations of intimacy—strong feelings which upset another person will rebound, and one's own emotional equilibrium will be disturbed. The result is that Javanese expect to have to read between the lines of other people's speech and attitudes, and have themselves come almost automatically not to say what they mean, with an instinctive dissimulation called *etok-etok*. 'Bluntness is simply not a virtue, and by the time one comes to the point in a well-modelled *priyayi* conversation, everyone should know what is going to be said, and often it is not necessary to come to the point at all—a great relief to everyone', writes Clifford Geertz. He describes a village politician saying in an election speech, 'I too never say what I really think, and you can't tell how I feel about things by what I say'. In the same vein, one must never directly refuse to do something which a person requests, as this is both impolite and likely to lead to unpleasant feelings. Rather, one agrees, and then uses various *etok-etok* excuses until the person realizes one wasn't serious in the first place. A common style of praise for someone is 'one can never tell how he feels inside by how he behaves outside'.

There are also certain stylized forms of politeness according to rank, which were so nicely observed that quite separate Javanese languages have evolved for speaking to your inferior, your equal and your superior (in addition to an ancient poetic language, a classical Javanese, and special vocabularies for the royal court and for the gods). One reason that is given for the colonial Dutch insistence on the mutual use of Malay as a lingua franca is that officials, used to dealing with Javanese royalty, knew only the forms of language used for equals or superiors, but would not allow Javanese to use these forms. (They would not allow Indonesians to address them in Dutch, because this also implied an unacceptable equality.) Another rule of etiquette is that it is impolite to have one's head higher than another's, especially when the other person is of higher rank. Geertz describes as impossible manners, to a Javanese, the typical American action of clapping someone on the back while towering above them and saying 'Let's go into town'—it is too direct, too intimate, and implies superiority. This overall control is expressed in language in another way also—'the higher social level of dialect one uses in Javanese, the more slowly, softly, and evenly in rhythm and pitch one speaks'.

Many westerners have noticed a tendency for Indonesians to laugh and behave with studied nonchalance. The hero figure is a casual, elegant stylist, with an unfurrowed brow and an air of confidence. A report in the press during one of the 'Maphilindo' meetings in Manila in August 1963, pictured the foreign correspondents—Australian, British, American, Malayan, Filipino and others— in a state of confusion, trying to establish what was going on inside the conference room. They turned to an Indonesian reporter named Charlie. 'Come on, tell us what your Indonesian officials are really out to do, huh? . . . Come on . . .' Soft-spoken Charlie just smiled. Whether Charlie knew about *priyayi* ethics or not, his behaviour was splendidly in the tradition.

The concept of outward and inner calm as an ideal state has been adopted by Javanese who are not of the *priyayi* class. So, an animist talking of spirits explained to Clifford Geertz that 'if a person is startled, confused, mixed up, and doesn't know where he is, he becomes empty and the djinn can enter him easily'. People who talk loudly, are aggressive, lack manners, dress sloppily and blurt out whatever they're thinking are considered un-Javanese, and like children, or wild animals. Most Javanese drink very little intoxicating spirits, not only because liquor is expensive, but because they intensely dislike the feeling of lack of control that drinking produces.

The traditional art forms, which include the *wayang* (theatre), the making of *batik* (patterned cloth), and classical music, dance and poetry, are all included within the framework of *priyayi* philosophy, although they were until recently—and in many places still are—the favourite arts and entertainments of the whole population. Thus, the famous *wayang* stories of ancient Indian and Indonesian kingdoms, wars and religious struggles, are to the peasants both an entertainment and a protection against the spirits (a *wayang* performance usually lasts all night, from 9 p.m. until 6 a.m., and while one is in attendance the spirits cannot cause harm), but to the *priyayi* they symbolize, in an elaborate interpretation, the conflict between *alus* and *kasar* feelings, the struggle between people's refined and base impulses, which, when successfully resolved, bring the ultimate mystic understanding, the merging of feeling and meaning, which is called *rasa*. In some views, the puppeteer or *dalang* is symbolic of god, the light which projects the puppets' shadows on to the screen represents eternal life, and the shadows themselves are people's souls, while the puppets are their bodies.

The making of *batik* was considered a spiritual discipline because of the months of 'great inward concentration' which it took to design and dye a piece, and a mystic experience is still described as 'drawing a batik design on the heart'. Certain batik patterns could only be made by *priyayi,* and in the pre-war period, many *priyayi* wives supported themselves and their families by making and selling batiks, their husbands seldom earning enough money through the prestige work of administration in the sultans' *kratons* (palace cities).

Much of the aloof social distinctiveness of the *priyayi* ethic disappeared after the war, especially in the Jogjakarta area, where the the sultan led the way in introducing democratic standards, and it is now possible to be considered a *priyayi* because of one's education, work or position. This has itself created difficulties, particularly in the new education. The 'white-collar' attraction is strong, buttressed by centuries of extremely formalized Dutch education habits. The struggle that science and technology had in western countries to be recognized as equal in status with the humanities is reflected in modern Indonesian education. It has been especially difficult to turn the genuine enthusiasm for learning, such as in removing illiteracy, toward practical benefits for an essentially agricultural community. Botany and biology are as useful to Indonesia at this stage of its development as the prestigious international studies of law and languages on the one hand, or nuclear physics on the other.

The *priyayi* influence in modern Indonesia should not be overstated. Obviously, the rules of etiquette are no longer formally followed as they were behind the walls of the king's *kraton.* But they remain, as a core of formality, in the attitudes and behaviour of official Indonesia, which has, if anything, become more bureaucratic than the old Javanese states. As the seat of government, Java's influence is paramount, and under Sukarno this influence has been given full rein. Moreover, *priyayi* attitudes, whether or not formally expressed, are popularly reinforced by Sukarno's cultural dependence on the old forms.

Many of the young intellectuals today would probably take the side of Sjahrir against Sukarno in the great debate: which way to turn? which course, which model, to follow? whose culture to adopt? Indonesians have already borne a strain in their search for values. First the Dutch, with their infallible European customs and air of rectitude. Then the Japanese, who, after showing that the Dutch had feet of clay, revealed their own civilization to be brutal

Dr Ali Sastroamidjojo
Leader of the Indonesian Nationalist
Party (PNI), and Vice-Chairman of the
Provisional People's Consultative
Congress (MPRS)

Mr R. Maladi
Minister for Sports

Professor Dr Prijono
Minister for Basic Education and Culture

Major-General A. Jani
Minister/Army Commander

Rear-Admiral R. E. Martadinata
Minister/Navy Commander

Air Vice-Marshal Omar Dhani
Minister/Air Force Commander

and, in the Indonesian setting, ineffective. Then came the international west. Seloesomardjan mentions how, because of U.N. intervention in 1945-9, all parties to the Dutch-Indonesian dispute had to use the English language. Indonesians who wanted to show that they followed the discussions had to master new terms in English like 'cease-fire agreement', 'status quo', 'background' and 'intelligence service'. He comments, 'The use of these terms among non-Dutch and non-English speaking groups of the society gave a feeling of satisfaction to the users, because of the intellectual flavour and the social prestige which they assumed they had gained by it'. Now come the Russians, with their language. Indonesians are adept as linguists, but it is not surprising that they have turned inwards and gone back to the traditional forms. Some artists, especially painters and musicians, have turned to the past for inspiration, as, for example, one young composer's sonata opus number one, entitled 'Shrivajaya Variations on a Gamelan Theme'.

There is already a tradition, however, among writers in particular, to work at the world they see and feel for themselves, rather than the shadow world of the puppets. In 1922 what is considered Indonesia's first 'modern novel' was published, *Siti Nurbaja (Miss Nurbaja)*, by Marah Rusli, which described the conflict of a Minangkabau girl caught between *adat* demands that she marry someone of her parents' choice and her love for a young 'modernist'. It was written partly in the old, stylized Malay poetic form *(pantun)*, but partly in modern Malay, which as Bahasa Indonesia was adopted by Indonesian nationalists as the national language at the All-Indonesian Youth Congress in 1928. Between 1922 and 1933 several other sociological novels were written, almost all of them, like the first, by young writers from Minangkabau, one of whom, Selasih, was Indonesia's first woman novelist. (The preponderance of Minankabaus among twentieth-century Indonesian writers is partly explained by the fact that their language is very similar to the Malay that comprises Bahasa Indonesia, and it was easier for them than for other Indonesian peoples to obtain a rapid fluency in the national language. But the Minangkabau excel in many fields and some observers believe that as monotheistic, mountain people they are tougher and more independently creative than the more verbal, stylized Javanese.)

The most influential of the groups of Indonesian writers that arose during the twenties and thirties was Pudjangga Baru or The New Writer, an organization which began to publish a magazine in 1933 dedicated to 'the new dynamic spirit' and the creation of 'the new Indonesian culture—the culture of unity in Indonesia'. One member, Takdir Alisjahbana, a Sumatran who became a lawyer, wrote a popular novel called *Unfurled Sails (Lajar Terkembang)* which argued for the emancipation of women, and was the first novel to insist that national progress could not be achieved unless women studied and worked along with men. He strongly opposed the work of another of the New Writers, Sanusi Pane, because his verse and drama concentrated on the Hindu-Javanese period (in, for instance, a play called *The Twilight of Majapahit*) which Alisjahbana called 'pre-Indonesian'. Pudjangga Baru was suppressed during the Japanese occupation, but the man regarded as the greatest poet of the young Indonesian Republic, Chairil Anwar, born in Medan in 1922 of Minangkabau parents, began to write during this time, although most of his work was not published until after the war. Another who began his work during the occupation was the short-story writer Idrus, a Minangkabau born in 1921, whose style has become a model of succinct vividness.

In 1946 Anwar and other writers and painters founded an association called The Arena (Gelanggang), which published two magazines and held art exhibits. It opposed the resurrected New Writer (which was dissolved as a group in 1954) as stereotyped and out of date, and, in its manifesto, declared itself the heirs of 'world culture', refusing to define Indonesian culture except as all the manifestations of the peoples' creative impulses. Its younger generation opponents, who included the poet Sobron Aidit, younger brother of the PKI leader, formed the Peoples' Cultural Institute (Lembaga Kebudayaan Rakyat), known as Lekra, whose aim was 'critical realism' and 'romantic revolutionism' and who denounced Gelanggang as interested in individuals rather than the social good.

Chairil Anwar died of typhus in 1949 at the age of twenty-seven, after a riotous life which reminds one of the romantic European poets of the nineteenth century. One of his poems, dealing with the guerilla struggle against the Dutch, became an Indonesian classic in the new style.

> We who lie between Krawang and Bekasi
> We are not able to shout 'Merdeka!' and
> take aim again.
>
> But who will not hear our coming?
> As a vision, we charge with beating hearts.
> We speak to you in the quiet of the night
> When the bosom is empty of feeling
> And the clock is clicking on the wall.

We die young. What is left is only dusty bone.
Remember, do remember us.

We have already tried what we can
But work is not over yet—far from it.

We have already given our lives
But work is not over yet, meaning has
not yet been given to four or five thousand lives.

We are only scattered bones
But they are yours
You have to decide the value of those scattered bones.

Whether we lost our lives for the sake
of Freedom, Victory and the Future
or just in vain,
We don't understand, we are not able to speak.
You have to speak now.

We speak to you in the quiet of the night
When the bosom is empty of feeling
And the clock is clicking on the wall.

Remember, do remember us
Continue, do continue our spirit.
Guard Bung Karno
Guard Bung Hatta
Guard Bung Sjahrir.

We are now dead corpses
Do give meaning to us
Do guard the border line between reality and dream.

Remember, do remember us
We who are only dusty bones,
Thousands—we lie between Krawang and Bekasi.

Recently there have been attacks in the Indonesian press on
'intellectualism and cosmopolitanism' in Indonesian literature, con-
demning Chairil Anwar, Takdir Alisjahbana and others. The life
of the creative intellectual in today's Indonesia, where the Great
Leader sets the standards and monopolizes the symbols, is likely to
be frustrating.

CHAPTER EIGHT

The Land

'From Sabang to Merauke', the geographical catch-cry of Indonesian nationalism, defines the nation by its territorial limits. The three thousand islands between the nation's western extremity, Sabang, an island off the tip of Sumatra, and its eastern limit, Merauke, a town almost on the border with Australian New Guinea, are so varied, however, in both land and people, that the following chapter is provided as a simple guide to one of the most complex countries in the world.

In the far west, closest to the Malayan peninsula, is Sumatra, or Sumatera, as it is spelled in Indonesia. When Marco Polo came there in 1290, he called it 'Java the less', but Sumatra (180,380 square miles) is in fact three times as large as Java (or twice the size of Victoria). Marco Polo's derogatory comparison has echoed down the centuries, with rebellious consequences that persist today. Sumatra is similar in climate to Malaya, and the narrow, shallow Strait of Malacca has been a point of contact between the two land areas rather than a factor of separation. More important as a barrier have been the swamps and marshes on the east coast, which contrast with the mountains of the west. Some of the most spectacular scenery in all Indonesia—which is saying a great deal—is found along the parallel chains of western mountains, punctuated with volcanic peaks, and the valleys lying between them, flooded with lakes. Lake Toba, the biggest, is 45 miles long, surrounded by cliffs up to 2,000 feet high, themselves split by deep gorges and watched over by dormant cones. The world's largest bloom, the Rafflesia, whose flowers may be more than a yard in diameter, luxuriates on the west coast. Much of central Sumatra is a jungle plain crossed by rivers and inhabited by some of the few remaining orang-utans, as well as elephants, tigers and rhinoceroses. It was in this region that the rebel colonels and economists fought their losing battle in 1958.

The most extensive cultivation is in the north, adjoining the Strait of Malacca. Here the Dutch established an elaborate plantation system known as the East Coast Residency, now run by the

Indonesian government, producing rubber (Sumatra's most important crop), tobacco, tea, palm oil and fibres. Medan, in this area, is Sumatra's largest city and a cultural melting pot, as a result of labour imported from China and other islands to work the Dutch estates. Wet rice is grown in the island's highland. The major mineral resource is oil, and Palembang in the south is one of Indonesia's two biggest refinery cities. Sumatra has more mining enterprises than any other Indonesian island. Gold and silver are mined, and the tin-producing islands of Bangka and Billiton lie off the east coast. So do the bauxite-rich islands of the Rhio archipelago, some of which can be seen from Singapore's harbour.

Sumatra is the second most populous island in the archipelago. Its sixteen million people are mainly small-holding rice-growers, living in strongly differentiated societies, whose patterns of *adat* and religion have been so strict that since the end of the last century successive younger generation intellectuals and traders have escaped to the relativism of Java, where they are noticeable for a direct outlook, open faces, and energy. Sumatrans have stood in disproportionate numbers among the forgers of the Indonesian Republic, as political leaders like Hatta, Sjahrir, Nasution, Natsir and Agus Salim, and as writers, among them Marah Rusli, Alisjahbana, the Pane brothers, Chairil Anwar, Idrus and Sitor Situmorang.

The Atjenese, in the far north-west of Sumatra, were the first to welcome Islam and among the last to succumb to the Dutch. The people are known for their martial spirit and sense of freedom, and during the police actions of 1947 and 1948 the Dutch significantly left them alone. Atjeh has been washed for centuries by the flow of peoples over the Indian Ocean and it has ancient associations with Arabia. In the sixteenth century many Indian craftsmen, including slaves, lived there. The Atjenese represent the strictest, or most fanatical, Muslim variant in Indonesia.

The Batak peoples live in the mountains around Lake Toba and part of the east coast. Batak was originally a derogatory Malay term, meaning 'robber' or 'blackmailer', and the tribes were traditionally repressed, squeezed as they are between the Atjenese and the Minangkabau. Not many of the Batak people are Muslim, having been almost isolated until the middle of the nineteenth century, when Dutch Protestant missionaries arrived. Now about half the Toba Batak are Christian, but most of the other Batak tribes are still animist. Batak clans lived in longhouses and warred with other clan-villages; the rivalry between the Toba and Karo Batak is still a factor of local politics. Rigid kinship ties and communal authority over land have caused extensive Batak migration to other islands during this century, and Christian Toba Batak are prominent in the army, education and commerce.

The Minangkabau, to the south of the Batak, live like them in the interior highland valleys centred around the towns of Bukittingi and Padang. Their language is closely related to Malay and in their border areas they merge with the surrounding coastal Malays. The Minangkabau people have been Muslim for three centuries, but have retained their matrilineal family structure, in which descent and inheritance are determined through the mother, not the father, with a woman's brother, rather than her husband, ruling the family group. Their elaborately decorated houses, with roofs curved like buffalo horns (*minang kabau* means 'our buffalo has won', which folk-stories say is how, in a challenge-fight with the buffalo of another people, the Minangkabau founded their homeland), testify to a high standard of culture and skill. When the Dutch stopped the system of forced coffee growing in 1910, cash-crop farming of copra, coffee, rubber and coconuts became a primary interest, and the Minangkabau's commercial shrewdness enabled them to exclude Chinese middlemen, which few other Indonesian peoples were able to do. Interest in education has always been high, and this, in combination with the tradition of a trip abroad by almost all young bachelors, to give them standing in the female-oriented society, has resulted in a migration of Minangkabau traders and intellectuals throughout the archipelago and into high positions in the government and civil service.

South Sumatra, in the area of the Lampung people, has a population of Javanese immigrant rice-farmers, as well as former plantation labourers from central and west Java. Sumatra is still short of labour for its rubber and tobacco plantations and its oil companies.

Moving in a clockwise direction, Kalimantan (Borneo) lies east of Sumatra. It is the third largest island in the world, and about three-quarters of its 286,969 square miles is Indonesian, an area slightly less than New South Wales. The island of Borneo has an active history, centred on Brunei, now a small, oil-fed sultanate, but once a maritime kingdom embracing most of the island. Han dynasty (first century A.D.) ceramics have been discovered in east Borneo, as have the oldest inscriptions in Indonesia, which are in Sanscrit and date from the beginning of the fifth century. During the seventh century China traded with Borneo, primarily for pearls, and birds' nests for soup. But with Brunei's waning power and the division last century into British and Dutch Borneo, the island is now known primarily for its natural resources and growth of tropical jungle quickened by an average rainfall of 150 inches a year. Ironwood is exported, as are tobacco, pepper and ivory. Gold, diamonds and coal are mined and oil is produced on the east coast near the town of Balikpapan (Indonesia's main refining centre in addition to Palembang) and on the east coast island of Tarakan. There are no active volcanoes in Kalimantan. In the jungle, the boiling rivers and south coast marshes and mangrove swamps, wild life flourishes, including the vanishing orang-utans, proboscis monkeys, gibbons, wild oxen (used on the Republic's crest to symbolize the people's sovereignty), crocodiles, honey bears and leopards. There are more than six hundred varieties of birds, and ferns, orchids and pitcher plants deck ground and trees.

The 4,200,000 people who live in Kalimantan are fairly sharply divided between the coastal people—Malays, Bandjars in the area around the south coast town of Bandjarmasin (the largest city in Kalimantan), and Chinese, most of whom live on the west coast nearest to Singapore and in the major town of Pontianak—and inland tribes. The coastal peoples are mostly Muslim and engage in commerce and plantation farming of rubber, coconuts and pepper. The peoples of the interior include Dyak, Punan, Kajan, Iban, Dusun and Murut. They are primarily animist, although some have become Muslim and Christian, and tend to live nomadic lives, dependent for their rice, maize, cassava and vegetables on the slash-and-burn method of *ladang* cultivation, clearing new areas of farmland every year. This sytem has resulted in serious soil exhaustion and erosion in several areas. Like Kalimantan itself, most of its people's resources have not yet been tapped.

Sulawesi (Celebes), lying west of Kalimantan across the Makassar Strait, is surely one of the most curiously shaped islands in the world. It has four tentacular arms, and was called 'the' Celebes by the sixteenth-century Portuguese, who thought that the arms were separate islands. The fourth in size of Indonesia's 'big five' islands (62,277 square miles, or somewhat smaller than Victoria), it is the most mountainous spot in the archipelago, with volcanoes in the northeast and south. Because of its rugged terrain, most of the island is still forest-covered, and there has never been an important estate agriculture. The interior peoples practice shifting cultivation, which in the Toraja area of central Sulawesi has led to serious erosion; they grow dry rice, maize, sugar-cane, tobacco, coconuts and breadfruit. In the south-west arm, both *sawah* and *ladang* rice is grown. The major export is copra, which is Indonesia's second most important small-holding crop, and corn, coffee, nutmeg, rubber and kapok are also exported, as are the horns and hides of the cattle raised on the rich pastureland of the interior plateau. Iron, nickel, gold, copper and lead are found in Sulawesi's south-east arm, but have not yet been intensively developed, and the adjoining island of Buton produces asphalt. Despite its extensive jungle cover, Sulawesi is poor in animal species compared with the rest of Indonesia, but some unique varieties are native, including the black-crested baboon, the dwarf buffalo and a pig called the pig-deer because of its long slender legs and curved, horn-like tusks.

There are 7,100,000 people on Sulawesi. The north-east and south-west arms of the island are the most densely populated, with peoples who have made their names known throughout the world for their seafaring activities. The Buginese and Makassarese, both ardently Muslim, live in south-west Sulawesi, the most fertile part of the island, which in parts has a population of over two hundred per square mile as compared with less than ten in most of the rest of the island, and during the fourteenth to eighteenth centuries was divided into many coastal kingdoms. The Buginese, whose name is still almost synonymous with 'pirates' in south-east Asia, were among the world's most intrepid ocean-going warriors, and their square-sailed, high-prowed ships still anchor in picturesque clusters in harbours throughout the region. Their principal kingdom was Bone (the Gulf of Bone between Sulawesi's two southern arms bears testimony to its fame) from which they warred with Makassar over the centuries, and they maintained colonies in the Rhio Islands, Borneo and elsewhere in the archipelago. Because of this and their extreme mobility, Buginese are now to be found in many parts of coastal Indonesia.

The Makassarese are centred around Makassar, which is Sulawesi's largest city, capital, and chief port and trading centre. From their kingdom of Gowa they used to sail and trade as far as China. Before the Dutch 'pacification' of 1905 they had large numbers of slaves, and an exclusive aristocracy. The Makassarese are a proud and competitive people, and their society is one of elaborate personal and political rivalry, with almost unlimited possibilities for individual achievement. Despite allegiance to Islam, their animistic ancestor-worship is a powerful force, and their towns usually support both a Muslim religious official and an animist priest, who conducts ceremonies which sometimes include animal sacrifices.

In the rugged mountains of central Sulawesi are the Toraja, who before 1905 were one of the fiercest and most isolated peoples in

Indonesia. They lived in small, walled fortress-villages, each atop
a hill, like the castles of medieval Europe, and warred almost con-
stantly with each other for heads and slaves. Headhunting was a
political, religious and social requirement; taking the head of an
enemy robbed his village of vital supernatural powers, and enemy
heads were a necessary offering to ancestral spirits at burials and
temple consecrations, ensuring the village's welfare and its agricultural and human fertility. Convicted sorcerers were sold to other
villages where they were beheaded. Only women and transvestite
men could become witch-doctors, but the villages were governed
by family headmen under one chief. People were buried at death,
and then again several years later, when their bones were cleaned
and their spirits transformed from devils to guardians. Each village
owned the jungle around it, where slash-and-burn agriculture was
practised. After 1905, the Dutch moved the villages down into the
valleys, with connecting roads, instituted individual money taxes,
and forbade headhunting, bone-cleaning and witch-executing. Most
Toraja are now Christian, with some Muslims—an agricultural
people whose staple crop is sago.

The Minahasans and Menadonese live in Sulawesi's north-east
arm, close to the Moluccas Islands. Because of their early and extensive contact with the spice islands' traders, they are racially mixed.
The Dutch East India Company gained control of north-east Sulawesi in the seventeenth century, and the Minahasans and Menadonese became Protestants. Throughout Holland's rule they supplied
mercenaries for the Dutch army. Many emigrated to other islands
and entered the colonial civil service, particularly on Java. The major
city of the area is Menado, which is the second largest on Sulawesi.

The Moluccas, called Maluku in Indonesian, lie between Sulawesi and West Irian. The chain of volcanoes which runs through
Sumatra and Java continues into the Moluccas, which are mostly
mountainous and densely forested, but contain some flat and swampy
islands. The total land area is about 35,000 square miles, and the
main islands are Halmahera, Obi, Sula, Seram, where oil is found,
Buru, Ambon, Ternate, Tidor, and the Banda, Kai, Aru, Tanimbar
and Wetar island groups. There are not many varieties of animal, but
birds, including the bird of paradise and, on Seram, cassowaries,
flourish, as do shellfish, including trepang, or sea-cucumber, with a
trade in mother-of-pearl. The main exports are, of course, spices,
primarily cloves and nutmeg, but include sandalwood, coconuts,
sago, coffee and copra.

The islands' agricultural riches, which made them an early focal point of world trade, and brought the Dutch to Indonesia, brought economic and social impoverishment to the people. From the fourteenth century on they were dominated in turn by Muslim Ternate, Catholic Portugal and Calvinist Holland, and the 800,000 population is of such mixed descent that its culture has been called 'creole'. There are more Christians in the Moluccas than anywhere else in Indonesia, although many people are Muslim or animist. Amboina on the island of Ambon is the largest city in the Moluccas, and was the islands' administrative centre under the Dutch. The Ambonese language no longer exists, having been replaced by Malay and Dutch during the colonial period. As a result of intense Dutch missionary activity, the level of education on Ambon was among the highest in Indonesia, and many Ambonese worked in the colonial administration and were an important and privileged segment of the Dutch army, like the Karens in Burma under the British. After the revolution, some Ambonese chose Dutch citizenship and went to Holland, but there are still large numbers in the Republic's civil service. On Ambon the village headmen are also animist priests, whose activities do not appear to conflict with the villages' Christian or Muslim religious leaders.

West Irian (Irian Barat), the easternmost part of Indonesia, comprises the west half of New Guinea, the second largest island in the world (Greenland is the largest). West Irian's 151,789 square miles is 22 per cent of Indonesia's total land area. It is nine-tenths jungle, and its interior is largely unexplored, ranging from steamy swamps to snow-capped mountains, as high as 16,000 feet, some renamed since the Republic's administration after slogans or people, as Trikora Mountain, Sukarno Mountain, Sudirman Mountain, Yamin Mountain. Rainfall is as high as 250 inches a year in places. Generally, soil is poor, and commercial agriculture is limited to coconut plantations for copra, mostly in the hands of Chinese in the Radja Ampat group of islands off the west coast. Nutmegs rank next in production value, followed by crocodile skins and copal. Oil was produced in 1948 near Sorong, and the following year nickel was discovered near Hollandia, the capital, now called Kota Baru, but expectations of mineral wealth have so far been disappointed. Pigs are the only important livestock, although wallabies are hunted. Sweet potatoes and sago provide the staple diet.

The population is less than a million, primarily Papuan, a people of stone age culture, and Melanesian (in the coastal towns), with a baffling variety of tribes and languages. No one language is intelligible to more than 150,000 people. Most of the West Irianese are animist, with some Muslim and Christian influences.

Bali is one of the islands of the Lesser Sundas, which stretch from the western tip of Java eastward to Timor, making up Indonesia's southern boundary. It is separated from Java only by a narrow strait, and is similar to Java in climate, flora and fauna, and in its configuration of west to east volcanic mountain chain, which includes Mount Agung. Like Java, Bali is intensively cultivated and *sawah* rice is a staple. Coconuts, sugar cane, tobacco, cocoa, indigo and peanuts are cultivated and some coffee is grown for export, although Bali has never had an export agriculture or exploited mineral resources. But the 1,800,000 Balinese, some of whom live on the western end of the adjoining island of Lombok, are not like the Javanese, nor like any other Indonesian people. The inheritors of a unique blend of Hindu, Buddhist and local animist religions, untouched by Islam as a result of their ancestors' fierce protection of their island from all invaders (including, until 1910, the Dutch), the Balinese remain creative in their ritual society, building new temples, inventing new music and dances and designing new sculptures and paintings in honour of their many gods and spirits as well as maintaining the customary purification rites, processions, offerings and cremations which fill their lives. Despite the twentieth century influx of tourists and a recent growth of commercial activity (conducted largely by the old nobility), Balinese society remains tightly knit, and few people migrate to other islands. There is a patrilineal kinship system, but all family groups overlap into the hundreds of temple associations, agricultural societies, and hamlet councils which interlock throughout the countryside. All land is privately owned. There is little trace of the old Hindu castes, although the Brahmin priests are the highest social class and there are still some marriage restrictions according to rank. Marriage is by consent or by pre-arranged 'elopement', and the young couple usually go to live with the groom's parents, unless the bride is the only daughter in the family. The capital of Bali is Singaradja on the north coast, and the largest town is Denpasar, in the south.

The other islands of the Lesser Sundas (called Nusa Tengarra, 'South-eastern Islands' in Indonesian) are influenced by the presence of the Australian continent. Timor, whose eastern half belongs to Portugal, has such Australian flora as the eucalypts, while Lombok has prickly pears and cockatoos. The people of the Lesser Sundas are very mixed, including Malay, Papuan, Polynesian and indigenous groups totalling about 3,800,000. The islands are largely agricultural, the main export items being sandalwood and horses. The major islands in addition to Bali and Timor are, from west to east, Lombok, on which is one of the highest volcanoes in the archipelago, Sumbawa, Sumba and Flores. The small island of Komodo is the home of the dragon lizards, the oldest living genus of lizard—about sixty million years—which reach a length of ten feet or more.

Java (Djawa), separated from Sumatra by the narrow Sunda Strait and lying south of Kalimantan across the Java Sea, is radically different in appearance from the other major Indonesian islands because of its heavy population and almost total cultivation. It is one of the most densely populated places in the world, with 50,604 square miles, or about a fourteenth of Indonesia's total land area (almost twice the size of Tasmania, or about the same area as England and Wales combined), and with Madura, the smaller island just south of its western tip which is usually included in its statistics, has a population of 63,000,000, or about 1,243 people per square mile. Java is also by far the most urbanized of the islands. Over one hundred volcanoes, fifteen of which are active, infest the mountain chain which runs from west to east close to Java's south coast, as a continuation of Sumatra's mountains, dividing the island into a narrow coastal strip on the Indian Ocean and a fertile plain which stretches north to the Java Sea. The climate is hot and wet, with some surprising variations—on the Dieng Plateau in central Java, the top of a 6,000-foot filled volcanic crater, the temperature may fall below freezing, and rainfall ranges from 165·94 inches at Bogor near Java's western tip, to 35·39 inches at Asembagus in east Java, where the pronounced wet and dry seasons are caused largely by the nearness of the Australian continent. A quarter of Java's land area is given over to *sawah* or wet-rice cultivation, in irrigated fields and stepping up the terraced hillsides, where food fish are also raised (only one per cent of the land outside Java and Bali is *sawah* cultivated). Very little dry rice is grown; in the drier areas of eastern Java, cassava and maize supplant rice. Sweet potatoes, peanuts and soya beans are also important crops, and the government-run estates, which are second only to Sumatra's in extent, produce tea, coffee, rubber, cinchona, cocoa, sugar and tobacco. But these export crops are not much help to the overcrowded peasant population, whose farming is almost entirely for subsistence, rather than the cash-crop small farming done on the other islands. The government land reform programmes are based on two hectares of land as a minimum holding for individual farmers, but in 1957, 78 per cent of Javanese *sawah*-owners had less than half one hectare, and 90 per cent less than one hectare, and much of this land was in fact under the control of rural moneylenders, because farmers with such small holdings cannot make ends meet. In any case, there is not enough land in Java to give all of its peasants the 'minimum' two hectares, and unless the government is more successful than it has been in persuading the rapidly-increasing Javanese population to migrate to the land-rich outer islands, the standard of living will become an even more serious problem than it is now. Another difficulty due to over-population is the over-clearing of land, which has reduced Java's forests to 23·4 per cent of the island, resulting in extensive erosion during the monsoon seasons.

Many Javanese are employed in the island's various industries, which range from cottage crafts like batik making and rattan weaving, to factories producing such commodities as cigarettes, textiles, soap, cement and paper (a 1958 survey of employees in major Indonesian industries compiled by the Central Bureau of Statistics states that 88 per cent of workers in plants with ten or more employees were employed in factories on Java). The most important mineral resource is oil, which is found near Tjepu, on the border of east and central Java, and at Wonokromo, close to Surabaya, which is Indonesia's second largest city and the capital of the province of East Java. Manganese, sulphur, gold and silver are mined, and there are extensive salt-works on Madura.

Despite the relative scarcity of forested land, a few one-horned rhinoceroses, and wild oxen, tigers, leopards and apes still exist on the island, as well as some four hundred species of birds, including peacocks and edible-nest producing swifts, and more than one hundred varieties of snakes, among them the great python. Seventy per cent of all Indonesian cattle and water buffalo are concentrated in Java and Madura, where they are used as work animals. Teak, bamboo, casuarina and many varieties of fruit trees grow prolifically.

The Javanese peoples are not as distinctively separate as those in most parts of the archipelago. The reasons are population pressures, the large number of towns and roads, the steady influx over the last centuries of people from other islands, and the Arabic, South Indian and Chinese traders and settlers which the spice trade of the fourteenth to eighteenth centuries brought to the many coastal kingdoms which rose and fell in west and north Java during that period. In fact the residents of Djakarta, the largest city in Indonesia, are so mixed that they have developed a Malay dialect of their own, and the Dutch considered them a separate people whom they called the 'Batavians'. The Sundanese, who are about 25 per cent of Java's population, live in the mountainous areas of west Java, except for the western tip of the island around the town of Bantam, where the Bantamese maintain some cultural distinctions of their own. The Sundanese language is still spoken, especially around Bogor, which was the capital of the twelfth-to-sixteenth-century Sundanese kingdom Pajajaran, and the people's historic rivalry with the central Javanese kingdoms and their intense dedication to Islam helped to make West Java a centre of the separatist activities of the Darul Islam ('Islamic State') which waged a rebellion from 1949 to 1962. Many Madurese, who are also strict Muslims, live in east Java as farmers and fishermen.

Central Java is the home of the Javanese proper. Although its capital is Semarang, the cities of Jogjakarta (whose area, under the governorship of Sultan Hamengkubuono IX, has the status of a Province) and Solo (formerly Surakarta) are the emotional and cultural centres, having both been capitals of former Javanese kingdoms, and frequently rivals. The Javanese have an individualistic kinship system, which centres on the small family unit, with descent traced through both mother and father, and inheritance the same for daughters and sons. Unlike most other Indonesian peoples, the Javanese have few organized communal features in their villages, such as landholding or ritual groups, and religion is a private affair. The divorce rate is very high—about 50 per cent—and the general tendency toward individual decision has inclined the Javanese toward membership in a variety of social, educational, philosophical and nationalist organizations and political parties.

CHAPTER NINE

The People

A. is in his forties. He lives with his wife and family in a suburban street in Djakarta. It is a pleasant house, its porch covered with bougainvillea and separated from the front fence by a small green lawn. The family car, a Volkswagen, is big enough, as they have only two children, a boy and a girl. They profess no religion. They are western in habits as well as in dress. The meals they serve are, except for the lack of meat in them, the thick Java coffee and red peppers, not substantially different from simple food in a middle class Australian family. The study is full of books, in English, Dutch, French, German and Bahasa Indonesia. They subscribe to European and American magazines, popular and seriously intellectual. He is a lawyer but his professional employment has been restricted, since he belongs to a party out of favour with the government. He is loyal to his country, but he is not fanatic about anything, including nationalism. He dislikes the trend under Sukarno with the deep instincts of a rational man, but he has accepted it as a—he hopes not fatal—stage in the country's evolution. I enjoy asking him the 'big' questions about Indonesia.

'Do you think Indonesia is becoming expansionist?'

'Not if by expansionist is meant the intention to expand. I think some of the leaders may be *historically*-minded, i.e., they remember the Indonesian, especially Javanese-based glorious empires of the past, and being intense nationalists may believe, in an emotional way, that it might happen again. But they don't think about it in a practical way, I'm sure. They somehow expect the rest of the world to fall down and recognize Indonesia's greatness, to accord her rights based on her past greatness, her sufferings under colonialism and her potential for the future: they don't plan it, however. They don't *plan* anything—that's my complaint.

'But if you are thinking that expansionism, of necessity, may follow the course our leaders are at present following you may be wise to think so. It is the duty of any country near Indonesia to pay attention to this. The fact is the Sukarno government has failed dismally to provide the Indonesian people with a reasonable minimum of economic welfare. While there is such potential unrest, fanned all the time by nationalistic slogan-shouting, you can never be sure what will happen, what the government will commit the country to abroad and then have to justify. It may not be territorial aggression as such; but it could be. It might well be the expansion of Indonesian *authority* in the South-east Asia region. They would have no trouble justifying this. There are many Indonesians who, in the state we are in, welcome the chance to do something definite, such as fight an enemy.'

'Would you say the Indonesian people are becoming militaristic?'

'No. There are deep currents of violence in the Indonesian make-up, but the people are not military minded. The trouble is that a nation has to *do* something. Even in settled countries, like Australia or the United States, there must be a raison d'être for the nation, which the government must claim, on behalf of the people, to pursue. At the very least, the government must convince the people that it can provide them with the security to go on living their private lives as they want. But, as the election of Kennedy in the U.S. showed, even this is not enough; people want to feel that their nation is playing a significant role in world affairs in some capacity or another. In Indonesia this desire is tremendously strong because the nation is still a matter of wonder and pride to the people.

'The removal of colonial rule has released the pent-up spirit of the people. Static for so long, they are now in a state of dynamism. They have a feeling of *power*, a feeling of being able to manage, manipulate, even to create their lives for the first time. They want to *do* something, to use this new sense of power. This is where the leadership becomes important. You cannot stop this urge, this dynamic movement of people. But you can channel it. You can turn it into productive channels. In Malaya, I think nationalism has been channelled into getting a high living standard. This is the way of the new Japan. In Indonesia nationalism has been directed *against* things, rather than *for* things. We are against subversion, rebellion, colonialism, capitalism, etc., etc. What are we *for*? The new emerging forces? Change everywhere, wherever or whatever it is? The President keeps talking about transforming the world, but what about transforming Indonesia? Nothing has been done here that a wind wouldn't blow over. The "revolution" in Indonesia is just a farce. The communists are quite right in their criticism that no *structural* reforms of significance have been introduced in Indonesia. Sukarno wants to change the world, because if he starts to change Indonesia, there will be trouble.'

'Do you think Sukarno has the makings of a military dictator, whether or not the people want it?'

'Good gracious, no. The Bung is no more a military dictator than I am. He wants to live in luxury, above reproach or criticism, mediating between God and his people (though not, I suspect, between his people and God), loved by all. He has no stomach for the harsh realities of dictatorship. He is an artist, creating his own reality. Unfortunately, we are landed with him—and it.'

'Do you see Sukarno as a real danger to the development of the kind of Indonesia you want?'

'I am beginning to think so, although I did not think so some time ago. In many ways, I have sympathy with Sukarno, although I do not want to go back to the Indonesian roots he keeps talking about. I can see that, at this period of nation-building, he has been a unifying force. Indonesian nationalism is necessarily anti-West, because it is from western colonialism that we have struggled free. We are in the western "sphere of influence"—like Cuba is, which is one reason why there is so much sympathy here with Cuba. So our revolutionary *spirit* is naturally anti-West, while our *situation* is western, in terms of trade, military logistics and so on. By going back to the pre-colonial Indonesia, to the traditions of village and family life as they have been practised here for centuries, Sukarno has avoided a split, which would have been disastrous. It may still come, but it will be less likely the longer Sukarno stays.

'What worries me, rather, is that there is no structure of restraint. Take the U.S. President, for example, perhaps the most powerful single political leader in the world. He is surrounded by a framework of critical restraint—press, pulpit, opposition parties, and a whole public philosophy to which his critics and advisers can refer in restraining or urging him. Even in communist countries, where power is more naked, there is a significant structure of restraint in Marxism-Leninism, which can be refined and revised, but only through persuasive argument, and by the party, which has its own long-term interests. Here, in Indonesia, we have no such restraints by which the satisfaction of power can be controlled. Everything—education, law, even religion—can be used in Indonesia to sanctify power. The restraints on Sukarno are negative and usually bad. For example, he cannot get rid of some of the incompetents in his cabinet because immediately the communists would clamour for admission.

There is no general framework which can be used, publicly, to define his authority and his tasks. All this ideology which he and the government propaganda machine produces—what does it *mean?* No-one can say, "But, Sukarno, that is contrary to *Pantja Sila*, or Manipol-Usdek, etc.", because these are only what the state and the government, at any given time, say they are. A while ago, the OK word was "retooling". Now it's "new emerging forces" or "self-sustaining growth" or some other nonsense. Nobody knows what these words are supposed to mean as a guide to action. Who and what is to be "retooled"? Who are "the new emerging forces" and what are they supposed to do? How do we develop "self-sustaining growth"?'

'But is this fantasy of meaningless symbols as you describe it, dangerous? Doesn't it keep people interested—make them believe something is happening? Indonesians keep telling me that the shadow is more important than the reality in Java, a legacy of the *wayang*.'

'I don't believe this. It is mysticism. I don't believe that the Indonesian "identity", whatever it is, can cope with the real forces at work in today's world. It is only child's play, nursery oratory, sentimental bed-time tales that a child must forget when it grows up and goes into the world or it faces destruction. The Indonesian's "identity" is just a joke to the rest of the world. We need to consolidate what we have gained—our independence as a nation. We need to strengthen our country, so that it can take its place in the world community. Sukarno is old-fashioned, wanting to revolutionize the world. Most people, in the east and west, as well as in the "non-aligned" countries, want peace and stability, in order to build and grow. Sukarno is never satisfied. He is always on the lookout for a fresh "concept", like a fresh ankle. As a revolutionary poet, perhaps, he could be properly honoured. But as a leader he is dangerous.

'What is dangerous is that Sukarno's rule is sanctifying the use of power without limits. At the moment this power is limited by his appreciation of the dramatic balance of forces under him, by his instinctive caution and by the inertia of our economic mess. But if any of these influences are removed, the danger increases that the power will run wild. Then it will have to be limited from the outside, which could mean war.'

*   *   *

B. is a Protestant Christian from the Minahasa region of north-east Sulawesi. Aged thirty, recently married, he has the look of a young warrior. His long, unruly hair frames an open, rough face, with a slow grin. He rides a motor scooter and, as his pillion passenger several times, I can vouch for his gay spirits. He is, I suppose, a religious man, although I have no direct experience of his sincerity as a Christian. We usually talk politics. He was disturbed by the rebellions in Sumatra and Sulawesi and at that time his loyalty to the central government was strained. His parents and close relatives now live in Java, but they maintain a regional loyalty. Younger and married to a Javanese, B. has adapted himself more easily. High spirits have helped him, turning his troubles into a wry joke. It was he who first told me the classic joke on Indonesian politics: 'If you understand the situation, you are obviously badly informed'. He works for Garuda Indonesia Airways, the national airline, and is a spare-time teacher.

'What attitude does the average Christian in Indonesia have to the present government?'

'We are quite satisfied. What we fear most is a Muslim theocratic state, as they have in Malaya. While President Sukarno stands by the *Pantja Sila*, which underwrites belief in God, without saying what kind of God, we support him. We have two Christians in the cabinet.'

'Where do Christians stand generally on political issues?'

'I would say in the middle, with the nationalists. The Muslims tend to be on the right and the communists on the left. The Catholics are perhaps more with the Muslims on political issues. On the issue of the secular state, however, Christians and communists were on the same side.'

'Do you think Christians in Indonesia feel free to live according to their beliefs?'

'Oh yes, there's no doubt about it. We don't feel restricted. One example, our newspaper *Sinar Harapan* [*Hopeful Beam*]. It was founded only a couple of years ago by a non-profit-making organization of some thirty Protestant groups. It has already reached a circulation of 25,000 and can't expect any more because of the newsprint rationing. The government does not discriminate against Christians. When West Irian was taken over, the government allowed missionary activity to continue. The Christians are responding to this by trying to adapt their activities to the basic feelings of the national revolution. For example, the Toraja people in central Sulawesi have very strong local customs, *adat* and so on. The Christians are now trying not to displace this culture, but to use it as a base for Christian beliefs. This produces some interesting problems. The traditional Torajas follow ancestor worship, so we have to adapt this to the Christian worship of God. The government is pleased with this approach.'

'Isn't this the famous syncretic approach to religion that you outer-islanders are always attributing to the Javanese?'

'It's not deliberately so. We—I mean Christians rather than Mina-hasans—don't favour relativism. You never know what the Javanese are thinking. Our beliefs are clear and in this case we decide, as a matter of policy, to do it this way. But perhaps in the long run it will amount to a syncretic religion of its own—Christian ancestor worship!'

'What do you think is the basis of religious tolerance in Indonesia? It is not common in the rest of the world.'

'A lot has depended on President Sukarno, who is not religious. Certainly he is not a religious fanatic, and has been able to hold the predominantly Muslim element at bay. And syncretism does come into it. So much has been taken in by the people of Indonesia—Hinduism, Buddhism, Islam, Christianity—that, although there has been some fierce fighting in our history, people now believe that we in Indonesia can absorb any new idea. This applies to communism. All these religions, including communism, have travelled a long way by the time they reach us in Indonesia. They are a long way from their original source and are probably weaker—so our basic culture has been able to withstand them.'

'I've often wondered what you Protestants, with the puritan strain of the Calvinists and Dutch Reformed Church in you, think of the oriental splendour of President Sukarno's court?'

'As you know, most Protestant Christians in Indonesia are middle class. We tend to come from the better educated groups in society, and we are interested in the professional skills and disciplines. We tend to discourage spendthrift finance, lax morals and a display of worldly things. President Sukarno has an artistic temperament, which does seem to please most of the people. We recognize that we are in a small minority, perhaps five million Protestants (and about one million Catholics) in a population of one hundred million. Sukarno works very hard for the country and he is not a ruthless dictator. Personally, I would rather have Sukarno's kind of government than a Catholic dictator like Ngo Dinh Diem, or Synghman Rhee and Chiang Kai-shek, who are Methodists.'

*   *   *

C. is a senior bureaucrat, an official of the foreign ministry. He has the deceptive appearance of many Indonesian men, and is probably

a good deal older than his boyish face suggests. He lives in a small
new house in Kebajoran, Djakarta's swanky suburb, with his wife
and three young children. They have lived abroad and have acquired
an American car, about 1957 model. He is ambitious, and his wife is
interested in his promotion. They are friendly to foreigners and I
have been, as their guest, the only stranger at small social gatherings
of his friends and their wives. Although most of his colleagues are
Javanese, C. is from Sumatra; a Muslim, though not a strict one.
Years of living in Djakarta and his professional concern with national
policies in the international setting have weakened any regional
loyalties he may have had. Dark-skinned, with short thick black hair
and an athletic figure, he has a military demeanour, but in fact he
has a subtle mind and a rather easy-going disposition, which make
him an ideal companion. He cooks, which is an unusual skill in a
land of servants and domesticated wives, but prefers, when enter-
taining, to go to a Chinese restaurant, where he orders a special kind
of hot-sour Szechuan soup which has become identified in my mind
with Indonesia. We have met in several places—at the United
Nations in New York, in Bali, for a moonlit walk on a beach, in
Jogjakarta, for a conference, in Manila, Tokyo and Singapore, also
for various conferences, and, of course, in Djakarta. We were together once in Hollandia, as it became Kota Baru, when the Indonesians took over the administration of West Irian. He went to look
at a Dutch political detention camp and became very emotional. He
has one grave fault: he takes foreign observers like myself far too
seriously.

'Do you think that the government is losing its authority in the
country because of the economic position?'

'You may as well ask me if I think the Indonesian ocean—the one
you call the Indian ocean—is going to dry up. Of course not. Economic hardship has been with the people for centuries. They will
bear it; now they can feel they have a reason for bearing it.'

'What reason?'

'A national identity. You laugh when we talk about national
identity as if it really means something. It does mean something to
us. You will never understand what it means for us to be able to
stand up in public and say, "as an Indonesian, I feel ... ". You take
your nationality for granted. But for us it is still a thrilling experience
to be able to use those words. The *meaning* of it—if you want concrete reasons, à la Marx or Freud or the balance sheet—isn't easy to
explain. Indonesians have always "belonged" somewhere, to family
or tribe. We do not need an "identity" to provide emotional security,

as you might say. We've always had custom or religion there, to explain things. But we were never able to achieve things for ourselves; there has always been someone in power over us, telling us what to do, telling the world what we were like, what we wanted, what we should be allowed to do. Now there is no-one over us. Our leaders have power, but it is our power. In the world, we are an equal with everyone else—no-one can order us about. That's why the foreign ministry is so important in everyone's eyes—it is the prestige service because when we are abroad we are in fact representing the whole nation.'

'Is it obligatory to wear the black cap abroad, to establish your Indonesian identity?'

'No, a matter of choice. So are sun glasses! But it isn't a matter of choice to know Manipol-Usdek and to understand what is implied in the return to the revolutionary 1945 constitution. And it is not a matter of choice to do everything we can, all the time, to advance Indonesia's interests. Your diplomats probably think of diplomacy as a career for themselves: what is in it for them. For us, it is not just personal satisfaction. We are entrusted with the sacred rights of the Indonesian people.'

'Other nations have rights, too, and other diplomats take them seriously. Why do Indonesians so often give the impression that they are not aware of this?'

'We are aware of it! Very much so. But it is our duty to look to our own. We do not believe that, having won independence, it is all over. We know we will have to defend this independence at every point. We are not so naïve as to think that Indonesia's struggle to survive over all these centuries is now over.'

'Who is going to take your independence from you?'

'Many would like to, especially the powerful western countries. They want capitalism to flourish in South-east Asia. They want anti-communism to flourish. Indonesia is non-aligned and socialist, so the western countries do not want her to succeed. Our environment is hostile, so we have to prepare to defend ourselves.'

'But don't you think the West has given up anti-communism? Socialist, non-aligned countries are now accepted happily. Surely, all the aid that has come from western countries to Indonesia is proof that the failure of Indonesia is not wanted.'

'Frankly, I think the aid is for the West's own benefit. I think it is hoped that aid will mean that Indonesia will open its doors to foreign capital—to capitalism in other words—that it will "buy western" and so on. It is self-interest.'

'And aid from the communist bloc is disinterested?'

'No. But one thing we do know. Economic aid from communist countries is a lot easier to accept. The terms are good and there are no pressures to conform afterwards. And there is not so much song and dance about it! Western countries, especially the United States, are forever talking about foreign aid. There are arguments in parliaments, the press takes it up: "Is this country good enough to receive our aid?" In communist countries, they give you the aid and shut up about it. Ever since we became independent the West, especially the press, which is hopelessly misinformed generally on Indonesian politics, has been sitting in judgment on us. The insults to us, as a nation, and to President Sukarno, who is our head of state, have been really unpleasant. We are not insulted by the communists. Why is this so? We are not communists and never will be. There are communists here. Why not? Is this sufficient reason for the West to insult us? No, it is something more, and deeply we suspect that while the communist countries want us to succeed, as we are, the West does not.'

'Perhaps it depends on what you mean by "succeed". If you mean succeed in stirring up trouble around you, it's not surprising the West is critical and the communist bloc is not. If Indonesia were in the communist "sphere of influence" Moscow would roast you, as they did—and Peking still does—Yugoslavia, for trying to be independent.'

'It's not geography. It's that three-quarters of the world is at present in the midst of changes, growing and developing out of backwardness and exploitation. One quarter is facing a decline from its peak of power. We are part of the three-quarters and so are the communists. The West is the one-quarter. This is what we mean by the new emerging forces and the old established powers.'

'What does this division mean? It is not a racial division, nor economic, nor political, nor religious, nor strategic. You put certain nations into one group and others into another, but this is like solving a problem by definition. "New" and "emerging" are not absolute references. Why is the Soviet Union, for example, a new, emerging nation? It has never been under colonialism. A revolution occurred in 1917, which replaced one form of government with another, but the nation did not emerge then, and if it had, it's getting on for half a century ago. Is that new?'

'The USSR is included, or all communist countries are, because they are in favour of revolution and change, because they are part of the three-quarters.'

'You are deluding yourself to think so. The communist countries are in favour of change only at someone else's expense. Any change directed against them is counter-revolution. Try it and see.'

'We do not want trouble with the communist countries. They have been our friends. If we are in trouble they will help us. They helped us over West Irian. The western countries did not.'

'It was an American, Mr Ellsworth Bunker, whose proposals brought the negotiations to a point where agreement on a treaty became possible.'

'But it was our policy on confrontation, backed by arms which the Soviet Union gave us, which made the Dutch agree to look at Mr Bunker's proposals.'

'And so you go on "confronting" for ever?'

'The President has said that our revolution is endless. We in the foreign ministry try to nail things down a little more. I would guess you won't find us settling down for, say, the rest of this century.'

*   *   *

D. is a grey-haired, laughing Sundanese. He has a large, growing family, all intent on serious education, which keeps him poor. We met at a friend's home and D. spent the entire evening talking of his children's education. Not that he was boring; he is a lively, charming conversationalist who expects you to contribute your share. But he is obsessed with the idea that Indonesia is going to pieces, morally and economically, and that the only chance for his children is to stay out of politics, learn as much as they can, and wait for the catastrophe to pass. He is cheerful about it and even a little excited at the prospect of a cataclysmic change. But he is basically a serious man, with a great love of his family and a strong code of honour and self-respect. Being Sundanese, he is suspicious of the Javanese, and he has a contempt for President Sukarno that is so insulting that it is almost familiar. He works as a clerk in a bank and has rigid views about money. The following monologue was discreetly jotted down in the back seat of a borrowed car while he drove me one morning for a visit to Punjak, the mountain resort outside Djakarta. One of his sons, who sat in the front seat with him, remained quiet throughout the journey. I managed only to murmur non-committal encouragements. He began by reading a slogan.

'*Hajo Pertinggi Produksi!* Come On, Let Us Increase Production! What is the use of increasing production if the leaders take all the money? They drive around in big cars, take wives left, right and centre, eat in expensive restaurants, and tell us we are lazy. The Indonesian people lazy! This is against my heart. The leaders are rich by privilege, not by work, rich by corruption.

'At least my children know their father is earning his living properly. We don't live well, but we are honest.

'I'd give them production! I'd give them the guillotine, like the French kings. But we have no power because we have no guns. It is as simple as that. If we had guns we would rise up against them and shoot them.

'They made lots of promises, but now they have good positions they have forgotten their promises. They say the people are looking fatter than under the Dutch. I tell you, my friend, it is beri-beri, from lack of vitamin B, eating too much cassava and not enough rice. Even *tjing tjao* [a green drink made from leaves] is going up in price. The leaves are still the same price, I suppose, but the man says he can't afford rice to eat.

'The President says we must sacrifice. What? Our lives, then we will be heroes. Heroes of the Revolution, so he can talk about us on Heroes' Day. Revolution! Now we've had our national revolution, we need a social revolution to get rid of our leaders.

'Oh, it's terrible, this country. Really terrible. The leaders are all going mad. Maybe Djakarta is too hot.

'Celebrations! They come to the *kampong* asking for donations for the August 17th celebrations. I told them, "The people are sick of celebrations". Let us have no more celebrations, but cheap school books instead. The students at the Bandung University booed the President when he said they were always complaining about the high cost of books. When he was a student he had to sleep on a rattan bed on the floor without cushions and read by an oil lamp—so he said. That was forty years ago, under the Dutch! Are we no better off now?

'Economic reform! Since they announced the economic reforms, the price of sugar has gone up four times. One kilogram of second class rice is twice the price, and going up. But the leaders go abroad and buy their wives jewellery and clothes in Hong Kong.

'Malaysia! We will confront the neo-colonialists! We will kill ourselves doing it. We should mind our own business and confront our leaders. The President is a colonialist—he dominates us! His police guard is full of Javanese. He wouldn't trust anyone else to guard him!

'I was better off under the Dutch. So were most people in the cities.

'My friends said to me: Tell the Australian journalist what you think. Maybe it will get into the foreign newspapers. It is the only way to stop the madness. So that I am doing. I hope you are not an intelligence agent.'

*   *   *

E. is a pretty Minangkabau girl in her early twenties, working as a receptionist in Djakarta. She always wears western dress. One of her ambitions is to meet a Hollywood film star. Failing that, she might be content to marry an ordinary American, Australian or Englishman. She does not like Asian men, especially Indonesians, because they are too short, too poor and because she wants to travel. She occupies her leisure in going to the cinema—only to American or European films; she never goes to Indonesian, Chinese or Indian films—in sailing, and in trying to meet western men. Her family lives in Djakarta and are a lively and interesting group. Her mother and father, who is in business, encourage the children to have independent views and they are not strict Muslims. Her brother is studying to be an engineer.

'I understand this Russian film is well worth seeing.'

'But if you're staying at the Hotel Indonesia, you can get tickets for the Tony Curtis film. Otherwise, I'll never see it. I don't like Russian films. They're communistic.'

'Aren't Hollywood films capitalistic?'

'Oh, they're just about people. They don't have propaganda in them.'

'Do you think the twist is out of step with the revolutionary rhythm, as President Sukarno says?'

'Oh, the President's old-fashioned, like my parents. I like the twist. *We* do it here at parties and nobody cares. We used to do the cha-cha, too, when that was banned.'

'Why did they ban the film *Never on Sunday,* do you think?'

'Because it's sexy. They don't like sexy things.'

'But they don't seem to mind sex in practice. I've always thought that Indonesian men and women treat the subject pretty calmly, and your President is noted for his mature interest.'

'People like to talk about having babies and that kind of thing, but they don't like sex in the movies because it's exciting, snappy. And they don't like looking at kissing.'

'Do you think western morals are decadent?'

'I don't know what all this about decadent means. I think it's just another way people have of trying to stop you from having a good time.'

'But surely you can have a good time "à la Indonésie"?'

'Where do you go in Djakarta to have a good time? No nightclubs. No shows or anything like that at the restaurants. The shops have nothing in them in the way of clothes. The young men are either trying to get on in the government, or are in some mad business. They're not sophisticated. When they look at you, they're either solemn and stupid-looking or they show off and whistle and that sort of thing. They're not sensible and dignified with you, like western men are.'

'Maybe the western men you've met and those on the screen are not the average. You'd find in their own countries they show off and whistle, too, and the girls think they're stupid.'

'But I'd be different, as a visitor. People say you can have a marvellous time.'

'What do you think about the youth groups that take part in demonstrations outside embassies and so on?'

'They're maniacs. It's just communist politics.'

'Is your brother interested in this kind of politics?'

'He's not interested in anything except studying. He's mad on building things.'

'Does he feel sure that when he's finished his studies, there'll be work for him to do?'

'My father says there'll be a lot of building to do in Indonesia for the next hundred years.'

'What do you think of the government? I know you don't care for politics, but would you rather have this kind of government or some other kind?'

'What other kind?'

'Any kind. Just a change.'

'Oh, the government's all right. But there are things all the time— one after another. There's always a crisis and yet things go on the same. I want to get away and see some of the world.'

*　　　*　　　*

F. is a member of the Indonesian Women's Congress (Kongres Wanita Indonesia). She has a large grown-up family. She is a doctor, although she has not fully practised for some years. I suppose she would be considered a 'feminist', but she remains intensely feminine, always wearing the traditional combination of *kebaya*, a filmy, tight-fitting, long-sleeved blouse, and *sarong,* an ankle-length skirt, usually of bright batik. Indonesian women are organization-conscious, due, they claim, to their *adat* background of participation in communal activity. The Women's Congress has many activities, ranging from child-care and health centres to marriage bureaus and adult education for women labourers. Its fundamental interest, however, is in removing discrimination against women, which, in a Muslim country, where men are technically permitted four wives, is even more of a task than in the West.

'Women in Indonesia seem more active and independent than in other Muslim countries?'

'Perhaps so. It is true that we have no Madam Pandit, but we have never had purdah either. We have women in the government and in the diplomatic services. We have twenty women judges, two public prosecutors. Seven per cent of the civil service is women. You'll find women in many municipal councils. On the whole, Indonesian women are politically equal with the men. Most discrimination is at the social and economic level.

'Since there's a surplus labour force, it's hard for women to claim their rights, even when they've got guarantees written into legislation. In some industries—batik, tea processing, cigarette, cocoa and chocolate factories, for example—about 60 per cent of the workers are women, but they're piece-workers without guaranteed rights.

'What we want more, though, is Article Sixteen of the United Nations' Declaration of Human Rights, which gives social equality, especially in marriage and divorce. When I tell you that the divorce rate in Java is as high as 50 per cent and that it is extremely difficult for a wife to get a divorce unless it's written into her marriage contract, you can see what a high time the men are having!'

'Does your *adat* act as a counter in marriage and divorce to the male-favouring Islamic law?'

'Yes, but mainly indirectly through the inheritance laws. *Adat* does not stop child marriages and it permits polygamy. The penal code, which is a combination of both customary and Islamic laws, is biased against women. For example, adultery committed by a husband with an unmarried woman is only punishable if his marriage law is based on monogamy, as it is if he's a Christian. So a Muslim husband committing adultery with an unmarried woman cannot be punished, while all married women committing adultery are liable to punishment, as are their accomplices. We would like an age limit for marriage—fifteen for women, eighteen for men—and the consent of both parties as a stipulation.

'We also want to do away with polygamy. Why should one man equal four women? Islamic law requires that all wives be treated equally! As if this were possible emotionally—and in any case, there is no punishment for non-fulfilment!'

'Do you think you have a chance of getting through such a law?'

'Why don't you add, "while Sukarno is President?" That's what most visitors say. Actually, the President does set a bad example as far as we are concerned. He talks about women being the glory of God's creation, like a beautiful flower, etc., but he isn't prepared to deprive himself of his right to pluck the flower when he feels like it. When he married Hartini, some of us refused to acknowledge her socially. If second wives are made to feel ashamed, fewer girls will be willing to marry a man who already has a wife. Also, some of our people on the Family Planning Associations have something to say about *Bapak* Sukarno! But the President isn't the only one to blame. Many of his ministers are just as bad.'

'Are you against Sukarno's kind of government?'

'That's a complicated question, as they say. It seems to me that women were better represented in some of the earlier governments, like the Sjahrir and Sjarifuddin cabinets in 1946-8. Women are particularly hard hit by inflation, too, which has increased tremendously since Sukarno introduced "guided democracy". Also I think we should benefit from regular elections. The right of franchise is given to all Indonesian citizens, male or female, over the age of eighteen, and there are more women than men. Undoubtedly most women would vote the way their men voted, as my friends tell me they do in Australia, but we—I mean the Congress—would have a chance to act as a pressure group for reform. As it is we are represented in the various bodies headed by Sukarno but we don't get far with matters that the men are united about—even if they won't openly admit it. They shake their heads and say, "Yes, yes, but the economic situation is difficult, as you know, and we are very busy at the moment".'

'Where do you think the best chances of improvement for Indonesian women lie?'

'Compulsory education is one field. Even before World War II we had some women medical doctors and lawyers. Now we have women engineers and technicians and women economists. Women with an independent livelihood and standing in the community can force through changes. Kartini, who is considered the pioneer for the emancipation of women in Indonesia, began in the field of education, but in her days only upper class girls could go to school. Until compulsory education is a fact—for probably a generation—we can't expect too much, I suppose; I'm told that Australia is still a man's country although the women have had their educational rights for years. But that doesn't stop us from trying.'

CHAPTER TEN

The World

Djakarta is one of the liveliest diplomatic centres in Asia. Compared with its capital city neighbours, Canberra and Kuala Lumpur, its diplomatic colony is noticeably large, like that of another non-aligned nation, India. At the end of June 1963, fifty-five countries had representatives in Djakarta, forty-three of them at embassy level. The political range is wide. Communist China is there, which has meant exclusion of Taiwan, but both North and South Vietnam maintain consulates, as does North Korea. East Germany has a consulate and West Germany an embassy. All the Soviet bloc countries except Albania are represented. Moreover, some of the missions are large. The United States' embassy, housed on Djalan Merdeka Selatan in a modern building which is one of the sights of Djakarta, lists fifty-three officials, excluding clerical and other administrative staff. The embassy of the USSR, situated in Djalan Imam Bondjol, which joins Djalan Diponegoro, the most fashionable thoroughfare in Djakarta, lists thirty-five. The United Kingdom, whose new embassy opposite the Hotel Indonesia overlooking Friendship Square was destroyed by rioting in September 1963, lists twenty, Australia (in the process of building a new embassy near the British) eighteen, Japan fifteen, China fifteen, West Germany and India nine.

The world's press is also represented, both in the major news agencies, like Australian Associated Press-Reuter, Associated Press (of America), United Press International, Agence France Presse, Tass, Tanjug and Hsin Hua, and by resident and visiting correspondents. Business and trading missions arrive on top of each other from both sides of the iron and bamboo curtains and the list of visiting heads of state and government includes the leading political figures of the mid-twentieth century world. After the restricted anti-communist atmosphere of other South-east Asian capitals like Kuala Lumpur, Manila, Bangkok or Saigon, Djakarta has an air of being in touch with the world at large.

In keeping with its status as a key international city, Djakarta, whose name means 'glorious fortress', is being given a face-lift. President Sukarno, an architect himself, has got to work on the flat, sprawling, hot and terribly overcrowded city (the population has increased from one to three million since the Dutch left in 1950). He flies about in a helicopter, observing progress. Djakarta is described in the tourist books as the biggest metropolis in South-east Asia, which may literally be true. But it has the appearance of a Dutch provincial town. It is one of Indonesia's least attractive cities and, until June 1962, when President Sukarno decreed that it should be rebuilt as 'an inspiration and beacon to the whole of struggling mankind and to all the emerging forces', there was speculation that Bandung might become the capital or that a Brasilia would be fashioned in the centre of Java, perhaps within sight of Borobudur. Djakarta is such a Dutch-looking city, with its tiled-roof villas and canals, and its value is not associated with the great exploits of Indonesian nationalism or with the ancient past. Its fame, as Batavia, was connected not so much with Indonesian history as with Dutch trading prowess. However, in 1928, the Indonesian youth made their famous declaration in Batavia calling for one nation, one flag, one language, and it was in Djakarta in 1945 that independence was proclaimed. In any case, it is conveniently situated for international traffic between Asia and Australia, the Indian and Pacific Oceans, and it has become, over the past decade, the nation's business centre, as well as the centre of government and politics. The city was chosen as capital by the great force of inertia.

The choice having been made, Djakarta is to be transformed during the next ten years. The fourteen-storey Hotel Indonesia has broken the skyline, and other hotels and multi-storied buildings are in progress. A six-lane highway from Merdeka Square to the outer suburb of Kebajoran runs past the Hotel Indonesia (built with Japanese reparations) and the impressive stadia built (with Russian money and an Indonesian army work force) for the Asian Games in August 1962. It has a clover-leaf overpass, which, second only to the hotel lit up at night, is one of the wonders of modern Djakarta. Another highway, providing a by-pass through the port of Tanjung Priok, has been completed. The President is planning a monument which will last a thousand years, a mosque which will be the biggest in the world, a department store modelled on one in Tokyo, a night-club, a supermarket and other projects designed to make Djakarta into the Cairo, Rome, Paris, Brasilia, etc., of Indonesia. Statues are springing up, designed in the heavy, exultant fashion of socialist realism. Djakarta is to be lifted into the cluster of symbols of the new Indonesia, alongside Manipol-Usdek, the biggest army in South-east Asia, the fifth nation by population in the world, 'socialism à la Indonésie' and the concepts of 'konfrontasi' and revolutionary diplomacy.

The old kampongs, once lost in the ever-growing greenery, are being replaced by concrete and glass shops and office buildings, and motorized pedicabs, keeping strictly to the left to avoid the constant stream of cars, are replacing the man-pedalled three-wheeled betjaks. But like the jungle, the ragged millions of crowded Java are hard to keep at bay. Already they blur the lines of these grand structures, setting up their portable stalls along highways, next to a concrete pillar, against a wall.

*   *   *

Indonesian foreign policies have been dominated by two considerations. One is the requirement that Indonesia should be independent of the cold war power blocs—that she should remain 'non-aligned' or 'neutral'. The second is fear for the territorial safety of the young Indonesian nation. Lately, a third element has been noticed—the claim that Indonesia should be recognized as the first power in South-east Asia and the leader, internationally, of what are called the new emerging forces.

The first full years of independence, under the Hatta (December 1949-September 1950) and Natsir (September 1950-April 1951) governments began Indonesia's 'active and independent' foreign policy with a decidedly pro-western slant. Foreign policy was not a demanding priority; the nation was beset with domestic problems. Diplomatic relations were established with all major western and non-committed countries, but no representatives were sent to communist countries except China. Peking sent an ambassador to Djakarta in August 1950; as he had worked as a communist organizer in Sumatra before being expelled by the Dutch, and had been publicly critical of the 'bourgeois' leaders Sukarno and Hatta, he was regarded with suspicion in Djakarta. Only an Indonesian chargé d'affaires was exchanged. Indonesia sought and received western economic aid, mainly from the Netherlands and the United States. It accepted western sponsorship for membership of the United Nations and its bodies. It abstained on the vote in the U.N. to brand communist China as the aggressor in Korea and Natsir blocked a move in the Indonesian Parliament to force recognition of Ho Chi Minh's government in North Vietnam.

In general, these were days of cautious and moderate pro-western policies, in which efforts were made to establish friendly relations with the Dutch, no fuss was made over West Irian and nothing spectacular was attempted. In fact, the period of these two cabinets was so unassuming that the parties in power came under strong attack, especially from the PNI, for failing to promote Indonesia's national interests. In Asia, Indonesia's closest relations were with India. President Sukarno and Prime Minister Nehru exchanged state visits in 1950.

The Sukiman government (April 1951-April 1952) was a Masjumi-PNI coalition. It continued the earlier pro-western policies, under the colourful direction of Foreign Minister Subardjo, who had been one of the leaders in Tan Malaka's attempted coup of 1946, and in fact fell on the issue of an 'active and independent' policy.

Two skirmishes preceded the collapse. The Sukiman government in July reacted against the assertive influence of Peking's ambassador in Djakarta by refusing sixteen Chinese embassy officials permission to land in Indonesia. On the whole the government came out of the exchanges with Peking quite well from the point of view of popular support in Indonesia, where nationalist sentiment did not usually include friendship with Chinese. At the same time, however, the government was embroiled in a more serious dispute over the signing of the Japanese Peace Treaty in San Francisco. Its decision to attend the conference, although without committing itself in advance to signing the treaty, became for its left-wing critics in Parliament and the press additional proof that Indonesia was settling down into a cosy corner in the western bloc. Critics pointed out that India had refused to attend and that there was a close connection between the treaty and a proposed American military agreement with Japan. Finally, after a series of dramatic delays, the Indonesian government signed, but PNI pressure from within the cabinet was so strong that the treaty was never sent to the parliament and ratified. (A separate bi-lateral treaty on reparations was negotiated later in 1951 between Japan and Indonesia but it was not finally ratified by Parliament until 1958.) The government offset its pro-American leanings in foreign affairs by strenuous solidarity with the anti-colonialist movements in Indo-China, Malaya and North Africa, and it firmly supported mainland China and spurned Taiwan for membership of the United Nations (while observing the U.N.'s ban on strategic material to communist China at some cost to its exports).

But it ran finally into trouble on a matter that seemed to be cut and dried—the acceptance of economic (including military) aid from America on the condition that Indonesia would make a 'full contribution' to the 'defensive strength of the free world'. Under the

United States' Mutual Security Act of 1951, certain assurances, including the one mentioned, were required and the Sukiman cabinet, after deliberation—mainly, however, by Subardjo, as there appears to have been no formal cabinet discussion—accepted them. The deal was arranged in secrecy, Subardjo committing Indonesia in a note to the American ambassador (Mr Merle Cochran) in January 1952. A month later the secret came out (it was never clear how it was expected to be kept) and in the uproar that followed, both the Masjumi and PNI withdrew their support of the government, which collapsed within three weeks. There was a certain resentment of 'secret diplomacy', which savoured of the tactics of colonialists, but the swift and strong reaction was primarily the obvious one—that Indonesia had strayed too far from the path of non-alignment. The retribution visited on the Sukiman government was not forgotten in the remaining years of cabinet responsibility and parliamentary government.

The Wilopo government (April 1952-June 1953), a mixed PNI-Masjumi-PSI affair, quickly asserted that it would receive only economic and technical, not military, assistance from the United States, and a new agreement was negotiated. The cabinet was absorbed in domestic crises, especially legislation for elections and deteriorating relations with the army which culminated in the 'October 17th affair'. Relations with the Netherlands became sharper, after the new Dutch government set itself against any discussion on the status of New Guinea. Indonesia during this period forced the removal of the Dutch military mission.

The first government of Ali Sastroamidjojo (July 1953-August 1955) was strongly PNI, with PKI support, and it followed a foreign policy of corresponding radical change in foreign affairs. Under the leadership of the ex-diplomat, Indonesia set out in this period to impress the world with the activity, as well as the independence, of its foreign policy. The first meeting of the Colombo powers—India, Pakistan, Ceylon, Burma and Indonesia—took place in April 1954, in an effort to bring the Indo-China war to a peaceful close. It was here that Ali Sastroamidjojo proposed the Bandung conference, which, held the following year, brought Indonesia into the forefront of world politics and into the leadership of the Afro-Asian bloc of nations. It was at the Bandung conference that Indonesia and communist China signed the Dual Nationality Agreement, which contained a major concession to Indonesia in China's waiver of the traditional claim that racial Chinese are national Chinese, wherever they are. Ali made a conscious effort to improve relations with China (a trade agreement was concluded in December 1953 and the prime ministers exchanged visits) and with the USSR (an Indonesian embassy was opened in Moscow in 1954). Unsuccessfully, he proposed a non-aggression pact of China, India and Indonesia as a counter to the South-east Asia Treaty Organization, formed in 1954. During this time, Indonesia also began its struggle for West Irian at the United Nations. It failed to gain the required two-thirds of the General Assembly vote at the 1954 session, but the issue was introduced into international diplomacy.

The Burhanuddin Harahap government (August 1955-March 1956) was largely a caretaker government for the general elections, the first and last to be held in Indonesia. It corrected to some extent the strongly nationalist image created by Ali's strenuous foreign policy. It developed cordial contacts with western countries, including Australia, whose minister for external affairs (then Mr Casey) visited Indonesia, and particularly it established with the Netherlands a fresh basis for talks on West Irian, which were held and failed. Its period was short and its authority refuted by the election results.

The second Ali Sastroamidjojo government (March 1956-April 1957) was able to pick up the threads of militancy without dropping a stitch. Its office marked the beginning of a swing away from factional political bargaining on the traditional assumptions of constitutional democracy that whoever held power in the parliament held power in the land, to growing mob activity, talks of coups and regional revolt and the beginning of President Sukarno's rise to power. Indonesia was a persistent critic of the British-French Suez action but was reserved in its comments on the Soviet suppression of the revolt in Hungary. It negotiated its first loan from the USSR. The Round Table Conference agreement with the Dutch in 1949 was revoked in stronger terms than previous governments had contemplated, and a large part of the debt Indonesia had accepted from the Netherlands was repudiated. Trade agreements with Czechoslovakia, Romania and North Vietnam were signed.

In May-July the President went to western Europe and in August-October to the Soviet Union and communist China. On his return, he announced he had long been unhappy about the way political parties were being used in Indonesia and now he had seen in the USSR and China how development was rapidly taking place, he had decided to speak out. 'I do not want to become a dictator . . . I am really a democrat. . . . But my democracy is not liberal democracy. . . . What I would like to see in this Indonesia of ours is guided democracy—democracy with leadership, but still democracy.' In

December, Dr Hatta resigned. On 21 February Sukarno announced his 'conception' in detail, calling for a *gotong royong* cabinet, including the PKI, and a national council of functional groups, headed by himself. Ali Sastroamidjojo returned his mandate to the President, who formed what he described as 'an emergency extra-parliamentary cabinet of experts' to introduce guided democracy. This was the so-called *kabinet kerdja* (working cabinet), with non-party Dr Djuanda, a veteran cabinet member, as prime minister, and Dr Subandrio, a diplomat, former ambassador in London and Moscow and secretary-general of the ministry of foreign affairs, as foreign minister. The cabinet, which comprised a balance of parties not unlike the last Ali cabinet, except for the inclusion of two ministers regarded as PKI sympathizers, lasted from April 1957 to July 1959. During its period regional elections were held in Java, with the PKI emerging as the island's strongest party.

The first priority in foreign affairs in 1957 was West Irian, and Dr Subandrio worked hard to build enough votes at the United Nations while President Sukarno threatened that if Indonesia were again defeated 'we will use a new way in our struggle which will surprise the nations of the world'. The two-thirds majority was not obtained, and tension rose quickly in Indonesia (the day after the ballot on 29 November an attempt was made to assassinate the President at a school bazaar). Strikes and demonstrations against the Dutch took place, with the government taking over all Dutch enterprises, which were formally nationalized in 1959.

In January 1958, as the rebellious mood of army commanders in Sumatra and Sulawesi grew, the President left for a forty-day tour abroad, visiting India, Yugoslavia, Syria, Pakistan, Ceylon, Burma, Thailand and Japan. After refusal by the United States to sell arms to Indonesia, purchases from Poland, Czechoslovakia and Yugoslavia were announced in April. Government statements criticizing the United States and nationalist China, in particular, for assisting the rebel government in Bukittingi (Sumatra) reached a pitch until May, when Washington formally denounced the rebels and released small arms and rice supplies to Djakarta. Indonesia began to take the initiative in a wide-ranging campaign for treaties of various kinds—scientific, educational and cultural co-operation with Czechoslovakia, trade with Bulgaria, an agreement with India on naval co-operation, a treaty of friendship with Malaya, and a cultural treaty with the Philippines. Tito and Ho Chi Minh paid state visits. Indonesia resisted, however, Malaya's prodding to join Seafet, later called ASA (Association of South-east Asia), which brought Malaya, Thai-

land and the Philippines into a loose association. In February 1959
Subandrio came to Australia seeking a softening of the Australian
attitude toward West Irian. The 'National Front for the Liberation
of West Irian' was formed. In April, before leaving for Turkey,
Europe, Latin America, Japan and North Vietnam, President Sukarno recommended to the constituent assembly (elected in 1955)
that it should adopt the 1945 constitution. After two months' debate,
the assembly failed to approve the President's suggestion by the
required two-thirds majority. In July, President Sukarno dissolved
the assembly and proclaimed the 1945 constitution by decree.

Djuanda returned his mandate and a second 'working cabinet' was
formed, with the President as prime minister and Djuanda as first
minister. In October, the annual Colombo Plan ministerial conference was held in Jogjakarta. In his address, President Sukarno warned
the west against assuming that Indonesia could be diverted from her
historic course by gifts.

During 1959 relations with Peking became strained as a result of
the Indonesian government's decision to ban 'foreign retailers' (meaning Chinese who had not taken up Indonesian citizenship) from
operating in rural areas. Subandrio visited Peking in October and
was unceremoniously treated. The communique issued with the
Chinese foreign minister (Marshal Chen Yi) referred to 'Chinese
nationals' in Indonesia. Indonesia expelled about 100,000 Chinese
before an agreement 'implementing' the agreement signed with Peking in 1955 on dual nationality was introduced, largely to Indonesia's advantage.

In December, Mr Menzies visited Indonesia, being assured by
President Sukarno that force would not be used to regain West Irian.
The Australian prime minister preceded by two months the Soviet
premier, Mr Khrushchev, who announced at the end of his visit a
U.S.$250 million credit for Indonesia. In April 1960 President
Sukarno left for a two months' mission abroad on which nine joint
communiques were issued and three cultural agreements, one trade
agreement and one friendship treaty were signed. In his 17 August
speech, the President broke off diplomatic relations with the Dutch
and banned the Masjumi and PSI.

In September, Indonesia sent troops to join the United Nations'
forces in the Congo (troops had also been sent for U.N. purposes to
the Middle East in 1957). Sukarno spoke at the opening of the U.N.
General Assembly. He suggested that Indonesia's *Pantja Sila* be
included in the charter of the United Nations and urged that membership of the Security Council and other bodies should be revised

to take account of 'international realities'. For the first time he spoke of the 'new emerging forces'. In December, Nasution visited Moscow for the first purchase of an undisclosed but estimated U.S.$1,000 million worth of arms.

The years 1961 and 1962 saw Indonesian policy preoccupied, indeed obsessed, with West Irian. As the military campaign against the rebels in Sumatra and Sulawesi ended, the nation's leadership turned toward the other major item of unfinished business. The Dutch began building up their defences in West Irian and in April 1961 opened in Hollandia the Papuan Council, which claimed the intention of preparing the West Irianese for self-government. Sukarno left in April for a two and a half months' tour abroad, during which he received from President Kennedy assurances that the United States was interested in a 'fresh approach' to the West Irian issue. Nasution came to Australia at the same time, also primarily to discuss West Irian, but received no such assurances in Canberra. In June, two Indonesian destroyers made a trip to the Soviet port of Vladivostock and in July the first aircraft from the USSR began to arrive in Djakarta. At the same time, there was a sharpening of general anti-foreign attitudes in Indonesia. In March, President Sukarno banned the Rotary Club, Divine Life Society, Masonic Lodge, Moral Rearmament and Mystical Order of the Rosy Cross (Rosicrucians). The Boy Scouts were dissociated from the international movement and placed under national leadership.

Indonesia was a leading participant in the conference of non-aligned countries at Belgrade in September. President Sukarno's relations with Mr Nehru were reported to be cool. In October, while Admiral Gorsjkov of the Soviet Union closed his ten-day visit with the presentation of ten gunboats to the Indonesian government, Dr Subandrio and Mohammed Yamin led the Indonesian team at the United Nations' debate on West Irian. Since 1957, after four unsuccessful tries, the Indonesians had not taken the West Irian issue to the U.N. The initiative this time was taken by the Netherlands, on a motion to transfer West Irian to an international body under U.N. authority. A variety of resolutions was introduced in the General Assembly debate in November, without reaching a conclusion. On 19 December President Sukarno announced the People's Triple Command for the liberation of West Irian (the Trikora). An Indonesian motor torpedo boat was sunk off the Aru Islands, to the south of West Irian, and the deputy navy chief of staff (Commodore Jos Sudarso) was drowned. Indonesian paratroops began dropping into West Irian.

Secret talks between the Netherlands and Indonesia proceeded in Washington along lines suggested by an American diplomat, Mr Ellsworth Bunker, and were eventually successful in reaching agreement on 15 August 1962. President Sukarno entitled his independence speech of 17 August 'A Year of Triumph'. The armed forces put on a model display in Djakarta to show that they were prepared for an assault on West Irian if diplomacy had not been successful. Public reception was not entirely commendatory, although the President's speech, before the critics could begin, placed the treaty in the category of Indonesian achievements. Later, while the response abroad tended to take the view that Indonesia had won its long battle, Indonesian press and political parties began to question the treaty's provision assuring self-determination—'an act of choice'—for the Papuans by 1969.

Before Indonesia had taken over the administration of West Irian, in May 1963, the country was entangled in another issue which promised to become more demanding than 'confrontation' of the Dutch over West Irian had been. In May 1961, the prime minister of Malaya (Tunku Abdul Rahman) broached an idea for a 'closer association' of Malaya with Singapore, the British protectorate of Brunei, and the British colonies of Sarawak and Sabah (North Borneo). In August, Lord Selkirk, British commissioner-general for South-east Asia, visited Djakarta and informed the Indonesians of plans for a federation of the five units, now known as Malaysia. On 20 November 1961, Dr Subandrio, in an address to the United Nations General Assembly on the West Irian issue, made the following observation to support his argument that Indonesia had no territorial ambitions beyond the area once covered by the Netherlands East Indies.

We are not only disclaiming the territories outside the former Netherlands East Indies, though they are of the same island, but —more than that—when Malaya told us of her intention to merge with the three British Crown Colonies of Sarawak, Brunei [sic] and British North Borneo as one Federation, we told them that we have no objections and that we wish them success with this merger so that everyone may live in peace and freedom.

This neutral, even permissive attitude by the Indonesian government toward the proposed Federation of Malaysia continued vaguely in 1962, although the PKI, in line with the international communist view that Malaysia was a British neo-colonialist plot, stated its opposition clearly at a conference on 30-1 December 1961. As late as

September, Subandrio, in written answers to a series of questions from the *Sydney Morning Herald,* said Malaysia was 'up to the people of those countries themselves'.

During the year, however, the leader of the Brunei Party Rakyat, A. M. Azahari, who opposed Malaysia, made several secret visits to Djakarta and urged government leaders, including General Nasution, to support him. A base was set up in Malinau, in Indonesian Kalimantan, to train the nucleus of a guerilla army—the Tentara Nasional Kalimantan Utara (North Borneo National Army—TNKU). Azahari also made contact with anti-Malaysia groups in Singapore and Malaya and made several trips to the Philippines, which had publicly stated its claim to sovereignty over part of North Borneo in June 1962. When the armed rebellion took place in Brunei on 8 December, it was from Manila that Azahari proclaimed himself 'Prime Minister of Kalimantan Utara'. It had never been clear what the rebellion hoped to accomplish politically. Azahari and his party had long sustained the dream of restoring Brunei's ancient sultanate over Sarawak and Sabah. He had also spoken of a 'Greater Malaysia' including Indonesia and the Philippines. But it was clear that the immediate purpose of the rebellion was to forestall the plan for Malaysia. Within five days, British troops flown from Singapore had quashed the revolt in the major towns.

Indonesian support for the Azahari rebellion was widespread—not only from the PKI and the '1945 Generation', but from the PNI and eventually Sukarno and Nasution. On 17 December Subandrio replied to what he described as 'offensive' statements from Kuala Lumpur linking Indonesia with the rebellion; he cited British army reports from Brunei that no evidence of Indonesian military intervention had been found. Diplomatic notes and protests were exchanged. On 8 January 1963, Sukarno emphatically rejected the Malaysia concept, and on 21 January Subandrio announced that Indonesia's patience was not inexhaustible and declared a policy of 'confrontation' toward Malaysia. On 1 February the army chief of staff, General Jani, speaking at Pontianak in Kalimantan, expressed moral support for the rebels and said the army only awaited 'the order to move'. The campaign mounted in Djakarta throughout February and March, with prominence being given to the Philippines' claim on North Borneo. In February, Azahari came to Djakarta, where he set up a government-in-exile. Statements by the Indonesian foreign office, including one that the Tunku was 'round the bend', became increasingly violent. The Tunku was also accused of having wanted to take Sumatra during the 1958-61 rebellion, of having gone golfing and fishing instead of meeting Dr Djuanda when the late first minister had visited Malaya, of having said Indonesia would join the Association of South-east Asia (ASA) before he had asked Indonesia—and of generally having caused Malaya to become an 'object of ridicule in South-east Asia'.

At a meeting of the Economic Commission for Asia and the Far East (Ecafe) at Manila in March, Australia took the initiative, in a series of private discussions between the minister for external affairs, Sir Garfield Barwick, and Dr Subandrio, to support a Philippine proposal for talks, provided it was clearly understood that Malaysia was not to be 'frustrated'. This was widely interpreted as an opportunity for Subandrio and Sukarno to be persuaded that Malaysia could be accepted. Shortly afterward—allowing for the visits of Marshal Malinovsky later in March and Liu Shao Chi in April—there was a lull in the exchange of propaganda, and at the end of May, Tunku Abdul Rahman and Sukarno surprisingly met in Tokyo. They reaffirmed their faith in the 1959 Malaya-Indonesia friendship treaty and captured the headlines with smiles and handshakes. On 7 June the three foreign ministers met in Manila and agreed to 'welcome' Malaysia provided the support of the Borneo territories was ascertained by 'an independent and impartial authority, the Secretary-General of the United Nations or his representative'. The three ministers concluded their conference with a resounding declaration of friendship and unity, formally encased in a project for a consultative council and eventual loose confederation of the three nations called Maphilindo. A summit meeting was prepared for 30 July. On 10 July, however, President Sukarno, in a speech on the occasion of the fortieth anniversary of the Indonesian Catholic party, reverted to 'confrontation', claiming that the Malaysia agreement signed the day before in London (after much financial argument between Singapore and Malaya and the eventual exclusion of Brunei) broke the undertakings given in Tokyo and Manila for ascertaining the wishes of the people. After weeks of apparent hesitation and some powerful rally oratory by Sukarno ('we'll crunch up Malaysia and spit out the pieces'), the President attended the three-nation summit meetings in Manila, which ratified the foreign ministers' agreement and proposed a detailed form for U.N. ascertainment.

Indonesian press and public response to the results of the meeting was cautiously favourable, encouraged by British criticism of the Tunku for having conceded too much. Djakarta comment stressed that Indonesia's position in South-east Asia had been recognized by the consultations on Malaysia. In addition, the chairman of the PNI

(Ali Sastroamidjojo) said he thought that Maphilindo was not contrary to Indonesia's 'free and active' foreign policy and that the
summit meeting was closer to the 'Indonesian conception' than had
been the foreign ministers' meeting. The first chairman of Nahdatul
Ulama (K. H. M. Dahlan) said the results could be accepted by the
Indonesian people. The deputy chairman of the PKI (M. H. Luk-
man) was reserved, as were the left-wing paper *Bintang Timur*
(*Morning Star*) and the Communist Party organ *Harian Rakyat*
(*People's Daily*), which urged that confrontation should be kept up.
The independent, nationalist newspapers were generally more optimistic. *Berita Indonesia* (*Indonesian News*) concluded that 'the
Tunku was finally forced to recognize the greatness and superiority of
President Sukarno as a Supreme Diplomat'. *Merdeka* (*Freedom*)
claimed that if the 'negative' aspects of the Manila agreements were
emphasized, 'Bung Karno's leadership in Afro-Asia will be reduced
to a role only in South-east Asia', and Seato and ASA would enter Maphilindo by 'the back door'. On the other hand, if the 'positive'
approach were taken—what the newspaper called the revolutionary
dialectical view—Maphilindo could become a supplement to the
struggle of the new emerging forces against imperialism, etc.

But it was evident that, whatever was said in public, the mechanics of confrontation were continuing. Joint navy and air force
manoeuvres were held in the South China Sea, involving some fifty
ships and squadrons of MIG-21's and TU-16's. General Nasution
visited Kalimantan and made several tough speeches, urging the
frustration of Malaysia 'by force if necessary'. Djakarta diplomatic
circles were convinced that Indonesia would not call off its opposition. A foreign ministry official, within days of the return of the
party from Manila, advised several correspondents, including the
author, that a showdown with Britain was planned. 'Malaysia is a
test of strength between Britain and Indonesia', he said. 'Britain has
valuable investments in Indonesia—that is our weapon.'

The arguments in the following weeks over the number of
observers to accompany the United Nations' team and the time given
to the team to complete its task seemed peripheral to the fact of
confrontation, which continued, especially in raiding on the Sarawak
border by guerilla bands trained in Indonesia. When the secretary-
general of the U.N. (U Thant) announced the team's finding, which
was a strong endorsement of the wish of the majority of the people
for Malaysia, Indonesia had an opportunity to accept Malaysia
without loss of face, as the conditions of her public concern for the
wishes of the people of the non-independent territories had been

met. But she chose otherwise. When Malaysia was proclaimed on 16 September, Indonesia and the Philippines refused to recognize it and the new government of Malaysia broke off diplomatic contact, bringing political relations of the South-east Asian neighbours to the lowest point since they achieved independence.

* * *

As diplomacy was practised in the early days of the Indonesian Republic, its object was to avoid a commitment to either of the two major power blocs, led by Washington and Moscow. An over-commitment created the danger—which became real in the case of the Sukiman cabinet—of rejection by a parliament of sensitive nationalists. A minor parallel might be found in Australian government efforts to avoid the impression that either of the country's allies, the United Kingdom or the United States, is favoured. Since 1957, when President Sukarno introduced his guided democracy, and particularly since the reorganization of government in 1959, Indonesian 'non-alignment' has become more dynamic. It has become less a matter of finding a mean between the positions of the great power competitors and more a matter of deciding what are Indonesia's particular interests. This is a normal maturing process, but it has been accompanied in the case of Indonesia by an ideological development which has created around the idea of the national interest conceptions of moral grandeur. The policy has been implemented, also, with dash and cunning. Indonesia's military strength has been transformed in the process and xenophobia has increased. Add to this the fact that internally Indonesia is uncertainly balanced, with an élite cluster of leaders around the President while the country at large struggles with basic problems that have scarcely been touched in the years of independence, and it is true to say that Indonesia represents, to its neighbours, friends, and enemies, an unpredictable hazard.

Dealings between countries are made easier by knowledge of two things—the definition of each other's 'vital interests', which is the area only to be disturbed in the expectation of serious trouble, and the certainty that the government is 'responsible', in the sense that it can be relied on to stand by whatever commitment its representatives make. In both these respects Indonesia has created doubts in the international community. One reason is the system of government, which relies on President Sukarno's ability to satisfy the power groups supporting him. These groups pay their respects to the concepts and symbols which the President has created to identify the Indonesian nation, but some of them are opposed on fundamental questions and on the distribution of power within the state. To satisfy these competitive courtiers, the President has devised even more abstract theories with little practical application except aggrandizement abroad. Another reason, which applies especially to foreign affairs, is that Indonesia's interests, so vehemently pursued, are so broadly and emotionally defined that their limits cannot be perceived. The long crisis over Malaysia revealed all these factors.

While President Sukarno is the great brewer of Indonesia's revolutionary spirit, Dr Subandrio has become one of its leading dispensers. Born at Kepandjen in east Java in 1914, Subandrio graduated in 1942 from the medical college in Djakarta and became assistant in the operating theatre at the central hospital. He practised privately as a surgeon in Semarang, central Java, during the Japanese occupation, keeping in touch with the nationalist underground. In 1946 he became secretary-general of the ministry of information. In 1949, he was appointed as the Republic's first ambassador to the Court of St James. In 1954 he was accredited to Moscow as ambassador and in 1956 was recalled to Djakarta to become secretary-general of the ministry of foreign affairs. Appointed to Sukarno's first cabinet in 1957 as foreign minister, he has risen steadily and, in the reorganization following Dr Djuanda's death in November 1963, he was promoted, with Dr Johannes Leimena and Chairul Saleh, to a triumvirate of chief ministers (now called vice-ministers) forming in effect a four-man presidium with President Sukarno, who remains prime minister. Subandrio belongs to no political party, but his attitudes suggest a sympathy with the PNI. He is a volatile and voluble man, with a quick mind and abundant energy. Diplomats respect his skill and experience, which has proved itself in several encounters, especially the issues of war reparations with Japan, dual nationality with communist China, and West Irian with the Netherlands. But because he has no party or group behind him, as Nasution has, nor clique support, like Chairul Saleh, Subandrio is more dependent on achievement and the President's goodwill.

He has grown more revolutionary with the President. On 20 July 1959, Dr Subandrio briefed some of his officers on the significance of the return to the 1945 constitution. He foreshadowed restrictions on (or what he called 'nuances of') Indonesia's 'active and independent' policy, in the following points: 1. Indonesia was isolated, being surrounded by nations which either were members of the South East Asia Treaty Organization (Seato) or of the British Commonwealth of Nations. If Indonesia were 'able to grow', these surrounding nations might come to have an attitude like hers—

namely 'independent and active', or non-aligned. Therefore it was in the interest of the nations in Seato and the Commonwealth Strategic Reserve that Indonesia should remain weak; 2. in the 'struggle against imperialism', Indonesia could not be independent. 'Whether we like it or not', the Minister said, 'we must exert pressure upon or urge or be hostile to imperialist states. . . . We must also be friendly with states that are anti-imperialist.'; 3. Indonesia was not free in its relations with Asian and African states. 'We cannot evaluate one of those states as our enemy if its system is different and resembles that of our enemy. . . . Willingly or unwillingly, we must seek bonds of friendship with these states . . . '; 4. Indonesia must make a 'compromise' on a 'good neighbour policy . . . because, although consistent with our independent policy a state that is a member of Seato should be regarded as an opponent, in the context of our good neighbour policy we must take into account that we wish to offer our friendship to our neighbouring countries for the sake of the safety of our own nation. . . . '

On 8 February 1962, Dr Subandrio gave another lecture to foreign ministry personnel—in this case undergoing special military training for the West Irian campaign. On this occasion he distinguished between 'conventional' diplomacy—'quid pro quo' diplomacy, which sought agreements of advantage to both parties—and 'revolutionary' diplomacy, in which a state's diplomacy was an instrument of revolution. Indonesia practised both kinds, he said, but without an understanding of the meaning of the Indonesian revolution ('without an understanding of the direct connection existing between the national interests and the principles of the National Revolution') Indonesia's diplomats 'will be drowned in the mere formalities of conventional diplomacy'. The Minister then added, probably ominously for some of his audience, that if he had to choose between a 'candidate diplomat' who was only technically skilled and one who understood only revolutionary principles, he would choose the latter, since 'technical knowledge can be learned in six weeks'. Career diplomacy was 'beside the point' to Indonesians at this stage of history.

In April 1962, Subandrio addressed a congress of the Union of Indonesian Police, held in Bali, on the theme of counter-revolution and subversion. He spoke of Indonesia's difficulties in accepting international law.

> For example, according to international law, colonialism is a legal condition, and, for instance, if the question of West Irian were to be brought before the International Court of Justice, Dutch sovereignty over West Irian would be justified. Similarly also with

other agreements which, for instance, regulate the investment of foreign capital, regulate the economic relations between two sovereign states; no matter how unjust they may be considered, they will be recognized as legal by international law if an agreement in a past age can be proved. To alter this situation we need to base our measures upon the law of Revolution, both in the international and the national field.

Confrontation (*konfrontasi*) is the instrument of this revolutionary diplomacy. Its range of manual techniques includes the hot-and-cold press (an alternation of friendly enticements with harsh and inexplicable punishment, described by a member of the Singapore government as the 'Pavlov technique') and a cynical and brutal use of popular emotion, shown in mobbing embassies and intimidation of diplomatic personnel. Confrontation proved effective against the Netherlands over West Irian, and some of the manual techniques have been used in Djakarta against the Americans, Japanese, Indians, British and Malaysians.

In the case of West Irian, confrontation worked well because the Dutch position was untenable. Indonesia had genuinely tried to reach agreement, with mild resolutions at the United Nations. Also, in the United States and Australia, the two other countries mainly concerned, for strategic reasons, to support the Dutch position, there was public sympathy for Indonesia and a general political need to make friendships among the Afro-Asian supporters of Indonesia's claim. Over Malaysia, however, Indonesia took on stronger adversaries than the faraway Dutch. The British, Malaysia itself and Australia, backed by the approval of the United Nations and the influence of the United States, provide a formidable line-up. The political reasons for this marked failure of policy—a failure in the sense that it will not achieve the destruction of Malaysia and may bring more hardship to Indonesia—are undoubtedly complex. Sukarno, having been finally convinced that economic reforms along western lines were necessary, offset hostile leftist reaction by proving his anti-imperialism abroad. Nasution is concerned to preserve the strength of his newly-armed forces and needs a sense of crisis to regain some of the army's influence under the war emergency regulations. He also distrusts political diplomacy. There has been for some time a dislike of Tunku Abdul Rahman in the Indonesian foreign ministry, where he is viewed as an upstart with international ambitions. Malaya's economic successes are not popular in Djakarta, where they are explained as a capitulation to western interests, and Abdul Rahman is haughtily characterized as the Tshombe of South-east Asia. Indonesian government leaders are also convinced that their country's riches bear a fatal fascination for other nations. They may have reasoned that, when the British had been properly humiliated, they would return, chastened and friendly, like the Dutch, eager for trade, and that, in any case, the Japanese and West Germans were waiting to take their place. The sequence of events itself may have had an effect, the tough line from Kuala Lumpur (fixing Malaysia Day as 16 September before the United Nations' survey had been made) leading to a point of no return.

But the fact remains that Indonesia, given several opportunities to accept Malaysia in a spirit of regional friendship, declined to do so. As a deliberate act of a sovereign nation, its confrontation of Malaysia must be given face value. It accords with President Sukarno's theory of inevitable conflict between the 'new emerging forces' and the 'old established forces'. It illustrates Dr Subandrio's principles of revolutionary diplomacy. It documents General Nasution's fundamentals of guerilla warfare.

It also represents a claim by Indonesia for supremacy in the region. 'We must realize that we are a nation of one hundred million, which means five times the Philippines and ten times Malaysia', said the minister for information (Mr Ruslan Abdulgani) in a speech to the National Front in Medan in August 1963 on the Malaysia crisis. 'It is our role to lead. Because of this we must be prepared to oppose every form of neo-feudalism and neo-colonialism which supports the conception of Malaysia. And we will win . . .' This bid for hegemony makes necessary a fresh assessment of assurances, often repeated, that 'Indonesia has no territorial claims whatsoever outside the borders of what used to be the Netherlands colony of the East Indies' (Subandrio, in September 1962). This kind of assurance obviously does not mean that Indonesia is renouncing the right to see that the people of Portuguese Timor, Australian New Guinea, Brunei, or people in the grip of Malaysian neo-colonialism like the inhabitants of Sarawak and Sabah, should not be given 'social justice' as defined by the Indonesian revolution, which, as President Sukarno has frequently pointed out, is part of the revolution of mankind. General Nasution expressed this viewpoint on 25 December 1963, on his return from a trip to the Soviet Union, the United States, Yugoslavia, France, Turkey, the Philippines and Thailand, during which he signed another arms agreement in Moscow. 'In the countries we visited we explained that Indonesia has no territorial claims anywhere, but will keep supporting North Borneo and other struggling nations anywhere to drive out the colonialists. We will always be prepared to train their soldiers and we will not stop our young men from joining them.' The essence of the Malaysia conflict is that Indonesia does not believe that the decolonization of the Borneo territories has been properly carried out and feels justified, to the extent of military intervention, in reversing the process. The same objections could later apply to any of the other territories mentioned.

This responsibility which Indonesian foreign policy seems to have accepted, has obviously serious ramifications. As a generalized expression of interfering goodwill in the world, it may have been harmless enough. But to convert it into a tangible foreign policy in the region of South-east Asia seems inevitably to invite real conflict.

CHAPTER ELEVEN

The Region

Australia and Indonesia are as diverse a pair of neighbours as it is possible to find. One is a large, flat continent, thinly populated with Caucasians professing Christianity and capitalism, essentially materialist, rational and scientific in outlook, instinctively part of the western world. The other is an archipelago of mountainous islands, populated with Asians professing Islam and socialism, essentially mystic and irrational, instinctively opposed to western values. The effort each made to get along with the other after Indonesia hurtled into the world in 1945 holds out some hope for the survival of reasoned self-interest in the affairs of the twentieth century.

There have been times when the cry has gone up in both countries for 'tougher' attitudes. But until recently there had seemed a broad, popular interest in friendship, supported sometimes by prudence, sometimes by charity, sometimes by incapacity to do anything else. The negative reasons may have been more influential than we would like to admit. In Australia, the post-war preoccupation with rising prosperity left little scope for serious consideration of foreign policies backed by an independent defence capability. Some Australians were interested in Indonesia, but their voices tended to be too reasonable and placatory to be heard or too strident and alarmist to be heeded. In Indonesia, Australia was not of pressing interest. Indonesia was more concerned with the larger world, especially with issues affecting the Afro-Asian nations. If pro- or anti-western positions needed to be taken up, the United States was there for the asking. Radio Australia, with its popular musical requests, and the flow of Indonesian students to Australia, were more typical of the vague friendliness and neighbourliness of the two countries than disagreement or agreement over issues of foreign affairs. Australia started out right with Indonesia by backing her in the days when her independence of the Dutch was not assured. In spite of the long struggle over West Irian, when the two countries were on opposite sides, the influence of this initiative remained.

As an exercise in constructive international relations, it brought benefits to the people of both countries. The abstractions of race, religion and colour were surprisingly melted in personal relationships of warmth and charm. Some Australian scholars benefited from the chance to rediscover Indonesia at its roots rather than from Dutch records and research. Some Australian journalists benefited from having to consider the meaning of events as well as their appearance. Some Australian diplomats benefited from being regarded as representatives of an individual country rather than an obedient minor of the Anglo-Saxon family.

The courtship tended to be unequal. Australians were more concerned about Indonesia than Indonesians were about Australia. Partly this is a matter of geography: it is more natural in the southern hemisphere to look north than to look south. But reinforcing this were political factors. Indonesia, under Sukarno's influence, regarded its large population, nearly ten times Australia's, as a status symbol rather than an embarrassment. The obvious corrective to this is Australia's productive capacity, but few Indonesian leaders were aware of it. Most of what Australia offered as an industrial nation was more interestingly available in the United States or Europe.

Australians, for their part, were confused in their attention to Indonesia. They felt themselves to be superior to Indonesians because their living standards were higher and because they were more stable, prosperous and experienced as a nation. Dr Subandrio detected this when he told the Australian cabinet during his visit in 1959, 'Your ancestors could have understood Indonesia better than you do'. At the same time, Australians felt themselves to be weaker than Indonesia, because more peaceful. The threat of a huge, underprivileged Indonesian population, evidently ready to sacrifice itself for national glories which Australians could not understand, was delicately balanced in the minds of many Australians with an awareness that they were not prepared to undertake these sacrifices themselves. There was uncertainty over the right to restrict immigration on racial grounds and over the effect this would have in antagonizing Indonesia. Australians were also divided over Indonesia's historic role. For some, Indonesia represented the 'Asiatic hordes'; to others it provided a northern tier of protection against the 'Asiatic hordes', in this case 700 million Chinese.

One of the curious omissions of this period was that President Sukarno, who has become one of the most travelled heads of state in history, never managed to get to Australia, a few hours' flying away. Special reasons have been given by Indonesians for this, one of them being that there is no Australian head of state to return the visit. The Queen, residing in London, is thought of primarily as the head of state of the United Kingdom (another of the few countries Sukarno has not yet found time to visit). It can probably be assumed, however, that Sukarno is not especially interested in Australia. His tastes are sensual rather than intellectual, and the Australian technological assault on its land mass has no parallel to interest him in modern Indonesia. Also, of course, Australia did not offer itself as a source of credit. It was part of the stable, prosperous quarter of the world, according to the theory of the new emerging and old established forces, but it wanted foreign capital itself.

Both countries are still feeling their way toward policies in the region they live in. Geographically, each is South-east Asian; emotionally, each is attracted to wider horizons. Indonesia took its place in the world before its position in South-east Asia had been settled. As a rich country, with a large population, having won an early victory over colonialism, it was quickly recognized as a leader of the new voices at the United Nations. Because it was non-aligned, both the U.S.A. and the USSR saw it as a potential convert. Its relations with its regional neighbours, however, were necessarily restricted. With the exception of Singapore, in the first flush of self-government, Indonesia's immediate neighbours were all pro-west and anti-communist. A little farther afield, Burma, Cambodia, Ceylon and India were non-aligned, but difficult to organize. While its neighbours were either members of Seato or ASA, Indonesia stayed away from any regional associations, joining only those organizations, like the Colombo Plan and Ecafe, which seemed large and general enough not to enforce an identity on their members. It cultivated emotional affinities with some of the left-wing African nations.

Australia's experience was similar to Indonesia's in that it looked beyond the region for its support. But its military links with Seato Asian countries, like Thailand, Pakistan and the Philippines, and its Commonwealth connections with Malaya (now Malaysia), Ceylon, India and Pakistan, brought it into intimate relations on a government-to-government basis with Indonesia's neighbours. So, although Indonesia felt itself to be a leader of the Asian-African-Latin American group—and therefore a world leader—Australia, an outsider, came into a closer relationship with some countries of the region.

With the spectre of South Africa and Pan-Africanism to haunt her, Australia was assisted in her careful and uncertain involvement with Asia by the fragmented rivalries of Asian nationalism. Her special concern with Indonesia lay in the fact that the archipelago cut across her path to the north. Yet Indonesian nationalism, the most sustained and demanding in the region, became the cause of a deeper Australian involvement than either country seems to have bargained for.

*   *   *

The group of nationalists who proclaimed Indonesian independence on 17 August 1945 quickly commanded respect in Canberra, which regarded them more favourably than did London or the Hague or, for that matter, Moscow. This Australian support is surprising in retrospect. From the outside, the Republic of Indonesia was an unknown quantity. The names of some of its leaders were known, but their pre-war record of nationalism against the Dutch had become confused with their deliberately misleading collaboration with the Japanese. For Australia, the Dutch were allies in the global fight against German Nazism and Japanese Fascism, which was still an emotional issue although the war had technically ended. In addition, Australians, like other European-centred people, were not able to appreciate at that stage the long-range advantages of Asian nationalism. Few Australians had any interest in the Indonesian struggle against the Dutch. It seemed safer for the Dutch to return, as was their 'legal right', just as the British were expected to return to their colonial possessions in Asia.

On 24 September 1945, just five weeks after the proclamation of independence and a few days before the first British troops landed in Indonesia, the Brisbane branch of the Waterside Workers' Federation took the initiative by announcing a ban on ships carrying arms to Indonesia. The decision had a startling effect, drawing attention not only to the issues involved, but to the political sophistication of the waterside workers. (It is interesting to speculate whether they may have been educated by some of the six hundred political evacuees from Boven Digul, in New Guinea, including a number of communists under Sardjono, former chairman of the PKI who took up wartime propaganda work in Brisbane.) Neither the Chifley government nor the Australian Council of Trade Unions supported the ban, but it drew attention to the cause of the Indonesian nationalists. In the prevailing sentiment of the times, which was hopeful and democratic, especially among Labor Party supporters, the union's actions made it difficult for the Labor government to oppose the nationalists on behalf of the colonialist Dutch, some of whom, coming to Australia from Indonesia during the war, had made themselves unpopular in official circles. Certainly, the ban was not lost on the Indonesians. The date—recorded as 28 September—

has an honoured place in the diary of events in the official history of the revolution.

Looked at from the viewpoint of Australian security, which was at that time still recovering from the failure of the colonialists—Britain, France and the Netherlands—to hold South-east Asia against the Japanese, there was something to be said for the Indonesians if they could prove that they had popular support and real qualities of determination. This was shown during the battle against British and Indian troops in Surabaya in November. The Indonesians lost the battle but they proved, by bravely resisting superior forces, that their independence was not just a political stunt. They did not prove positively to the Australians by this that they were prospective allies, but they showed convincingly enough that the theoretical advantages of Dutch occupancy of the archipelago—commercial and defence arrangements—could not be guaranteed. A government less inclined to be guided by ideals on foreign affairs than was the Chifley administration (with Dr H. V. Evatt as minister for external affairs) might not have been moved to support the Indonesians. Subsequent events showed, however, that Australia's role in the period of the 1945-9 conflict between Indonesians and the returning Dutch was correct.

The first Dutch 'police action' on 21 July 1947 brought a sharp reaction, removing some of the cautions in Canberra's mind during 1946, when the British were engaged in the thankless business of restoring order and trying to bring the Dutch and Indonesians together. On 30 July Australia and India each brought the matter before the Security Council and Australia was nominated by Indonesia to the three-man United Nations' Committee of Good Offices established on 25 August. (Belgium was the Netherlands' representative and the United States took the decisive third place.) For the next two years, Australian diplomats and military officers attached to the committee played an important part in the complicated negotiations leading, after the second Dutch 'police action' on 19 December 1948, which brought open Australian criticism of Netherlands' duplicity, to the transfer of sovereignty and international recognition of Indonesia in December 1949. During this time Australia was active in supporting Indonesian independence, despite European backing for the Dutch and growing United States' concern over the uncertain place of Indonesia in the approaching cold war. In January 1949, Australia took part in the New Delhi conference—otherwise entirely Asian—to discuss the Indonesian conflict. Mr J. A. C. Mackie, in his chapter on Australian-Indonesian relations in

Australia in World Affairs, 1956-1960, notes that Australia had a moderating influence on the resolution finally passed, and prevented a non-white alignment. But the decision to attend was opposed within the Labor party and attacked by Liberals.

The Labor government was replaced by Mr Menzies' Liberal and Country Party coalition in December 1949, too late to change Australian policy toward the transfer of sovereignty to the Indonesians, if that—suggested by Liberal party sympathies with the Dutch—were wanted. However, some reaction against the Evatt policies became evident. The new minister for external affairs, Mr P. (now Sir Percy) Spender, visited Djakarta in January 1950 and the Indonesian government learned, apparently with surprise, that Australia did not look kindly upon its claim to New Guinea. One field correspondent, Arnold Brackman, claims that 'baited by the nettled press' on the White Australia policy as well as on West Irian, Spender 'within two days had drained the store of good will that Australia had accumulated during the Indonesian revolution'.

As the year progressed, with an attempted armed uprising led by Captain 'Turk' Westerling, which received a lot of attention in Australia, proclamation of the unitary state on 17 August, and various extravagant statements by non-government nationalists like Mohammed Yamin, opinion in Australia began to harden against Indonesia. Some members of the Labor party, especially Mr Calwell, criticized the government for not being tough enough with the Indonesian leaders over West Irian. The government's view, which had the official support of the Labor party, was put by Mr Spender on several occasions throughout 1950. These reasons, in varying emphasis, were to dominate Australian thinking on this issue during the next decade. First was the fear that if Indonesia were given West New Guinea 'it would be but a matter of time . . . when the claim will be pushed farther so as to include the Trust Territory of Australian New Guinea and its people'. Second was the determination to keep communism, which was believed to be rising in Asia as shown by the war in Korea, from gaining a foothold among the New Guinea people. Third was the belief that New Guinea was 'an absolutely essential link in the chain of Australian defence'. Self-determination, which became a frequently used argument later, was not popular at this stage.

When Mr R. G. (now Lord) Casey became minister for external affairs in 1951, he urged that the West Irian question be kept 'in cold storage' as a means of damping down emotions. By this time, however, opinion was hardening in both Djakarta and the Hague, and when the succession of moderate Indonesian governments ended in 1953 with the first Ali Sastroamidjojo cabinet, the prospect of putting the issue on ice had become remote. Whatever flimsy basis the Indonesian claim had in the eyes of anthropologists, historians and western defence experts, its source in popular Indonesian sentiment and international politics was not neglected under Ali, who had strong nationalist and communist support in Parliament. This was the period of the abrogation of the Netherlands-Indonesian union, the first appeal to the United Nations on Irian (1954) and the Bandung conference, 1955. Australia opposed the Indonesian request at the U.N. to place the West Irian issue on the agenda. The assembly agreed to the request, but the resolution, which asked no more than that the two parties should get together, did not gain the necessary two-thirds majority. The following year, in October, Casey visited Djakarta, during the office of the caretaker Burhanuddin Harahap government, which was a temporary reversion to moderation pending the elections. Casey announced Colombo Plan aid, and a communique urged the 'greatest possible degree of co-operation' between the two countries, while maintaining their respective views on the West Irian issue.

Australia continued to oppose Indonesian efforts to bring West Irian before the United Nations. Despite the admission of new members to the U.N., especially from the so-called Afro-Asian bloc, Indonesia's vote did not show a marked improvement, due mainly to strong lobbying by Australia and the Netherlands' Nato allies, which had success in Latin America. Indonesia's political instability began to alarm Canberra. In 1956, when the second Ali Sastroamidjojo government was installed, regional dissatisfaction with the central government in Djakarta was becoming evident. Hatta's resignation reinforced Canberra's belief that a showdown was imminent.

When President Sukarno established his first emergency cabinet in April 1957, under the late Dr Djuanda, the 'return of West Irian to the jurisdiction of the Republic of Indonesia' was one of the five points of its programme. The new foreign minister, Dr Subandrio, told the twelfth U.N. General Assembly session at the end of 1957 that another adverse vote might force Indonesia to 'embark upon another course, even at the risk of aggravating conditions in Southeast Asia. . . .' On 6 November, the Dutch and Australian governments released a joint announcement on administrative co-operation for New Guinea as a whole, which made its point clearly enough. Next day, President Sukarno stated that if another attempt for a United Nations' settlement failed, Indonesia would take 'measures which would startle the world'. The U.N. appeal failed. A state of war was proclaimed in Indonesia, and Dutch enterprises were taken over. In February 1958 the rebellions in Sumatra and Celebes broke into civil war.

The 1958 rebellion and successive events had a maturing effect on thinking in Canberra and perhaps on Australian public opinion generally. At first it was widely believed that the central government would be forced to make concessions to the rebels and there was little doubt that Australian sympathy lay outside Djakarta. The government, although it may have been tempted, steadily followed a non-interventionist policy. It was probably less restrained by a desire to maintain friendly relations with the Indonesian leaders in Djakarta than by a fear that intervention (as the rebels sought from Seato) would bring a major war to Australia's shores. This fear was confirmed by communist political support for Djakarta during the rebellion and reported sale of communist arms to the central government. Australian policy, however, took no initiatives on the other side, maintaining very much a 'wait and see' attitude. The deciding factor became the speed with which the rebels were defeated. The first landing of government paratroopers took place on 7 March in the oil areas of east central Sumatra. Padang fell on 17 April and Bukittingi on 5 May. By the end of May, the Sumatran rebellion was reduced to guerilla action. By the end of July no major town remained in rebel hands. In north Sulawesi the end of the rebels' military effectiveness was in sight by June. By May, United States' policy was showing signs of a change, with the new ambassador in Djakarta, Mr Howard P. Jones, personifying a more favourable attitude to the Sukarno régime. In August, Washington announced the sale of light arms to the Indonesian armed forces. Australia did not follow America's lead immediately. Mr Casey in September was at the Hague for two days of talks with Mr Luns, which raised comment in Djakarta on the possibility of an Australian-Netherlands military alliance. However, in December, Britain reversed an earlier decision not to sell military aircraft to Indonesia, over the protest of the Netherlands and the 'regrets' of Australia.

Subandrio's visit in February 1959 was not the first visit by an Indonesian foreign minister (Subardjo having unexpectedly dropped in when returning from his controversial visit in 1951 to San Francisco to sign the Japanese peace treaty), but it was the most heartily publicized and it showed, for all the mixed public reception Subandrio received, a clear indication of official respect toward the Djakarta government. The five-day visit was capped by a joint announcement which contained an important qualification of the Australian position on West New Guinea—'that if any agreement were reached between the Netherlands and Indonesia as parties principal, arrived at by peaceful processes and in accordance with internationally accepted principles, Australia would not oppose such an agreement'. The government ran into heavy criticism from newspapers and some of its members, notably Sir Wilfrid Kent Hughes, for appearing to provide Indonesia with an incentive to put pressure on the Dutch for a settlement. Both Mr (now Sir Robert) Menzies and Casey denied a change in policy, and pointed to Subandrio's acceptance of peaceful means for the settlement of the issue. If the Dutch and Indonesians did in fact reach agreement without duress, Australia had no alternative but to accept the agreement, it was said—but the situation was claimed to be hypothetical, and it was specifically denied that Australia had any intention of urging the Netherlands to negotiate.

The sophistication of this position, which had some difficulty in being interpreted by press and Parliament, was maintained cautiously by the government throughout 1959, and was the informing element in the visit by Menzies to Djakarta in December. An effort was made in Djakarta to establish a favourable atmosphere for the Prime Minister's visit; advance references were made to 'a common enemy from the north', which sounded plausible in view of Indonesia's entanglement with Peking over its Chinese citizens, and unusual measures were taken to see that the visitor was not upset by the tropical climate. The visit produced some poignant good-neighbourly behaviour, including one newspaper's description of the guest as 'an hospitable old man', but no dramatic results. Menzies was impressed by the intelligence and authority of President Sukarno, who did not thump the table, as he did once with Casey, and he extracted from the Indonesian leader absolute assurances on the question of force over West Irian. The two men stood behind the Subandrio-Casey communique of February, but Menzies laid emphasis on self-determination for the Papuan people.

Mr Menzies was followed by Mr Khrushchev (February 1960) and a year of rising tension. The Dutch developed a crash programme for Papuan independence. The aircraft carrier *Karel Doorman*, visiting West New Guinea in June, embarrassed Canberra by requiring harbour facilities in Australia. On 17 August, Indonesia broke diplomatic relations with the Dutch. The prime minister of Malaya (Tunku Abdul Rahman) made an effort to mediate on West Irian in October, after the Dutch had reported the arrest of armed Indonesian groups there. The effort failed and the situation worsened as the Tunku was bitterly attacked by Dr Subandrio on the grounds of having exceeded his mandate. This important incident, which ushered in stronger Indonesian policies and later provided a context for Indonesian attacks on the Tunku over Malaysia, has never been clearly explained. Australia's attitude to the Tunku's mediation was not disclosed. In any case, by November the Dutch announced their decision to strengthen the defences of West New Guinea; Neptune bombers were bought from the United States for possible use there. What the Hague had meant by its willingness, according to the Malayan prime minister, to subject its West New Guinea policies 'to the scrutiny and judgment of the U.N.', was forgotten as the Indonesian cabinet took its fateful decision to request Russian military aid and Nasution left for Moscow on 28 December. January 1961 saw an intensive 'confrontation' propaganda from Djakarta and, as rebel armed forces 'returned to the fold of the Republic', a build-up of Indonesian forces in the eastern waters of the archipelago.

In December 1960, President Ayub Khan visited Djakarta, and in January, returning from Moscow, Nasution visited Delhi. Both Pakistani and Indian officials advised Indonesia that the hard core of Commonwealth resistance to Djakarta's intentions on West Irian came from Canberra. During March 1961 vague suggestions of a non-aggression pact with Australia were aired by Indonesian leaders and, in April, General Nasution paid a visit to Australia, leaving Djakarta two days after President Sukarno left—as part of two and a half months abroad—for Washington. Nasution maintained in public and in his confidential discussions with Australian government leaders the theme that Indonesia repudiated 'force' over West Irian. He sought, as Subandrio had done, Australian neutrality. The visit failed to gain a response; on 27 April Mr Menzies restated the Australian position in uncompromising terms. In June, Nasution joined the President in Moscow and spent the next six weeks touring Europe and the Middle East. Indonesia's foreign ministry was active during this time in suggesting that, following Sukarno's talks in Washington, the United States was willing to adopt a 'fresh approach'. A private message from Kennedy to Sukarno, in which the late American president said he would be assisted by a 'calm atmosphere' and urged Sukarno to 'maintain tranquillity' in the region, was taken to mean that America intended to mediate. Indonesian officials said at that time that six months had been set aside for American mediation to bear fruit. They also singled out Australia for criticism, saying it had become 'tougher' on West Irian than the Dutch.

In his speech of 17 August, President Sukarno mentioned approvingly the idea of a gradual transfer of authority and through the rest of the year there was a noticeable edging toward areas of agreement. At the United Nations in November, an American suggestion that the principle of self-determination should be endorsed but that Indonesia should be allowed entry to West Irian to campaign for a vote in favour of union with the Republic was described by Mr Ruslan Abdulgani, vice-president of the Supreme Advisory Council and now minister for information, as 'rather progressive', and he talked about 'internal self-determination' as a prospect. The Dutch proposed 'internationalization' by the United Nations.

From this time until 15 August 1962, when the Netherlands and Indonesia finally signed a treaty under the firm mediation of Ellsworth Bunker, there was an atmosphere of unreality in Australia's calm response to the mounting tension in its near north. On 10 December, the Australian chief of the general staff, Lieutenant-General Sir Reginald Pollard, visited Indonesia a few days after the New Zealand defence minister (Mr Eyre). Two days later Sukarno was appointed 'Commander in Chief of the Liberation of West Irian'. On 19 December, he issued the People's Triple Command (Trikora) for the liberation of West Irian which, following on the Indian action in Goa, suggested that if there was any negotiating space left in Indonesia's position on West New Guinea, it was fast disappearing. Two Indonesian motor-torpedo boats were sunk by the Dutch south of West New Guinea on 15 January 1962. The activity of mobilization was now widely emphasized. Volunteers were pictured enlisting from all corners of the island Republic (including some from Malaya) and the armed forces kept asserting their readiness. On 22 January U Thant began a series of talks with the Indonesian and Netherlands representatives in New York. On 23 January some sections of the Australian press, following a visit to Melbourne by senior officials of the external affairs department, began speaking of a change in Australian policy, which was denied officially in Canberra. (In December 1961 the Menzies government had been returned with a much reduced majority of two after a campaign in which an unusual combination of the Labor party and the *Sydney Morning Herald* had protested against what was described as appeasement of a dictator, drawing lessons from Hitler's expansion in the 1930s.)

Australian press comment became increasingly sharp as the In-

donesians announced parachutist landings on islands off the West
Irian coast, and finally on the territory itself. The Dutch rushed
reinforcements to the territory and Indonesia used diplomatic pressure on Japan and the United States to prevent landing and transit
rights for Dutch planes in the airlift. A fifth assassination attempt
was made on Sukarno in May, followed by U Thant's appeals to
both countries to stop hostilities. On 4 June, the Australian defence
minister, the late Mr Townley, visited Indonesia where, according to
the official record, he 'displayed an understanding of Indonesia's
rights with regard to West Irian'. In Australia, however, the visit
only intensified public reaction, especially as the Minister, caught
without his baggage on a visit to a Siliwangi training camp, wore
Indonesian 'uniform' (variously described as 'jungle greens', 'fatigues',
etc.) decorated with his own war medals.

   The agreement of 15 August was not warmly received in Australia, although it was recognized as having brought to an end a
long and bitter argument which had affected relations with Indonesia. It was realized that although technically the agreement had
been gained by diplomacy and that the rights of self-determination
for the indigenes of West Irian were explicitly safeguarded in the
agreement by United Nations' participation in the 'act of choice'
before 1969, Indonesia had gained effective occupancy of the dis-
puted territory by a mixture of diplomatic bluff and military threats,
based on her acquisition of an estimated U.S. $1,000 million worth
of arms from the Soviet bloc. This was demonstrated when the armed
forces held a display in Djakarta to show how, if Subandrio's diplomacy had been unsuccessful, plans were in gear for a large-scale
invasion of West Irian in November. President Sukarno's repudiation
of force to Mr Menzies three years before became a quaint memory.
Sir Garfield Barwick, now the minister for external affairs, made the
most of the agreement as a victory for diplomacy, as did spokesmen
in Washington. In Barwick's hands Australian policy toward Indonesia retained its friendy composure during the transfer of West
Irian to the Indonesians from October 1962 to May 1963. But before
any benefit from the removal of this thorn in Australian-Indonesian
relations could be tested, the Malaysia crisis had taken precedence
and Australian attention was diverted from the newly-shared five
hundred mile border on New Guinea to the nine hundred mile
border in Borneo that the new state of Malaysia would share with
Indonesia.

   Australian opinion had been generally favourable to Malaysia
from its beginnings in 1961. This had been encouraged during 1962

by Indonesia's apparent lack of concern. By the end of the year, however, the Brunei revolt had opened up a possibility of active Indonesian opposition and the Australian government was faced with the prospect of trying to maintain friendships in the opposing camps. Popular suspicion of Indonesia was revived, which was not comfortable for a government with a working majority in the House of Representatives of only one. After the holiday period had been properly observed, Australian diplomacy began to apply itself to preventing a clash. On 14 February 1963, the secretary of the External Affairs Department, Sir Arthur Tange, went to Washington, without official explanation, but with the generally understood purpose of seeking U.S. diplomatic help in restraining Indonesia. President Kennedy made a declaration of American support for Malaysia, hitherto assumed. After Tange's return to Australia, a series of conferences took place in Canberra attended by the chief of the Imperial General Staff (Sir Richard Hull) who flew out from London, and the British commissioner-general for South-east Asia (Lord Selkirk) from Singapore. Australian diplomats were recalled from Asia. The high commissioner in Kuala Lumpur (Mr T. K. Critchley), well-known and liked by Indonesian leaders in Djakarta for his role as Indonesian nominee on the United Nations' Good Offices Committee, stopped at Djakarta for informal talks with Sukarno and Subandrio on his way to Canberra.

Compared with definite British military commitments on Malaysia, Australian statements at this time were cautious. On 28 February, the government announced that Australian forces would remain in Malaya after the scheduled Malaysian birthday of 31 August, but when the Malayan prime minister, Tunku Abdul Rahman, announced on 10 March in Malacca (where the Commonwealth brigade is stationed) that 'the British and Australian governments have pledged to support us in the event of war resulting directly from Indonesia's policy of confrontation toward Malaysia' he was forced to make a hasty apology. He claimed to have said only: 'Australia is a member of the Commonwealth and has openly said that she supports Malaysia. She too would rally to our help.'

Sir Garfield Barwick used the occasion of the Ecafe meeting in Manila in March to introduce, in a series of private discussions with Subandrio, the proposition that Australia could help Indonesia —if it were interested—to satisfy its honour over Malaysia. These talks were a delicate exercise in diplomacy. They were not recorded; Subandrio was alone and Barwick was accompanied by the Australian ambassador in Djakarta (Mr K. C. O. Shann). It is unlikely that a full version of the discussions will ever be available, although they represent an important event, backed as they were in Manila by Australia's application for regional membership of Ecafe, in the development of a more confident attitude by Australia toward its role in South-east Asia. In effect, Barwick took up a suggestion by the president of the Philippines (Mr Macapagal) for a meeting between Malaya, Indonesia and the Philippines, on the assumption that the Indonesian government would be prepared to accept an appearance of consultation of this kind to enable it to 'get off the hook' on Malaysia, the hook being its support for the Brunei rebels and loss of face in not being consulted by Kuala Lumpur. Australia was undertaking, on the assumption of its good relations in Kuala Lumpur, to bring Malaya to the party, despite British opposition. Subandrio's job was to convince Sukarno. Barwick's performance at Manila impressed diplomats, including the British, who were not happy about its intention.

It seemed likely throughout April and May that, backed by American reminders in Djakarta that aid was needed to finance Indonesia's economic reforms, the initiative was holding. The meetings in Tokyo and Manila appeared to be leading to a successful summit conference of Abdul Rahman, Macapagal and Sukarno, scheduled for 31 July. On 10 July, however, Sukarno, reacting to the signing of the Malaysia agreement in London, renewed confrontation. On 14 July, Sir Robert Menzies, returning from London, stated at a press conference, in relation to Australia's defence commitments: 'Now that Malaysia becomes a fact, the time arises when we have to determine what we are prepared to do.' He was criticized by Subandrio for 'provocation'. The summit meeting in Manila was held, the three leaders adopting the Maphilindo declaration, but Indonesia did not drop confrontation. Subandrio advised Shann after a meeting on 26 August that Indonesia was interested in implementing the Manila agreements and the Minister made a press statement in which he said he understood the Australian government 'wants to help seek the best solution to the Malaysian issue'.

But when Barwick visited Djakarta on 12 September, on his way to Kuala Lumpur for the Malaysia Day celebrations on the 16th, he gave the clear impression that Canberra was no longer interested in 'solutions'. During his visit the results of the United Nations' ascertainment—an effective clean bill of health for Malaysia—became known. Barwick told the Indonesian leaders that Australia would choose Malaysia in the event of a choice being forced by Indonesia. (He also apparently knew, or strongly suspected, that an Australian election was pending; he made it clear to Indonesian leaders that any Australian government which tried to do more than his had done to accommodate Indonesia's point of view would risk defeat at the polls.) The delicacy that Barwick had shown in Manila was not now in evidence. He spoke bluntly, even critically, to Sukarno and Subandrio. On leaving Djakarta he told a press conference that he had made clear to Indonesian leaders 'the possible repercussions upon Australian opinion of continued Indonesian intervention in the affairs of neighbours'.

On 25 September, Menzies made a 'definitive' statement to Parliament on Malaysia, which included the following key sentence:

If, in the circumstances that now exist, that may go on for a long time, there occurs, in relation to Malaysia or any of its constituent States, armed invasion or subversive activity—supported or directed or inspired from outside Malaysia—we shall to the best of our powers and by such means as shall be agreed upon with the Government of Malaysia, add our military assistance to the efforts of Malaysia and the United Kingdom in the defence of Malaysia's territorial integrity and political independence.

Foreign affairs and defence, with emphasis on Australia's 'grave responsibilities' in South-east Asia, were the central theme in the Menzies government's campaign for the precipitately-called elections of 30 November 1963. It won an unmistakable vote of confidence.

* * *

In the files of a certain embassy in Djakarta, the following item appeared in a list of countries whose relations with Indonesia were assessed in 1963. 'Australia: relations with Indonesia are best characterized as civil. They are marked by a growing, if grudging, recognition by Australia that it has an important role to play in Asia. The sudden realization that the insular dominion now shares a common border in New Guinea with the biggest and most populous Southeast Asian country is an important factor in this awakening.'

To anyone who knows the anguish behind some of the private and public debates in Australia over Indonesia, the truth in this appraisal will seem irritatingly detached. The interesting fact in retrospect, however, is that it was not the long-pondered New Guinea problems which brought relations between Indonesia and Australia to a head, but Malaysia, which burst late on the scene and seemed at first to be harmless. By 1962, if not before, the Australian government had accepted the inevitability of Indonesia's occupancy of the western part of the New Guinea island and, despite misgivings over the use of 'confrontation', there was public sympathy for Indonesia's claim and a tendency to regard her patriotic extravagances over West Irian as a special case. In terms of power, perhaps, Canberra's acceptance of Indonesia as a land neighbour was negative. Australia was not prepared to fight for the Dutch. She was not able to dissuade the United States from a tolerant interest in an Indonesian victory. She did not have the military capacity to support an independent policy. But it was still true that a reservoir of friendly attitudes toward Indonesia remained in Australia. Barwick's attempt to reach an understanding with Subandrio on Malaysia expressed this friendliness, as it expressed also a growing confidence in the Department of External Affairs that Australia could devise its own diplomatic strategies in South-east Asia. The attempt failed, but the cause of its failure lay outside Australia.

Indonesia had determined to remove the British from South-east Asia as she had removed the Dutch. As far as Australia was concerned, this was too high a price to pay for a friendship that was untested and unstable. The traditional links with Britain, the Commonwealth defence arrangements with Malaya and the general support for Malaysia as a solution to the political future of the peoples of Singapore, Sarawak and Sabah, made Australia's choice inevitable, although not easy to make when the time came.

Indonesia's immediate neighbours—Australia, Malaysia and the Philippines—were faced with the simple problem of balance of power in the region. They had been given enough notice of Indonesia's ambition to dominate the region. The civilized idea of co-operating with their large, undisciplined neighbour became impractical when Indonesia made one of its first conditions the removal of the United Kingdom's military presence from South-east Asia. Whatever reservations may be held in Kuala Lumpur and Canberra about Britain's position in the region, neither country was able—and will not be for some time—to match Indonesia militarily. Manila may be attracted by the prospect of replacing Malaysia as an entrepôt for Indonesian trade, but there is no guarantee in Indonesia's policy of confronting the old established British presence that American power, on which the Philippines depends, is not next on the list. On the contrary, President Sukarno has often enough indicated that it is. There has long been a tendency to suppose that Indonesian leaders do not mean what they say, that they talk big to cover their country's inadequacies. While this is often true, there is enough now on record of what Indonesia does, not only what its leaders say, to show its three neighbours that precautions are necessary. Until Australia, Malaysia

and the Philippines are themselves better armed they cannot dispense
—even if they wish to—with outside Western military support without acknowledging Indonesian leadership in the region. This obviously poses fundamental issues of policy.

Indonesia is highly sensitive to its security. From the beginning
it has been a shaky national union, with a centrifugal tendency. The
regional rebellions confirmed the suspicion that covetous eyes were
cast on the outer islands, especially rich Sumatra. The British naval,
air and military bases in Singapore, and the American air base in the
Philippines, as well as the roaming presence of the American seventh
fleet, can be seen as a threat to Indonesia's security. As Nasution has
pointed out, Britain and America are too big for Indonesia to handle;
they may be friendly now, but Djakarta cannot be sure what kind of
policies will prevail in London and Washington in the future. Its
freedom of action in the region is undoubtedly curtailed. Because it
is non-aligned and antagonistic to the interests of western capitalism,
Indonesia may well feel that she is surrounded by the enemy and
must therefore double her guard.

One way, of course, to remove a sense of encirclement is to join
the encirclers. This does not seem likely; Indonesia has grown steadily
more anti-western. Another way is to fight your way out, crushing
your opponents with the help of powerful, distant friends. There is a
third way, which is that Indonesia should be given guarantees that
her security is not threatened. This was the assumption of the Maphilindo talks in Manila; Malaya and the Philippines provided the
guarantees. Why Indonesia did not accept the Maphilindo declaration as satisfaction for her protest on Malaysia is a mystery whose
solution would probably throw useful light on the workings of the
Sukarno régime. The British view on Maphilindo was that it went
too far in Indonesia's direction. To what extent did the Indonesians
lose the chance to benefit from Maphilindo because they were bustled
by the British and to what extent because the Maphilindo grouping,
with Seato-member the Philippines, and anti-communist Malaya
(Australia also waiting in the wings), was too obviously directed
against Peking for Djakarta to accept? American initiatives, such as
the visit of Mr Robert Kennedy to the area early in 1964, revived
the idea and Indonesia showed interest.

But it is hard to see that either Britain or America would be prepared now to negotiate with Indonesia their rights in the bases concerned. The kinds of restrictions which Indonesia would place on
their use of the bases would make them difficult to operate for the
defence purposes of Malaysia and the Philippines, not to mention

Seato. Indonesia, in deciding to confront Malaysia, was really deciding to confront the western position in South-east Asia. She decided on a test of strength.

There is no way by which the Indonesian government can be forced to recognize that its regional policies are mistaken except by their failure. The proof of this may be a long and costly process. The Indonesian leaders are convinced, with some evidence to support them, that their powerful friends are more powerful than their neighbours'. They are convinced that the long-range policy of establishing Indonesia as the primary power in the region will succeed.

The Australian-Indonesian courtship is now over. If the countries are to remain friends, the terms will be more realistic. If they are not to be friends, issues between them will be argued and perhaps forced with the usual exertions of national power, including military strength. This is a normal state of affairs. Most countries, especially if they are neighbours, live together on assumptions of war as well as of peace.

A decision to be realistic about Indonesia means, however, for Australia, something more than a decision to be belligerent. Indonesia cannot be made to sink beneath the waves. It is the only country in South-east Asia with the potential of a major power. There is no guarantee that the present leadership in Indonesia will be succeeded by more accommodating men. One way or another, Indonesia will continue to lay claim to rights in the region.

Malaysia provided the immediate commitment for Australia, but its relations with Indonesia are still likely to be tested in New Guinea, where the quality of fighting men and weapons is not as decisive as the quality of the political decisions behind them. Indonesia has embraced the West Irian Papuans as 'brothers'. Australia's attitude toward the East New Guinea Papuans is at best paternal. The difference between these two attitudes provides the classic basis for the kind of military-political subversion which Indonesia introduced on the Borneo border.

Australia's 'powerful friends' in Seato and Anzus would certainly deter any would-be aggressor from declaring his intentions in New Guinea, but they are unlikely to be effective against armed infiltration, with political unrest as its objective. In the twilight zone of undeclared war Australia would realize that it was not enough to be a tough fighter in the Digger tradition. The techniques of counter-guerilla warfare, with their associated political awareness, would need to be learned.

CHAPTER TWELVE

The Future

The real political problems of Indonesia are problems of what the late Aldous Huxley called the Politics of Ecology. At the current rate of growth, there will be twice the present population in thirty years —200 million Indonesians before the end of the century. Unless there is a radical change in the style of political leadership, the chances of these Indonesians being represented in the world by a nation which is peaceful and productive are remote.

Indonesia is underdeveloped now. It lacks the trained personnel and the capital resources to create the kind of industrialized society able to meet the demands of its present population. It cannot meet their primary needs; it cannot feed them properly, although it is naturally rich in foodstuffs. While the people increasingly demand greater satisfactions than the age-old privilege of subsistence, the trend in the world is that the rich, developed countries are becoming richer and the poor, underdeveloped countries are becoming comparatively poorer. The gap between the affluent societies and the underprivileged societies is widening. Disappointment and frustration, coupled with resentment, point to unrest among the underprivileged. It may be directed against the leaders. But the leaders have all the power in their hands—the power of the armed forces and police to prevent an uprising, the power of propaganda to convince the people that the reasons for their predicament lie elsewhere, and, above all, the mystical authority of the nation, symbol of the people's freedom from colonialist slavery. It is more likely to be directed against other nations and other people.

Under Sukarno, Indonesia has taken a deliberate step away from the Politics of Ecology, of which some of the early Indonesian leaders seemed aware. It has engaged itself, rather, in the Politics of Psychology. Here, the indices of population and production have not as compelling a reality as the measure of the notice one can attract— the extent to which one's *identity* is recognized by others.

I am not underestimating the importance of this in determining people's needs. Indonesians do not live by rice alone. When they are given evidence—as they frequently are—that their country is a force to be reckoned with in world affairs, they feel pride and satisfaction. And they may say to themselves, when new equipment arrives for the armed forces or the head of state of an important country comes as a guest or an international conference is held in Djakarta or a new loan is announced or even when Sukarno is criticized in another country: 'Things may be bad but at least Indonesia counts for something these days.' Sukarno has even created for them a new ideology, which idealizes their suffering, identifies their enemies and channels their energies into revolutionary tasks directed away from the failures and compromises of the government.

Politicians cannot be expected to operate in the impersonal, statistical style of the Politics of Ecology. The myth-makers must first work the long-term interests of the land and the people into symbols as fascinating as those which represent the short-term interests of the State and the nationalism it expresses. There has not yet been time for this in Indonesia.

The history of the modern world has shown that nationalism unifies the will of a people more emphatically than any other cause, including those extremes of human self-interest, economic welfare and religion. Nationalism exists today as a powerful force in countries as disparate as the U.S.A. and the USSR, both international leaders with an interest in national interdependence within their groups, in France and China, representing two world cultures, and in Australia, one of the most unprovocative nations in the world.

The Nation demands a loyalty above all others—those of religion, politics, social or economic class, which divide a country. Its demands, moreover, are those of security; if your country is conquered, you become someone else's property, whatever your beliefs. When editorial writers describe an action by one of their country's leaders as 'statesmanlike' they mean that it is above self-interest, whether of person, party, region or religion. But if his action were so elevated as to be above the national interest, he would be condemned as a traitor.

So Sukarno can hardly be blamed for idolizing the Indonesian nation. It is still new and still uncertain and there is scarcely an Indonesian who is not sensitive to its survival. This sensitivity, occasionally doubling as arrogance, has naturally increased with the nation's failures. 'Now you mustn't laugh', a foreign ministry official prefaced his remarks to me one day about his government's determination to drive the British from South-east Asia. One reason, perhaps, for the early relationship between Indonesia and Australia was that the Australians, accustomed for so long to the superior judgments which the British passed on their speech, their clothes, their houses and other characteristics of their national life, felt an instinctive sympathy for the Indonesians, struggling with their pride.

In today's circumstances, however, the chances for democracy in Indonesia are slight, while tyranny's chances are excellent. An underdeveloped country with a high population growth can hold off catastrophe by wise policies, hard work and population control. With luck—I don't think anyone knows the answer to these problems of the future—it might win through and its large population become a symbol of strength, as it is in developed countries. Population control is costly, but not nearly as costly as battleships and jet bombers. There seems little prospect while Sukarno remains, and even beyond him, that this approach will be taken by Indonesia. How the dangers of this can be brought home to the Indonesian people, without inflaming suspicion, is one of the major hazards of responsible diplomacy.

Sukarno is not a tyrant in the mould of recent European dictators, who transformed their societies into police states enforcing a single philosophy. He does not have a party machine to carry out his will. Nor is he cruel and sadistic. He errs on the side of pleasure rather than pain. Many Indonesians who have opposed him are living free lives, provided they do not engage in politics. There are ten political parties and several functional bodies which are able to organize themselves into pressure groups. Newspapers are not as outspoken or as powerful as they are in India, Japan or the Philippines, but neither are they as submissive as in Thailand or Vietnam. Indonesians know how to read between the lines and there is a balance of political news with the propaganda.

Yet Sukarno has increasingly shown lately many of the attributes of dictatorship. He has cut through constitutional processes to increase presidential power, which is now practically unlimited. He has encouraged xenophobia and has shown signs of megalomania, both in policies and in private life. He can claim to have the overwhelming support of the people, but this, as Hitler and Stalin showed, is almost a qualification of a successful dictator. Guided democracy pays lip-service to the principles of popular rule, but it contains none of the safeguards, especially the people's ability to change its government peacefully, and its right to an independent judiciary. Indonesia's democracy is less an instrument by which public opinion can exercise influence on the government and more an instrument by which the government can shape public opinion.

The President complains that he is not a free agent, that he must pay attention to what his people say. To the extent that this is true, it is more true of almost every other national leader. Every president or prime minister has a cabinet, a committee, a parliament, a party, an impending election or some other check on his authority to commit the nation. The restraints on Sukarno imposed by *musjawarah* and *gotong royong* may be genuine, but, especially in the areas of foreign policy and national security, the President has an operating licence which does not have to be renewed.

It is true that, as a matter of politics, Sukarno is affected by the distribution of power groups which support him. Since the Masjumi and the PSI were banned, however, and the army and the PKI have entered the competition for presidential approval, there is no group which on foreign affairs can brake or redirect his policies. The President is increasingly surrounded by like-minded men. On confrontation of Malaysia, there appears to be unanimity among the government leadership. Yet until recently—and even now not to a crucial extent—the Indonesian élite, and, further, the Indonesian people, were not interested in being hostile to the new federation. They will be eventually, of course, if the consequences of confrontation build and propaganda increases, but certainly, at the end of 1963, many Indonesians who had been wholehearted in their support for confrontation of the Dutch over West Irian were not behind the Malaysia policy.

The fact that Sukarno needs to balance carefully the support of his contending courtiers does not mean that he will be less belligerent abroad. It could mean the opposite. The connection between tyranny at home and expansion abroad is not simple. A weak tyrant may need to be more adventurous than a strong dictator. There is a strong presumption in the Malaysia developments that left-wing criticism of the economic reforms, introduced at the height of the negotiations, weakened the diplomacy undertaken by Subandrio.

In some respects—setting aside the glaring differences in attitude toward communism—Sukarno's Indonesia resembles the authoritarian models of Latin America: a flamboyant leader, backed by the military, popular with the masses, including the trade unions, supposedly progressive but, in fact, conservative, in that no radical domestic reforms are introduced. He also sponsors an ideology which successfully blames someone else for the national ailments.

It is well known that there are able and loyal Indonesians who disagree with what is happening in their country, but the evidence suggests they are not increasing in number. Sukarno's influence has grown, and the present trend will continue for the rest of his lifetime.

It might be expected that Indonesian nationalism would become more sophisticated in time. There is nothing in Sukarno's theory of the inevitable clash of the 'new emerging' and 'old established' forces to support this, however. As he grows older, Sukarno seems more than ever concerned to establish Indonesia as a military power, and that cannot be done without conflict.

What of the succession? Until the death of Dr Djuanda, it was possible that, as first minister and as acting president when Sukarno was absent from the country, Djuanda would inherit the presidency as a compromise, stop-gap candidate. A solid administrator, without much interest in Indonesia's ideological or military status abroad, he would not have been popular with the PKI nor, probably, with some elements in the army. But because the mechanics of the succession are still unused (Sukarno has never been elected and the 616-member Provisional People's Consultative Congress—MPRS—has the task of electing his successor), Djuanda might have filled the post as a measure of mutual distrust by the stronger candidates. In that event, it is possible that in time, moderate, rational elements in Indonesian political life would have moved again to the surface.

On Djuanda's death, a new line-up was established with the appointment of three vice-ministers under Sukarno: Leimena, Subandrio and Chairul Saleh. As a Christian, Leimena would probably not be acceptable as president; in addition he has shown no political ambitions on this scale. Of the other two, Subandrio is the better known internationally and is a Javanese, which may be a domestic asset. He has no backing, however, independent of Sukarno. Saleh is technically non-party, but he has close links with the 'national communists' (Partai Murba), and he has a strong following in the National Front, the Veterans' Legion, and among the group which has been called the 'youth' or '1945 generation'. If it came to a vote of the MPRS he would seem a likely choice.

Born on 13 September 1916 (in Sawahlunto, a small central Sumatran town), Saleh is about the same age as Subandrio (chapter 10) and Nasution (chapter 5). The son of a doctor, he was a law student when the Japanese occupied Indonesia and he developed as a professional revolutionary, first in the underground (he was one of the students who kidnapped Sukarno and Hatta to force a declaration of independence) and later as a lieutenant of the rebellious Tan Malaka. Arrested by Sjahrir in 1946, released without trial, re-arrested in 1950 and exiled until 1956, Chairul Saleh has risen quickly under Sukarno, as minister for basic industries and also veterans' affairs. He has modelled his oratory on the President's and has the same success in his public relations. He is well-groomed, lives stylishly, and is controversial and amusing in conversation. His left-leaning, anti-western views, coupled with confidence and energy, mark him as a man who could follow Sukarno without any appreciable change in the present direction of Indonesian policies. The army's long conditioning under Sukarno would ease his way.

As long as Sukarno and his successors know that they can unite the country by external confrontations, the temptation in such a diversified and troubled nation as Indonesia is likely to be constant. In addition, Indonesian leaders have developed a healthy respect for the authority of military success. They learned during the revolutionary war with the Dutch in 1945-9 that military victories provide diplomatic strength. This was tested again in the case of West Irian, and the technique of confrontation, as it developed in the West Irian campaign and has been used over Malaysia, combines military and diplomatic pressures.

The use of military pressure on external affairs is perhaps made easier by the kind of warfare involved. Guerilla tactics are cheap and can be used without a declaration of war for which the nation must openly accept responsibility. They illustrate the famous Clausewitz definition of war as 'a continuation of political relations'. Nasution's special interest in guerilla warfare, which he sees as a weapon suited to Indonesia's terrain, its politics and the technical level of the army, may in fact act as a corrective to one status symbol as yet beyond Sukarno's reach—that of a nuclear capacity. This prospect may be difficult seriously to imagine, but the example of Cuba is clear enough.

Certainly, the Australian decision to offer facilities for the United States to establish a communications base for nuclear submarines makes it easier for the Indonesians and Russians, if they wish, to agree to a similar arrangement. (Although if Indonesia were looking for provocation, the fact that the British V-bombers based in Singapore are able to act as a nuclear strike force would be enough.) It is hard to see, however, what advantage the Russians would gain from setting up nuclear bases in Indonesia on the Cuban pattern. Russia improved and diversified its America-pointed attack with Cuba, but in the case of Indonesia the only target with similar appeal would be Australia. It seems unlikely that either the USSR or Indonesia would take such a step for such a result. In Indonesia's frame of mind, however, and with the crisis of her affairs continuing to mount, as I am supposing it will, we cannot rely too much on rationality in Djakarta. We may be better advised to rely on good sense in Moscow. One thing is sure—and it needs to be borne in mind by some hot-heads in Malaysia. The danger of a Cuba situation in South-east Asia is much greater if there is a regionalist breakaway from Djakarta, say in Sumatra and Sulawesi. Java, isolated, overwhelmingly left-wing and incapable of feeding itself, would be forced into a predictable reaction.

What sort of policy should be adopted toward Indonesia, seemingly intent on disturbing the peace? There has been argument about 'hard' and 'soft' attitudes, about the need to encourage friendliness and the need to provide scope for improvement. Foreign affairs are actually played as a much tighter game, especially by the Indonesians. The opportunity for moral initiative in deciding a policy toward Indonesia seems to me to have passed. It is necessary to assume that Indonesia is doing in foreign affairs what she has chosen to do.

Sukarno has plainly said that he expects the result of his policies for Indonesia to bring conflict. He appears to welcome the prospect. The choice of diplomatic initiative becomes dangerous when a nation has so clearly chosen the techniques of force to make its policies succeed. Assuming that it will 'win' without a negotiated settlement, Indonesia may place a high price on calling off confrontation, even if its leadership can be persuaded to engage in 'quid pro quo' diplomacy. In these conditions, diplomacy runs the risk of always appeasing, never satisfying.

Contemporary history is hard to write with assurance. The history of Hitler's Germany or Mussolini's Italy are today deceptively simple, filled with the anguish and knowledge of later events. But at the time people were confused about what was happening; one of the confusions was their hope that it would not turn out the way it did. From the time Indonesia entered the world as a new nation, it attracted hope and sympathy. Some aspects of its policy, including those unpopular among conservatives in the west—such as the tight grip on foreign investment—are useful to Indonesia. If Sukarno were a socialist in deed as well as word, combining non-alignment with a determination to get on with the task of developing the intellectual and physical standards of his people, he would undoubtedly find wide support in the west as well as in communist countries.

It is unlikely that anyone would be disappointed if Indonesia turned out to be a great nation with new ideas which would really startle mankind with their freshness. A new idea for feeding and clothing the Indonesian people would be welcomed not only in Indonesia but by impoverished people all over the world. No-one would be unhappy if the creativity of the Indonesian people, which the present leadership is so eloquent about yet also distrusts, were given more interesting challenges than the old-fashioned demands of power politics.

But the idea of the 'deferred good' which has an appeal in rational and secure societies has found no receptive ground in the new Indonesia. The people's needs are so great and the justification of their suffering under colonialism so strong that there is an assumption, fostered by the leadership, that now Indonesia is entitled to whatever it needs. The gap between desire and expectation is emotionally narrow, although realistically it is widening. There is an air of feverish attainment in Indonesian politics, although the record of actual achievement is slight.

The situation has now been reached where Indonesia, which once thought of itself as a peaceful influence on the power-hungry great nations and once had the sympathy of its neighbours, has promoted nationalism to a point of conflict with its environment. New theories about Indonesia and the world have been created to explain this, but their effect, in the constricted atmosphere of Sukarno's leadership, is to intensify the conflict.

GLOSSARY

adat	gradually developed body of customary law; like common law
agama Djawa	'religion of Java'; a syncretic blend of religious beliefs
alus	refined, smooth
bapak	father
betjak	a three-wheeled pedicab
bung	brother
dalang	*wayang* puppeteer
dukun	native medico who uses herbs
etok-etok	dissimulation as a form of politeness
gamelan	Indonesian orchestra
gotong rojong	traditional village practice of mutual assistance
kampong	village; in cities a poor-man's enclave usually without paved roads or electricity
kasar	base, coarse
konfrontasi	'encounter' or confrontation
kopiah	black velvet cap, similar to a fez
kraton	ancient palace-city of kings and sultans
kris	sword with undulating blade; also traditional magic symbol
ladang	unirrigated arable land, often prepared by slashing and burning jungle
Manipol-Usdek	manipol stands for 'political manifesto' and usdek is an acronym of the five points of the manifesto: return to the 1945 constitution; socialism; guided democracy; guided economy; Indonesian identity. The slogan was coined by President Sukarno in 1960.
marhaen	literally 'proletariat' but used by Sukarno as the basis of a 'little people' kind of socialism

177

mufakat	consensus; agreement; unanimity
musjawarah	mutual discussion
Nasakom	an abbreviation of Nas (nationalist) A (*agama* or 'religion') Kom (communist), indicating the three political streams supporting Sukarno's government
Pantja Sila	the five principles enunciated by Sukarno in 1945 to provide the philosophical basis of the Republic
pantun	an old-style Malay quatrain
priyayi	old Javanese official class; now used to describe a cultured person or cultured behaviour
rasa	Javanese term for 'meaning' or 'feeling' or a mystic blend of the two
sandang pangan	'food and clothing'; traditional expression of economic welfare
santri	devout Muslim
sawah	irrigated rice field
tjotjog	Javanese word meaning 'to fit'
Trikora	three-pronged plan to secure West Irian
wayang	Indonesian theatre either of human actors, puppets or shadow images

BIBLIOGRAPHY

Abdulgani, Ruslan, *The Bandung Spirit and the Asian-African Press*. Department of Information, Djakarta, 1963.

Aidit, D. N., 'Dare, Dare and Dare Again!' (Report to PKI central committee), *Harian Rakyat*, 11 February 1963.

Ardjasni, 'My Life', *Eastern Horizon*, January, February, March (three issues) 1962.

Bell, Coral, 'Non-Alignment and the Power-Balance', *Australian Outlook*, August 1963.

Boyce, P. J., 'Canberra's Malaysian Policy', *Australian Outlook*, July 1963.

Brackman, Arnold C., *Indonesian Communism*. Praeger, New York, 1963.

Calder, Ritchie, *The Inheritors*. Heinemann, London, 1961.

Calhoun, John B., 'Population Density and Social Pathology', *Scientific American*, February 1962.

Cantril, Hadley, 'A Study of Aspirations', *Scientific American*, February 1963.

Clark, C. M. H., *A History of Australia*, vol. i. Melbourne University Press, Melbourne, 1962.

Compulsory Education in Indonesia. Ministry of Education, Djakarta, 1961.

Crozier, Brian, *The Rebels*. Chatto and Windus, London, 1960.

Cunningham, K. S., 'Final Report of UNESCO Mission to Indonesia on Teacher Training and Educational Research' (mimeographed paper), 1957.

'Diplomatic and Consular List', Department of Foreign Affairs, Djakarta, June 1963.

Dobby, E. H. G., *Southeast Asia*, University of London Press, London, 1958.

Far Eastern Economic Review Yearbook, 1962, 1963, Hong Kong.

Feith, Herbert, *The Decline of Constitutional Democracy in Indonesia*. Cornell University Press, Ithaca, New York, 1962.

——————— 'Symbols, Ritual and Ideology in Indonesian Politics' (paper presented to the Australian Political Studies Association conference), August 1962.

————, and Lev, Daniel S., 'The End of the Indonesian Rebellion', *Pacific Affairs*, Spring, 1963.

Fischer, Louis, *The Story of Indonesia*. Hamish Hamilton, London, 1959.

Fish, Hamilton, 'The Troubled Birth of Malaysia', *Foreign Affairs*, July 1963.

Geertz, Clifford, *The Religion of Java*. Glencoe Free Press, Illinois, 1960.

Greenwood, Gordon, and Harper, Norman (eds.), *Australia in World Affairs 1956-1960*. Cheshire, Melbourne, for Australian Institute of International Affairs, 1963.

Gunther, John, *Inside Asia*. Hamish Hamilton, London, 1939.

Haar, B. ter, *Adat Law in Indonesia*. Bhratara, Djakarta, 1962.

Handbook on the Political Manifesto: two executive directions of Manipol. Department of Information, Djakarta, 1961.

Hanna, Willard A., *Bung Karno's Indonesia*. American Universities Field Staff, Inc., New York, 1961.

Harris, Richard, 'Communism and Asia: Illusions and Misconceptions', *International Affairs*, January 1963.

Higgins, Benjamin, *Indonesia: The Crisis of the Millstones*. Van Nostrand, Princeton, New Jersey, 1963.

Hindley, Donald, 'Foreign Aid to Indonesia and its Political Implications', *Pacific Affairs*, Summer, 1963.

The History of the Armed Forces of the Republic of Indonesia. Ministry of Information, Djakarta, 1958.

Huxley, Aldous, 'The Politics of Ecology' (paper), Center for the Study of Democratic Institutions, Santa Barbara, California, 1963.

Indonesia, 1961. Department of Foreign Affairs, Djakarta, 1962.

Indonesia, 1962. Department of Foreign Affairs, Djakarta, 1963.

'Indonesia Today', special issue of the *Bulletin*, Sydney, 14 December 1963.

Johnson, John J. (ed.), *The Role of the Military in Underdeveloped Countries*. Princeton University Press, New Jersey, 1962.

Kahin, George McTurnan, *Nationalism and Revolution in Indonesia*. Cornell University Press, New York, 1952.

Kroef, J. M. van der, 'Two Forerunners of Modern Indonesian Independence: Imam Bondjol and Thomas Matulesia', *Australian Journal of Politics and History*, November 1962.

Legge, J. D., 'Indonesia since West Irian', *Australian Outlook*, April 1963.

Leur, J. C. van, *Indonesian Trade and Society*. Sumur, Bandung, 1960.

Lockhart, R. H. Bruce, *Return to Malaya*. Putnam, London, 1938.

Lubis, Mochtar, *Twilight in Djakarta*. Hutchinson, London, 1963.

Macdonald, Malcolm, *Angkor*. Jonathan Cape, London, 1960.

McVey, Ruth (ed.), *Indonesia*. Human Relations Area Files, Inc., New Haven, Connecticut, 1963.

Modelski, George, *The New Emerging Forces: Documents on the Ideology of Indonesian Foreign Policy*. Australian National University, Canberra, 1963.

Moerdowo, R., *Reflections on Indonesian Arts and Culture*. Permata, Surabaya, 1959.

Myrdal, Gunnar, 'Economic Nationalism and Internationalism' (Dyason Lectures for 1957), *Australian Outlook*, December 1957.

Nasution, A. H., *Fundamentals of Guerilla Warfare*. Indonesian Army Information Service, 1953.

Njoto, 'Develop the Manipol-Offensive in the Field of the Press' (Speech on twelfth anniversary of *Harian Rakyat*), *Harian Rakyat*, 8 February 1963.

Palthe, P. M. van Wulfften, *Psychological Aspects of the Indonesian Problem*. Brill, Leyden, 1949.

Pauker, Ewa T., 'Indonesia: the Year of Triumph', *Current History*, November 1962.

Pauker, Guy J., 'Indonesia's Eight-Year Development Plan', *Pacific Affairs*, Summer, 1961.

Rose, Saul (ed.), *Politics in Southeast Asia*. Macmillan, London, 1963.

Selosoemardjan, *Social Changes in Jogjakarta*. Cornell University Press, New York, 1962.

Shrieke, B., *Ruler and Realm in Early Java*. W. van Hoeve Ltd, the Hague and Bandung, 1957.

Sjahrir, Sutan, *Out of Exile*. John Day, New York, 1949.

Subandrio, *Indonesia on the March* (collection of speeches, 1957-63), Department of Foreign Affairs, Djakarta, 1963.

Sukarno, President of Indonesia. Ministry of Information, Djakarta, 1958.

Thio, *Indonesian Folk Tales.* Tunas, 1962.

Tjoa, Marianne, 'Survey of the History of Java and Sumatra' (private paper), Djakarta, 1963.

Tregonning, K. G., 'Australia's Imperialist Image in Southeast Asia', *Australian Quarterly,* September 1961.

Veur, P. W. van der, 'The Irian Changeover', *Australia's Neighbours,* July-August 1963.

Vlekke, B. M. H., *Nusantara, A History of Indonesia.* W. van Hoeve Ltd, the Hague and Bandung, 1959.

Wedding Ceremonials, Prapantja, Djakarta.

Wertheim, W. F., *Indonesian Society in Transition.* W. van Hoeve Ltd, the Hague and Bandung, 1959.

Woodman, Dorothy, *The Republic of Indonesia.* Cresset Press Ltd, London, 1955.

INDEX

Abdulgani, Ruslan, 23, 40, 149, 161
Adat, 3, 94, 95, 96, 97, 103, 107, 129, 130
Adityavarman, 7
Adjitorop, Jusuf, 64
Afro-Asia, 45, 135, 136, 137, 144, 147, 151, 153, 157
Agriculture, 2, 95, 96, 102, 106-15 *passim*
Agung, Sultan, 12
Aidit, Dipa Nusantara, 26, 54, 58, 61, 63, 64, 65-6, 74
Aidit, Sobron, 104
Albuquerque, Alfonso d', 9, 10
Ali Sastroamidjojo, 42, 62, 73, 136, 137, 138, 144, 157
Alimin Prawirodirdjo, 41, 56, 59, 61
Alisjahbana, Takdir, 104, 105, 107
All-Indonesian Youth Congress, 103
Alus, 99, 101
Ambon, Ambonese, 10, 11, 29, 69, 111, 112
Amir Sjarifuddin, 22, 23, 26, 28, 57, 59, 60, 70, 131
Amok-running, 12
Animism, 3, 93, 94, 107, 109, 110, 111, 112, 113
Anti-colonialism, anti-imperialism, 135, 147, 148, 150
Anwar, Chairil, 104-5, 107
Anzus, 168
Arena, The (Gelanggang), 104
Aristocracy, 4, 5, 7, 13, 18
Armed forces, 29, 31, 59, 68-80, 89, 91, 141, 144, 145, 148, 158, 160, 162, 168
Arms and equipment, 65, 69, 75, 140, 149, 162
Army, 32, 45, 52, 55, 60, 61, 65, 66, 67, 68-80, 134, 136, 140, 142, 158, 172, 173
Art, 3, 4, 36, 101, 113
Aru Is., 111, 140
Asian Games stadium, 34, 133
Association of South-east Asia (ASA), 138, 143, 144, 153
Atjeh, Atjenese, 8, 10, 11, 13, 14, 97, 107
Australia, 27, 28, 55, 63, 68, 151-68, 170-1; communism, 63, 66, 154, 156, 158; defence, 156, 164-7; economic aid, 84, 88; geography, 113, 114; historic relations, 8; Labor Party,

154, 156; Liberal and Country Party, 156; Malaysia, 143, 162-8; Papuans, 97, 168; regional rebellions, 158; U.N. Good Offices' Committee, 155; West Irian, 139, 140, 156-62; women, 131; World War II, 58
Australian Council of Trade Unions, 154
Azahari, A. M., 80, 142

Babad Tanah Djawi (*The Clearing of Java*), 12, 13
Badan Penjelidik Kemerdekaan Indonesia—BPKI (Body for Investigation of Indonesian Independence), 25
Bali, 6, 7, 11, 13, 14, 27, 95, 113
Balikpapan, 109
Banda Is., 111
Bandjarmasin, Bandjars, 14, 109
Bandung, 27, 133; conference, 45, 136, 157; Study Club, 41
Bangka, 107
Bantam, Bantamese, 10, 12, 116
Bapakism, 96
Barisan Tani Indonesia—BTI (Indonesian Peasant Front), 54
Barwick, Sir Garfield, 143, 162, 163-5, 166
Batak, 78, 107-8
Batavia, 11, 12, 116, 133; *see also* Djakarta
Batik, 101, 102
Belgrade conference, 46, 140
Berita Indonesia (*Indonesian News*), 144
Billiton, 107
Bintang Timur (*Morning Star*), 144
Body for Investigation of Indonesian Independence, *see* Badan Penjelidik Kemerdekaan Indonesia
Bogor, 47, 116
Borneo, 3, 7, 13, 14, 25; territories, 143, 149, 150, 162; *see also* Brunei; Sabah; Sarawak
Borobudur, 1, 2, 5, 52, 133
Boven Digul, 20, 21, 57, 58, 63, 154
Brackman, Arnold C., 26, 61, 66, 156
Britain: Atjeh, 14; confrontation, 148, 167-8; early trade, 11; Malaysia, 88, 141-4, 146, 147-9, 162-8; military aid, 158; military bases, 77, 166, 167, 170,